Planning
in Rural
Environments

John R. Campbell
Department of Dairy Husbandry
University of Missouri
Consulting Editor in Animal Science

Carl Hall
College of Engineering
Washington State University
Consulting Editor in Agricultural Engineering

Lawrence H. Smith
Department of Agronomy
University of Minnesota
Consulting Editor in Plant Science

Planning
in Rural
Environments

WILLIAM R. LASSEY

Rural Sociologist
Professor of Sociology
and Environmental Science
Washington State University

McGRAW-HILL BOOK COMPANY
New York   St. Louis   San Francisco
Auckland   Bogotá   Düsseldorf   Johannesburg
London   Madrid   Mexico   Montreal   New Delhi
Panama   Paris   São Paulo   Singapore
Sydney   Tokyo   Toronto

Planning in Rural Environments

Copyright © 1977 by McGraw-Hill, Inc.
All rights reserved. Printed in the United States of America.
No part of this publication may be reproduced, stored in a retrieval system,
or transmitted, in any form or by any means, electronic, mechanical,
photocopying, recording, or otherwise,
without the prior written permission of the publisher.

1 2 3 4 5 6 7 8 9 0 K P K P 7 8 3 2 1 0 9 8 7

This book was set in Times Roman by National ShareGraphics, Inc.
The editors were C. Robert Zappa and James W. Bradley;
the cover was designed by Anne Canevari Green;
the production supervisor was Charles Hess.
Kingsport Press, Inc., was printer and binder.

Library of Congress Cataloging in Publication Data

Lassey, William R
    Planning in rural environments.

    Bibliography: p.
    Includes index.
    1. Regional planning. 2. Land use, Rural—Planning.
I. Title.
HT391.L35   309.2'63   76-56157
ISBN 0-07-036580-6

Contents

Government. Obsolescence of Rural Institutions. Natural
Resource Depletion. Social and Economic Costs of Space.
Leisure and Recreation. Transportation Systems. Functional
Specialization of Activities and Towns in Rural Areas.
Legislative and Legal Inadequacies. Financing. Education for
Rural Planning.

Physical Factors. Biological Factors. Cultural-Historical
Experience. Government-Political-Legal Factors.
Social-Psychological Factors. Economic Factors. Design
Factors. Development of Environment and Institutions.
Relationship Analysis. Projections of the Future. **Key
Processes.** Educational, Communication, and Public
Involvement Processes. Alternatives for Decision and Action.
Goals. Implementation: Management, Monitoring, Feedback,
Evaluation.

Rural and Regional Distinctions. Delineating Boundaries for
Planning Regions. Coordination as the Key Regional
Function. Basis for Regional Collaboration. Major Obstacles
to Effective Collaboration and Integration.

Emerging Concept of Land. Redefinition of Property Rights.
Role of the States. Alternative Forms of Social Organization
for Land-Use Guidance. Social and Organizational
Implications of the Alternatives. The Basis for Greater Public
Control of Land.

Definitions. Constraints and Conflicts in the Role of State and
Local Government. Interactions with Physical and Land-Use
Planning.

Preface

The principal goal of this work is to offer a body of basic concepts, research-based information, planning procedures, and management tools which can help strengthen the capability and effectiveness of planning units having responsibility for rural regions. As society has become more complex and large-scale, federal and state governments have been increasing their budgets and power, often at the expense of local government. In large part this is because local governments have not had the capability or foresight to plan and institute changes demanded by changing technology, new public values, and environmental deterioration.

The critical missing ingredients usually include: (1) adequate understanding and appreciation of planning as an approach to solving problems and realizing opportunities and (2) the resources—both human and financial—to undertake needed adaptations. Similarly, local officials have not understood how to locate the critical knowledge, nor how to link the knowledge with effective action, so as to deal with the multiplicity of issues with which they are constantly confronted. The material presented here is intended to be useful in illuminating rural and regional policy issues, while introducing the central considerations which must permeate adequate guidance of societal and environmental change.

A well-conceived planning system can create effective dialogue between citizens, elected or appointed public officials, and planners while guiding the resolution of crucial public issues. Such dialogue can draw upon the collective wisdom of citizens, public officials, and planning professionals, each equipped with unique knowledge and skills with applicability to problems or opportunities. The evidence from research and experience in Europe and the United States suggests that the alternatives offered in these pages are potentially productive in allowing local government to achieve greater initiative and effectiveness. State and federal governments and large private organizations relentlessly use advanced concepts of planning and action to further their public and private aims; local governments must gain access to more enlightened procedures and professional talent if they are not to be overwhelmed.

Although the concepts introduced here may in many instances have general applicability to urban settings, I have chosen to emphasize rural populations and territory; in the context of the current environmental and resource "crisis," rural territory and its human-guidance system are crucial in maintaining a viable life-support system for the planet. The rural environment has an integrity of its own, apart from urban and metropolitan territory and population—but this integrity has been ignored or neglected while the public preoccupation focused on the growth of population in cities and the profound problems associated therewith. In a real sense, the urban conglomerates are much more dependent on rural-based resources than are rural regions dependent on urban centers; rural areas are the principal source of food, air, water, and other raw materials on which life depends. Moreover, the rural environment is increasingly appreciated for its contribution to mental health, for its aesthetic values, and as a locale for recreation and refreshment apart from the noise, pollution, and constructed environment of cities. It seems of supreme importance to preserve and enhance areas where the rural amenities can be enjoyed in the context of a delightful, natural setting.

However, many of these natural and constructed rural settings are in the process of deterioration or are being put to uses which may be destructive both to the ecosystems which support life and to the aesthetic values which many of us treasure. A planned approach to preservation, conservation, reconstruction, and appropriate use of rural-based physical, biological, and human resources seems only sensible if not profoundly necessary.

Preparation of this manuscript began in the summer of 1972 when I was director of the Center for Planning and Development at Montana State University. Background reading and research in Europe, particularly in the

Netherlands and the United Kingdom, was undertaken as part of a sabbatical leave granted by Montana State University for the 1972–73 academic year. I am particularly grateful for the strong support and encouragement from Dr. Roy Huffman, Vice President for Research; Mr. Ernest Ahrendes, coordinator of extension and community services; Professor Anne S. Williams, coordinator of social science research, Center for Interdisciplinary Studies; and Dr. Joe Asleson, dean of agriculture. My work as a co-principal investigator in a National Science Foundation funded study, "Impact of Large Recreational Developments Upon Semi-Primitive Environments" (Grants #GI-38, #GI-29908, #GI-29908X1, and #GI-39592), of the Gallatin Canyon in Montana contributed substantially to my appreciation and understanding of a need for better concepts and strategies in rural-based regional planning.

While on sabbatical, I was a visiting scholar at the Agricultural University in Wageningen, the Netherlands, where I enjoyed extraordinarily hospitable surroundings. Dr. A. W. van den Ban, professor of extension education; Dr. Adrian Constandse, professor of sociology; Dr. E. W. Hofstee, professor of sociology; Dr. Bruno Benvenuti, professor of sociology; Dr. J. P. Groot, professor of sociology; Dr. D. B. W. Dusseldorp, professor of non-Western sociology; and Dr. B. F. Galjart, professor of non-Western sociology were all exceedingly helpful in directing me to materials, contact people, and observable rural planning programs, while hosting me in their homes and in the university.

While in the United Kingdom, I was a visiting scholar at the University of Reading and at University College, University of London. Professor Gwyn Jones offered innumerable kinds of personal assistance and support through the Center for Rural Development; Professor Morris Rolls, director of the Center, kindly permitted me full access to facilities of the Center and Reading University. Dr. Gerald Wibberly, professor of countryside planning, University College, University of London, was both hospitable and extremely helpful in locating literature, contact people, and consulting with me on substantive questions about rural planning. Numerous other individuals were helpful in providing access to information and first-hand contact with rural planning problems in the United Kingdom; my experiences with the residents and administrators of the town of Mapledurham and Mapledurham Estate, near Reading, were immensely interesting and useful.

The final work was completed at Washington State University. My administrative colleagues Dr. Don Dillman, chair of the department of rural sociology; Dr. Harry Cosgriffe, associate director of the cooperative extension service; Dr. Charles Bowerman, chair of the department of sociology; and Dr. Frank Scott, chair of the program in environmental science were each helpful. Viki Dahlkvist, Pat Hatfield, Jan Cyr, Elizabeth Sundell,

Loralee Lindsley, Linda Kinney, and Cindy Devary were responsible for manuscript typing and preparation for publication.

Financial and resource support for the work came principally from the Agricultural Experiment Station and Center for Interdisciplinary Studies (now the Center for Applied Research), Montana State University; from the Agricultural Research Center and Departments of Rural Sociology (through ARC Project 0207) and Sociology, the Cooperative Extension Service, and the Program in Environmental Science, Washington State University; from the European institutions noted above; and from personal resources.

A very large number of students and faculty who offered bits of help here and there shall go unnamed here, but my thanks and appreciation are gratefully extended.

William R. Lassey

Planning
in Rural
Environment

Chapter I

Introduction:
Rural Planning in Perspective

Until very recently, systematic planning to deal with the potential negative consequences of change in most rural areas has somehow seemed unnecessary and inappropriate. The consequences of modernization in agriculture, increased technology in harvesting natural resources, the rush of affluent urbanites to reside and recreate in the countryside, and numerous other impacts have been left largely to chance.

Rural population has been decreasing, although a reversal is now under way in many regions (Beale, 1975); quality of services for many rural people is lower than for urban areas (Carruthers, Erickson, & Renner, 1975); exhaustion of some natural resources is occurring; pollution of streams is evident; and a clear decrease in quality of certain pristine areas is under way (other examples are noted in Chapter II). Formalized "planning" as an appropriate mechanism to counteract such a state of decline has not been clearly perceived by many government officials or other rural leaders.

Much of the urban "problem" in most countries can be traced directly to rural inadequacies; poor and uneducated people who cannot survive in small towns and cities or on farms have moved in large numers to inhabit the slums and draw on the social services of the cities. Meanwhile, the crowded accommodations within the more scenic and attractive rural terri- tory attest forcefully that affluent urbanites are increasingly seeking out the rural environment for leisure or recreational activities, often leaving their artifacts and effluent notably evident. Agriculture continues to serve as the principal use of rural land, but new industries and new land uses often leave deserted farmsteads as a symbol of change (see Figure 1-1). The conse- quences of these parallel movements in opposite directions is becoming clear: parts of both urban and rural environments are becoming less hospi- table as repositories for the realization of ideal human values. There is frustration in the city because of crowding, air pollution, noise, filth, trans- portation tie-ups, and a multitude of other assaults on the senses; the es- cape to the country, or residence therein, is often equally frustrating be- cause existing rural populations and institutions are not prepared to deal with the influx.

The basis and requirements for systematic rural planning are therefore in need of articulation, as a means of applying what we understand *and* as a supporting mechanism for rural enhancement. Enlightened planning for rural regions, accompanied by vigorous development guidance tools, could help reverse the negative trends.

However, it is most difficult for planning and guidance to occur when there is limited public knowledge about planning organization or process and few well-conceived guidelines for effective action. Planning for rural regions is primitive indeed as a body of integrated concepts; it seems very much in order to begin systematizing and generating new knowledge, filling knowledge gaps, testing applicability of planning concepts in varied circum- stances, training citizens and professionals in use of the knowledge, and developing planning institutions capable of systematically working toward preservation and improvement of the rural environment.

Rural Planning: Definitions and Dimensions

In its broadest sense, planning can be defined as the process of identifying the complex of factors which contribute to the creation, change, or devel- opment of a social and/or physical entity (i.e., community, region, business, etc.); studying the interrelationships and interactions of those factors in terms of their relative or specific influences; determining as precisely as possible the degree to which a specified unit of change in any one factor contributes to change in one or more other factors; predicting how changes in one factor ought to be made so that future society will achieve an im- provement in human welfare without destruction or deterioration of the life-support system (environment) on which later generations must depend;

(a)

Figure 1-1 Changing rural America. The deserted farmstead is one of the chief symbols of change in rural America. Agriculture was long the principal occupation of rural residents; it will continue to serve as the principal use for large expanses of land, but now directly employs only a very small proportion of the total rural population. New industries and new land uses are converting the countryside into a vastly different and more complex socioenvironmental system. Systematic application of knowledge to these complexities, through a well-conceived planning and decision process, may be the chief device by which new opportunities are realized and destructive misuse of land and people is avoided. (a) Deserted farmstead. (b) Wenatchee, Washington, and vicinity (see next page). Wenatchee is sometimes characterized as the Apple Capital of the World and serves as a major regional center for rich agricultural, recreational, lumber, and mineral-extraction activities in north-central Washington. (*Washington State University, College of Agriculture photos.*)

(b)

finally, acting on these predictions to achieve a more satisfactory human and physical-biological system.

A general model of the role planning can play in ecosystem mainte-nance is displayed in Figure 1-2. This conception assumes that the basic

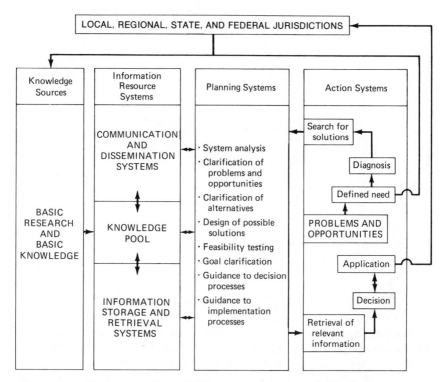

Figure 1-2   The role of planning in social and ecological system maintenance.

rationale for planning is to facilitate the systematic application of knowledge to establishing and achieving publicly defined goals. Planning becomes the linking mechanism and the series of processes which help to assure that information will be applied to action projects. It also assumes that much existing scientific or experience-based knowledge is not directly translatable by the potential users into usable forms. Knowledge is often "stored" without useful application. (The planning content and process as briefly illustrated in Figure 1-2 is elaborated in greater detail as the major thrust of Chapter III.)

Figure 1-3 illustrates in somewhat more simplified fashion the potential relationship of planning to knowledge sources and the various dimensions of government activity—such as policy and decision formation, coordination of various program activities toward common goals, monitoring and measuring program activities, facilitating design of better systems for knowledge use, and evaluating the results of program applications. The complex relationships in the diagrams are fully discussed in later chapters.

The focus of rural planning activity includes all jurisdictions outside

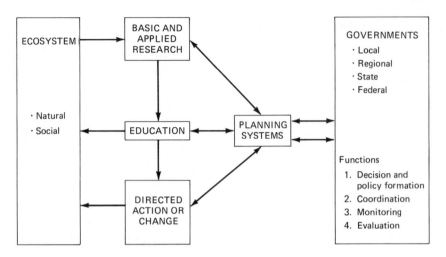

Figure 1-3 Planning linkages.

the incorporated limits of urban responsibility. Obviously, however, a high level of interaction exists between urban and rural populations and environments, particularly in proximity to urban areas; therefore, urban impact on rural environments must be a central input to rural planning. Technically, it might be appropriate to limit the size of "rural" towns to populations of 2,500 or 5,000, but such an arbitrary exclusion based on numbers gives too much weight to demographic factors when in fact other variables are often more important.

Need for an Improved Knowledge Base

An improved understanding of rural and regional planning is important if we are to help policymakers marshal the tools to deal systematically and rationally with the issues confronting rural territory and rural people in the United States and in other parts of the world. Literature is needed for instruction of students who have become conscious of the rural planning "problem" but who cannot find the courses nor professors to guide their learning. Scholars need direction and points of departure if they are to undertake the conceptualization process and devise research to test and verify concepts, while expanding the knowledge base. Professional practitioners need conceptual guidelines and tested knowledge on which to base their planning and action programs. Legislatures and government officials must have sufficient knowledge of rural planning to design and administer the rules by which it is undertaken. Finally, citizens must understand planning if they are to participate in its implementation and support taxation adequate to provide the professional staff, tools for developing plans, and resources to make planning functional.

The Slow Evolution

Rural planning has been slow to evolve in the United States, in part because the huge territory (and relatively sparse population) was able to absorb the assaults upon it without highly visible scars. More importantly, there has been a strong ideological bias against public or "government" infringement on private property rights. We have operated under the assumption that individuals can make better decisions about the use of the land than can government, and further, that collective decisions of landowners or controllers of land will result in improved total welfare. The social value systems have not been conducive to considering rural territory as a "public" good in danger of misuse by private decision makers. Only with the advent of serious pollution and environmental despoliation has this ideology of individualism begun to change, and then only to a very limited degree as yet in many rural locales.

In certain other parts of the industrialized world rural planning has been much more widely accepted. The Netherlands has been devising and implementing rules to maintain or increase the adequacy of rural land use for decades, with a continuing series of changes in direction as policies have been tested and proved faulty; more than half of the rural territory in the country has been "reconstructed" to increase the size of farm units and improve the physical system supporting more efficient land use. Development of the polders (reclaimed land from the sea) is probably the most highly organized and complete rural planning process in existence, although clearly a unique kind of enterprise in most respects (Hofstee, 1972; Constandse, 1972). Countryside planning in the United Kingdom is a long and honored tradition, although it has until recently been confined to physical planning of recreation areas or regions of great natural beauty. There is a clear consciousness among British political leaders, intellectuals, and much of the general public of the potential deterioration facing the countryside. In both the Netherlands and the United Kingdom this "consciousness" arises in part because of much more dense populations and greater pressure on rural territory than has existed in most parts of the United States (Wibberly, 1973; Clawson & Hall, 1973).

Implementation of planning for rural regions in the United States is made difficult by a second ideological perspective: a preoccupation with local control and autonomy. In most rural areas there has been no tradition of periodic evaluations of institutions affecting land, economic activities, social organization, or cultural traditions. Most human institutions have grown from historical tradition and are not part of any rational, long-range conception of what ought to be. There is relatively little experience with planning as a formal governmental process, and no widely acceptable institutional structure exists to support systematic public approaches to problem solving and preparation for the future. The requirement of compulsory plans for each level of governmental region, as is the case in many European and most socialist countries, is not generally understood nor accepted, although it is now required for many federally supported programs (Ditwiler, Lassey, & Barron, 1976).

Possibly of most crucial importance is the divergence between rural and urban populations on goal priorities. Physical and social planning is somewhat familiar to and accepted (if grudgingly) by many urban dwellers; in most rural areas, planning of land use and social institutions is largely foreign and appears to directly contradict the individualistic decision-making processes which many rural dwellers tend to idealize. In the urban setting, government officials usually understand the planning process with reasonable sophistication and find it an essential tool for effective governance; many rural government officials often do not understand even the basic rudiments of the planning process and are accustomed to thinking of their primary task as maintenance of some minimum level of services, with little mandate nor inclination to think systematically about the desirable future character of their domain.

Many state, regional, and federal planners assume that "rural" planning can easily be derived from standardized urban or regional planning approaches. However, the character of rural territory and populations suggests this is inappropriate; rural planning may require a radically different conception and approach. For example, urban planning usually assumes systematic and condensed or compact growth of the constructed physical environment, while rural planning must often contend with declining population, widely scattered growth, and creation of new towns based on specialized industries, such as recreation or natural resource development. The knowledge, institutional structures and constraints, and required resources are different in many respects from that which is familiar to most professional urban or regional planners. Trained "urban" planners who move into a rural situation are often frustrated and ineffective because they are unable to apply the sophisticated concepts that fit the urban setting. To be effective, they feel a need for additional understanding of rural society, institutions, and environment.

The Urban Bias
The most prestigious professional planning association in the United States, the American Institute of Planners, has helped to achieve a major increase in the sophistication of planning since its inception in 1916. However, when visionary planners discuss planning priorities, they do so almost exclusively in terms of the urban environment and the constructed or adapted physical components of it. The rural regions have not (at least until very recently) been overtly recognized as having distinctively different characteristics and planning requirements.

The consequence of this urban bias has been a serious neglect of professional preparation for planning in rural regions. This situation is further aggravated by the tendency to divide the rural environment into sectors—such as agriculture, forest, water, parks, etc.—with very little provision for an adequate overview of how the total rural ecological system functions as part of an interrelated whole *and* in the context of the various human populations inhabiting (either permanently or temporarily) each of the sectors.

Predominance of Concern with Rural "Economic" Development

Most legislation at the federal and state levels contains implicit (or occasionally explicit) biases suggesting that the bulk of activity and funds ought to be focused on means to increase the economic viability and productivity of rural regions, so as to raise employment and income levels, thus stopping out-migration. Most research in agricultural experiment stations of the land-grant college system and the federal rural research establishment has (at least until very recently) been focused on finding higher-yielding products, better means to control weeds and insects, or the development of more refined economic criteria for improving agriculturally oriented government agencies; this may be both expected and appropriate. However, the consequences of such policies have in some respects been perceived as inappropriately directed (Hightower, 1972).

The development of agricultural technology has been among the most spectacular achievements of the American system and has contributed to highly significant improvements in food production throughout the world. (Figure 1-4 illustrates some of the agricultural research processes which have been developed to implement rural agricultural development.) Such achievement cannot be criticized on the basis of ill intent. However, the consequences for many rural people in the United States and abroad have been decrease in welfare, decline of communities, and migration to locations where displaced skills can be applied only at menial tasks; *or* rural out-migrants are required to radically change their occupational proclivities through retraining.

Rural development policies have often served to concentrate land and wealth in the hands of fewer individuals who have acquired the management skills and resources to use the new technology to its optimum. Such individuals tend to operate much like successful business executives, ranging far outside the local community to seek the lowest cost inputs and highest prices for outputs; this often means that the small town entrepreneur, who formerly supplied inputs and purchased outputs, gets bypassed on both ends of the marketing process.

Of greatest concern (for purposes of this analysis) is the failure of rural programs to design and implement functional and future-oriented rural

(a)

Figure 1-4 Agricultural research. Agricultural research programs of land-grant universities have contributed substantially to improvement of productivity in rural areas. The research emphasis in recent years has shifted to include a broader range of rural issues. However, additional programs of research may be needed which deal more comprehensively with rural planning and development than has so far been the case. (a) Walt Hendrix checks wheat growing in a greenhouse at Washington State University. Dr. Hendrix is a plant pathologist at the university. (*Washington State University, College of Agriculture photo.*) (b) Dairy cattle research center at Washington State University. (*Photo by W. R. Lassey.*) (c) Experiments with dairy cattle feeding. (*Photo by W. R. Lassey.*)

(b)

(c)

planning institutions. The potential value of more deliberate linkages between planning and development activities in urbanizing or declining rural regions now seems eminently clear. The assumption of need for "economic growth" as the basic priority may be replaced by public values focused on the long-term suitabilities of land, resources, and rural institutions.

Per capita income criteria as measures of human welfare and development level may be increasingly inappropriate as levels of public service increase (such as universal medical service and other forms of social security); standards of living measured in monetary income terms are often misleading. This issue is illustrated forcefully in certain European countries (such as the Netherlands) where income levels are somewhat lower than in the United States: because many services are now publicly provided or guaranteed, the visible evidence of low or poverty-level living standards is almost nonexistent, while in the United States deprivation is highly visible. The conservation and care of resources is much more persistent and effective in countries such as Denmark and the Netherlands, where a very high proportion of material inputs to well-being must be imported. Likewise, the proportion of national income expended to maintain ecological balance, and to repair intrusions on the environment, is substantially higher than in resource-rich nations such as the United States and the Soviet Union.

The Ecological Basis of Planning

Concern with "ecosystem" as a basis for planning is now very much in vogue, particularly in reaction to recent literature on the impending doom of the universe if ecological "laws" continue to be disobeyed (Commoner, 1971; Meadows et al., 1972). A wealth of books, articles, and television documentaries has served to highlight the potential destruction of the life-support system on which we depend for survival.

Studies have been undertaken to document the damage under way in agricultural areas as a consequence of ignorance in the use of chemicals; stream pollution has occurred from livestock feed yards; despoliation of vegetative cover, air quality, and water quality has been caused by recreation in rural locations. Research projects of major proportion are under way in nearly every field of academic endeavor to further document damage and to search for a better understanding of the requirements for ecological balance. In fact, the evidence of imbalances is already sufficient to make environmental impact studies essential for any major disturbance of the rural landscape. Ecological balance requires an exchange between ecosystem components: animal life, plant life, and physical or inorganic elements. Human activity has had a profoundly upsetting impact on the balance of exchange because we have failed to appreciate the limitations of these natural processes.

Much of the damage resulting from inappropriate applications of technology is a consequence of misunderstanding or lack of knowledge about human and nonhuman systems. However, it becomes increasingly clear that the tendency to damage the physical-biological environment results in major part from lack of sufficient understanding about how to reorganize human systems to guide behavior in less destructive directions. It is common practice for us to constantly reorganize nonhuman systems—to increase productivity of food plants, to improve the weight-gain of livestock, or to increase the heat productivity of coal—but application of comparable scientific and technical skills to human organization is still an underdeveloped enterprise.

The Need for Adequate Goals

Part of the basis for predominant emphasis on economic and physical elements of rural development arises from a limited image of what we want the future of rural people and rural regions to be (Groot & Dusseldorp, 1970). The goals have seemed to focus on increased productivity in agriculture, more industries in rural areas to employ displaced residents, more physical amenities in small towns and on farms, improved services to small town and rural people, and of late, avoidance of pollution. A potential goal arises from the massive problems of managing large urban concentrations: the need for decentralization of population and industry.

Explicit and operational goals are needed if we are to solve rural problems and realize the potential of rural regions. Maintenance of open space, preservation of wilderness or primitive areas, preservation of national parks, avoidance of agricultural pollution, avoidance of subdivision proliferation, and avoidance of ill-conceived recreation or second home developments are each readily accepted at the national and state levels. But locally, the acceptance and implementation of such goals runs headlong into special interests and value conflicts which engender vociferous and powerful opposition, often most vigorously from the local officials who would presumably be responsible for implementing the goals.

Although much of the rural American countryside remains unspoiled (see Figure 1-5), adequate policies and goals must be developed to avoid wanton misuse and arbitrary development. The following list is not intended to be exhaustive, but rather suggests some of the major values which are derived from the countryside, and which a high proportion of citizens might accept as desirable ends.

1 *Preservation of ecological integrity so as to provide a continuing supply of life-supporting resources*: We are in danger of seriously damaging or destroying the life-giving processes on which we depend for survival. These processes occur primarily on rural land and involve complementary resources: vegetation, water, and air. It is crucial that we discover what must be done to assure continuing renewal of the essential ecological processes

(a)

(b)

(c)

Figure 1-5 Rural countryside. The countryside remains largely unspoiled in much of rural America. Increasing population and urbanization place heavy pressures on public and private property owners to convert land to other uses, unless policies and rules are established to assure that arbitrary and destructive development is avoided. (a) Wheat-growing country in the Palouse Hills of eastern Washington. (*Washington State University, College of Agriculture photo.*) (b) Dairy farms and timbered hills of western Washington. (*Washington State University, College of Agriculture photo.*) (c) Rural residence in northern Idaho. (*Photo by W. R. Lassey.*)

and proceed systematically and vigorously to undertake the necessary preserving or enhancing actions.

    2 *Efficient and appropriate land use*: Rural land now tends to be used according to the individual interests and tastes of its owners, even though it might be much better suited for some other use. As land and associated resources become increasingly scarce, the larger society has a greater stake in assuring that land is not misused for private gain to the disadvantage of present and future generations. The geological foundations, topography, underground and surface water, soil conditions, vegetation, and other factors have much to do with best potential uses of land. It should be possible to develop basic rules to circumscribe what should and should not be done with certain kinds of land.

    3 *Healthy living conditions*: The healthfulness of living conditions is obviously very much related to ecological integrity; a constructed physical environment is required which minimizes the dangers of physiological and mental disease and maximizes the potential for comfort and security of home and family. The present tendency is often to dispose of waste in such a manner as to preserve health and sanitation in our immediate surroundings, while seriously polluting the land and water which surrounds us—thus decreasing global health conditions. Healthy living conditions in the broadest sense must include the total environment which we affect.

4 *Aesthetically pleasing environment*: Aesthetic tastes of individuals vary widely. Yet most of us can differentiate degrees of beauty in natural and in constructed physical environments. We can define differences in purity of air, levels of noise, and in general attractiveness of the landscape. Given a choice between the noise of jet engines and the quiet of a deep forest, a fair proportion of the population would probably opt for at least occasional opportunities for the latter. Given a choice between a roadside on which billboard advertisements entirely hide the landscape and a rolling countryside with occasional farmsteads, a fair proportion of people would probably prefer fewer billboards. The general tendency in a technologically oriented society has been to put up with noise and billboards, as well as other aesthetically displeasing actions, in the interest of economic gain. Such values must be profoundly reexamined if our taste for an aesthetically pleasing environment is to be fulfilled.

5 *Effective social, economic, and governmental institutions*: The created institutions which serve rural areas are often inadequate or obsolete—if census statistics and studies of rural areas are sufficiently indicative. Health and welfare services are of substantially lower quality and more scarce in many rural areas than in urban places. Local government at the county and small town level is often less efficient, sophisticated, and effective as compared with governments in urban places and at state and federal levels. Most citizens would probably prefer improved functioning of the institutions responsible for guiding social, economic, and governmental activity.

6 *Improved human welfare*: The American goal has seemed to be "maximum" welfare for those who could effectively compete in the economic system as it has evolved. The concept of improved human welfare as currently interpreted suggests there should be some minimal economic and social level below which no human being would be allowed to live. Recent tendencies in federal and state legislation indicate that we are searching for a standard which provides a minimal right to health care, food, housing, and other basic physical needs, while encouraging those more fortunate individuals to achieve higher levels of affluence.

7 *Physical structures and adapted landscape of pleasing design*: This goal is obviously very much related to items 3 and 4 above, or might be considered an extension of them. It has been immensely disturbing to many individuals when forests are destroyed, soil piled in huge spoil banks from mining, or streams interrupted by structures or activity which is offensive to vision and often destructive to ecological integrity. A countryside in which structures are unique and interesting, where open scars are avoided, and where careful efforts are made to construct attractive spaces is probably considered desirable by a high proportion of citizens.

8 *Comprehensiveness*: If all major factors affecting human impact on the environment are to be considered in planning, a comprehensive or holistic viewpoint is necessary. National and state policies on air and water pollution are steps in this direction and seem to be well received by most citizens, but clearly, comprehensiveness of planning needs to include the full range of physical, biological, and human factors in rural regions.

Objectives of This Analysis

The following chapters attempt to develop an overview of the status of rural planning as a subject of research, education, and action; more specifically the intention is to:

1 Summarize and critique: the existing status of rural regions; social, economic, and ecological problems related thereto; recent efforts in rural development; and rural planning as a potential constraint on misuse of rural territory and society.

2 Examine organizational, methodological, and implemental schemes and processes, in a search for effective tools through which well-conceived planning can be translated into guidance systems, so that the fundamental objectives of rural planning can be realized.

3 Conceptualize tentative models, processes, and structures for regional, area, county, and local planning.

4 Review selected international, national, state, and local experiences with rural planning, in search of effective efforts which might be emulated.

5 Outline the process and potential content of educational programs for citizens, policymakers, administrators, and professionals in rural planning.

6 Finally, outline an adapted model for rural planning organization and process, while also emphasizing research needs that will help to generate additional critical knowledge for testing the model and increasing the knowledge base that could lead to more effective rural planning.

Chapter II

Key Issues:
A Rationale for Rural Planning

Many of the issues which lead to a rationale for rural planning have been briefly noted in the introductory chapter. The purpose here is a more detailed discussion of underlying problems, explanations of why rural planning has often failed, and a suggested rationale for development of a more adequate planning system. Understanding of the issues is a necessary background for appreciating the pervasive obstructions and difficulties in the implementation of a useful rural planning system.

Urbanization of Land and Society

The persistence of urbanization has been one of the clearest and most significant social, economic, cultural, and political changes of our time. It has altered the life-style and the welfare of millions of people, often for the better, but too often has created rural and urban ghettos with questionable improvement in life quality (see Figure 2-1). The persistence of mobility toward the city is now easing, and clear indications of increases in rural population within certain regions are now evident (Beale, 1975). Although urbanization might be counted as advantageous to members of rural society who remain behind or who migrate to rural areas—in fact, the process of urbanization has removed part of the population and tax base for provision of services. Loss of people, particularly the young and affluent, weakens the remaining social-economic-cultural-political structure in sparsely settled areas; meanwhile various and profound impacts coming from urban sources cause a multitude of adjustment problems with which rural institutions are not readily prepared to cope.

Increasing affluence, improved transportation mechanisms of many kinds, and apparent increasing tendencies of urbanites to use leisure time for escape from the city have caused tremendous pressure on rural environments for leisure and recreation space. Those with sufficient resources are buying up country property at a vigorous rate, while those with less ability to purchase are seeking space for campers or habitation of other kinds in nearly every attractive locale that can be approached (Price, 1972). Wealthy individuals and large companies are acquiring huge blocks of rural territory for long-term investment, as tax sanctuaries, for executive relaxation, and for further subdivision or other kinds of development. This phenomenon has not been fully documented, but examples abound in all parts of the least urbanized areas of the United States.

The proportion of Americans owning second homes increases annually; the second home often occupies more space, but is under less intensive use, than the first home. If it were not for the boom in mobile campers—purchase of which has absorbed an extremely high proportion of disposable income among increasing numbers of families in many industrialized countries—the pressure for purchase of rural property for second homes would quite likely be much greater.

The camping phenomenon leads to another kind of urban impact—the unfortunate tendency of many temporary users to treat rural areas as sewers and dumping grounds, particularly when such areas are ill-equipped for regular garbage disposal and purification of sewage. A dramatic example is the inability of some national parks to dispose of the sewage and waste from an increasing number of visitors; Glacier National Park officials have resorted to trucking or "muletraining" sewage or solid waste out of many parts of these magnificent natural areas. Although the problem is in focus and under careful consideration by park officials, as yet no clearly discernible solution is available to control or alleviate these problems for areas not under federal or state control. As the public locations overflow, the pressure on private providers of space increases, but often without the kind of long-range planning and financing that is possible (if not fully implemented) when rural territory is under state or federal control.

Conventional behavior patterns in the urban environment are often highly inappropriate for visitors to the rural scene; for example, the tendency to acquire and casually toss away numerous metal and plastic containers

Figure 2-1 Rural housing subdivisions. New housing subdivisions in rural areas are constantly under development, sometimes with adequate guidance and control, but often otherwise. Many beautiful wooded settings are destroyed by wholesale bulldozing of trees and soil to minimize the cost of development, at the expense of visual amenities. The new developments often use individual sewage disposal and water systems which prove inadequate as the development expands; introduction of sewer and water systems after initial construction, particularly if the development is remote from existing utility systems, can be enormously expensive to taxpayers in the responsible local jurisdiction. (*Photos by W. R. Lassey.*)

creates only modest problems when technology and personnel are available for collection and disposal, but it becomes a landscape blight of major proportion in remote areas. Rigid controls may be necessary for protection of all natural phenomena—plants, birds, animals, air, water, and the combination of these that makes them aesthetically pleasing—if these delightful amenities are to survive the human tendency to pull, shoot, touch, burn, dump, and generally ignore the wonders of nature.

Pollution and despoliation by urban or rural visitors to the countryside are a consequence of many factors other than deliberate inattention to ecological issues. Sheer numbers of automobiles, people, and accompanying technological devices add to air, noise, visual, and often serious water pollution. Facilities for dealing with these sources of despoliation are often not adequate, in part because consciousness of consequences has not sufficiently progressed. Private recreation entrepreneurs do not generate enough income on a seasonal basis for investment in the expensive control procedures that may be necessary—and local officials do not have the legal means (nor often the commitment) to force compliance to standards that will prevent environmental deterioration. The institutional and legal structures, funds, and processes of public education have not developed sufficiently (in most regions of the United States) to treat the problems with reasonable effectiveness.

Another urban impact of increasing significance in the more aesthetically pleasing rural areas is the overwhelming proliferation of rural subdivisions. Huge quantities of land have been removed from productive use (for agriculture, forestry, etc.) and converted for real estate speculation; a high proportion of the lots sold will not be occupied at all for many years, while other parcels will be "visited" for only a few days per year at best. Such subdividing activity is largely under the control of developers, often with minimal requirements for sewage disposal and sanitation, and with high potential for profits. One increasingly popular use of this land is the establishment of mobile home parks (see Figure 2-2), but careful planning is also needed here to provide the most propitious use of the rural landscape. It should be noted with emphasis, however, that many developers have assumed high risks and have in numerous instances been left holding the proverbial "bag," often to great public, as well as private, disadvantage.

A rationale for improved rural planning does not arise simply as a mechanism to increase the welfare of current rural residents. The urban outthrust is a national phenomenon likely to increase; unless its consequences are understood in great depth and detail and adequate planning and action are undertaken to add some vigorous measure of control, urban impact can only lead to a transfer of many of the highly visible problems of the metropolitan conglomerates to the rural locales, which already suffer from service inadequacy and despoliation of environmental amenities.

Industrializing Agriculture

The success of American agriculture in application of knowledge and technology to production of an abundance of relatively inexpensive food is surely one of the most impressive achievements in world history. Many agricultural scientists insist that maximum production is not yet in sight. (Figure 2-3 depicts some of the advances in machinery and specialization brought about by the industrialization of agriculture.) Agriculture services have become a major source of employment for some rural towns (Figure 2-4). With greater applications of technology, better management, and increases in scale, the potential for increased food production remains substantial, although energy and resource shortages could exert serious limits.

As technology and scale increase, the numbers of farmers and farm workers decrease. As farm population decreases, the communities which have depended on agriculture are depopulated, unless replaced by other business or industry. In many areas where agricultural land is the only natural resource of consequence, and distance to urban areas is substantial, population is likely to continue declining. The farmers and ranchers who remain on the land tend to be more successful and educated professional agriculturalists or individuals who are unprepared for any alternative vocation. The successful agriculturalists begin to identify with a "culture" and wider community that is not consistently supportive of those inefficient businesses and obsolete social institutions often found in small rural towns. The results are not difficult to visualize: small towns wither; young people (particularly the more capable) depart; services deteriorate or disappear; and a vicious circle ensues which is immensely destructive to many individuals and institutions.

Although the "ghost town" phenomenon has been with us for decades, we have not adequately understood the possible alternatives nor have we devised sufficient means to avoid the incidence of human casualty and environmental blight resulting from boarded up Main Streets; we seem to have assumed this to be a "natural" process and beyond our power as a civilized society to resolve. Federal programs designed to support agriculture have often only accelerated the difficulties (Hansen, 1970).

The National Farm Programs

Much of the federal attempt to deal with the problems of rural society has been channeled through a long series of special programs for farm commodities. These are illustrated particularly by the price-support programs for wheat, cotton, and other products for which there tend to be widely fluctuating market prices, depending on the supply level and nonmarket forces arising from public policy. Price supports are designed to stabilize incomes of farmers by protecting them to some degree from the price cycles. Such programs are also justified as a means to protect the so-called "family type farm" from absorption by larger "corporate" farms; price supports are also presumed to help stem the flow of out-migrants from agriculture.

However, decreases in numbers of farms and increases in farm size would seem to demonstrate that these programs have generally been to the greater advantage of larger and more efficient farm units. The overall impact appears to have encouraged major increases in productivity, through the application of increasing levels of technology and improved management. The smaller operators are less able to appreciate and finance the application of the new technology, and hence have steadily been compelled to leave their farms because of income inadequacies and failure to effectively compete.

The farm programs have become highly complex and involve a wide

Figure 2-2 Mobile homes in rural areas. Rural families are increasingly housed in mobile homes, in part because they are less expensive to purchase than an on-site constructed dwelling, but also because there is relatively little alternative housing available for new residents in rural communities. Mobile home parks of adequate design can be a comfortable and attractive situation, but lack of planning and control often leads to proliferation of mobile homes on the rural landscape without attention to aesthetic values. (*Photos by W. R. Lassey.*)

array of products and issues; but until recently they have been limited largely to the provision of assistance to individual operators and have not been directed toward alteration of the rural structures or institutions which might alleviate the stresses. Within the decade of the 1960s greater emphasis has been given to these latter issues, but with much less total investment than in the subsidy programs for individual producers. In the early 1970s the emphasis has shifted toward "rural development" in a broader sense than before—with less emphasis on farm residents and greater attention to the total complex of "rural" problems.

The proper emphasis and appropriate level of federal support for farm programs is a controversial issue—with direct consequences for, and applications to, rural planning efforts.

Subsidies, Revenue Sharing, and Rural Development

A major attempt to shift from a farm program emphasis to rural development in the broader sense is evident in the initiation of subsidies and

(a)

(b)

(c)

(d)

Figure 2-3 Industrializing agriculture. Agriculture is undergoing massive changes, as a consequence of advanced technology and industrialization of production. Large machinery and specialization have led to vastly decreased labor needs for food production but have also created major problems for rural towns. They have led to chemical pollution problems, erosion, and a variety of other environmentally destructive results. Environmental protection programs are in process to alleviate some of the problems, but these have tended to be piecemeal rather than arising from a broadly based planning perspective. (a) Crawler tractor spreading chemical fertilizer. (*Washington State University, College of Agriculture photo.*) (b) Sprinkler irrigation systems. (*Washington State University, College of Agriculture photo.*) (c) Ranch headquarters. (*Photo by W. R. Lassey.*) (d) Beef cattle in a 10,000-head feedlot. (*Photo by W. R. Lassey.*)

Figure 2-4 Agricultural services. Service to agriculture is a major source of employment in many rural areas. It provides the principal source of income and is the only basis for survival of many small towns. Many businesses are highly specialized in providing a single service to a large number of specialized farmers, such as crop spraying, purchase and storage of grain, or sale of farm equipment. (*Photos by W. R. Lassey.*)

revenue sharing to help rural communities improve certain basic services. There is much greater emphasis on "area" or "regional" approaches to rural development, as contrasted with earlier concentrations on "community development."

Since these programs are relatively new (as of 1976), they have yet to produce sufficient experience and results for reasonable evaluation. But the change in emphasis is a highly significant development and could deal much more broadly with rural problems than the farm programs described above.

Subsidies for medical facilities, sewer and water systems, maintenance of public transportation opportunities, housing programs, and other such support for rural areas have allowed some improvement in well-being with only modest investment of local tax funds; however, it must be quickly noted that such efforts have had only a marginal impact on maintenance of population and other services in many locations where the opportunities for productive employment have failed to develop. A variety of special programs for particularly depressed areas has been attempted, in some instances with considerable apparent success, i.e., resource conservation and development projects, economic development districts, and community action programs. But it seems quite clear that no adequate formula for reversing the negative effects of technology in agriculture, forestry, and mining has yet been discovered (Williams & Lassey, 1973).

Revenue sharing and the 1972 Rural Development Act are too new for any clear impact trends to have emerged. But both sets of policies are likely to have profound effects on the financing and support for rural services— since they require a new evaluation of local government decision-making processes and involve federal, state, and local government in new relationships (National Academy of Sciences, 1974). Revenue sharing provides funds to local governments which can be used to speed up the provision of traditional physical additions (roads, buildings, etc.), to expand social services, or to initiate innovative actions. The Rural Development Act expands the loan support for rural industrialization, community facilities, and other activities which could enhance the economic or social well-being of rural communities. The Act changes and expands the participation of the federal government in programs for improvement of soil and water quality and environmental conditions in rural areas. The intent of the act is to expand extension and research programs of land-grant universities toward solving rural development problems or searching for improved opportunities in rural areas.

Agricultural Land-Use Changes

Apart from the impact of changes in agriculture, there are a number of issues specifically related to agricultural land use toward which rural planning might be directed. Consolidation of farms and ranches has been under way since the very inception of land settlement, but often without any systematic pattern that increases the probabilities of better land use and improved productivity without damage to the environment. Many marginal farms remain in operation, and there is no assurance that the perpetuation of inefficiency and underemployment of marginal farmers will be halted.

As noted earlier, the large firms or wealthy individuals who continue to purchase large tracts of agricultural land are not necessarily committed to improving land use or productivity, but often invest in land for reasons which may not be in the long-range best interest of the local communities, the larger society, or ecological well-being. In fact, the land consolidation pattern is somewhat contradictory to values considered as central to democratic societies and indicates movement in the direction opposite to land reform efforts in many land-poor nations. The large firms or individuals with excess wealth are able to purchase land because they offer prices which are often inflated (by local standards) and which make purchase increasingly difficult for "legitimate" farmers or ranchers; high interest costs, increasing prices for most agricultural inputs, and the generally low return for agricultural labor as compared with other occupations make purchase of land for agricultural production a high-risk situation for individuals who must secure sufficient income to make mortgage payments while maintaining a reasonable standard of living.

These issues suggest the need to consider alternatives to the present system of land ownership—which generally places extraordinary emphasis on private land ownership rights. Many countries have instituted restrictions on use of particular kinds of land, have limited size of units, and are working at consolidation to achieve more viable agricultural units (notably in socialist countries, but including the Netherlands and the United Kingdom, *all* land is subject to public planning). In any case, it need not be assumed that the system of land ownership rights (at least as these rights have historically developed in the United States) is necessarily the optimum arrangement for the long-range interests of existing owners or the public (McEntire, 1972; Hofstee, 1972).

Alteration of ideological traditions surrounding land ownership rights will not be an easy process. Emotional attachment to land is a powerful force in most rural areas. Changes in the system may impose restrictions on freedom to profit from changing uses of land, which would also obviously interfere with freedom to sell land to the highest bidder, regardless of intended use.

Problems of the Small Rural Town

As general public affluence increases, we are becoming increasingly conscious of the unfortunate plight of citizens in declining small towns. The sons and daughters of older residents have often departed for distant places where jobs are more plentiful. The few businesses that do remain on Main Street in many of these small towns (Figure 2-5) survive because of their social function. The country store (Figure 2-6) sometimes remains as a center for everyday needs. The very services which become more crucial to the remaining (and aging) population—such as medical care, public transportation, modern housing, and stimulating and time-occupying activities—often tend to deteriorate or become accessible only at some distance and at relatively high cost. The problems of aged citizens are only one example among many other small town social issues (Hahn, 1970).

The difficulties of dealing with rural towns are a consequence, in part, of the increasing influence of external forces on local decision alternatives. As technology and scale increase, both within and apart from agriculture, there is a powerful tendency for political impact of larger urban centers to increase, at the expense of influence by smaller and rural places; larger businesses, such as chain grocery stores and lumber dealers, are increasingly controlled from outside the small towns, and their owners have little concern for the locale where they buy or sell—so long as a profit is generated to the satisfaction of stockholders and executives. The logical consequence is decrease in the ability of rural communities to control their own

Figure 2-5 Main Street in small towns. Main Street in many towns consists primarily of post office, general store, and tavern. None of the businesses would survive, in many instances, if it were not for the social function they serve, particularly for older people in the community. Buildings are often dilapidated and landscaping minimal, particularly if the local economy suffers from declining employment and low incomes. (*Photos by W. R. Lassey.*)

destiny; the significant decisions which they *can* influence decrease, and those decisions which do occur locally become increasingly less relevant to the survival and viability of the community (Warren, 1972).

Many rural residents who are employed by larger firms exhibit relatively little commitment to the local community but, rather, devote their energies and abilities to the institution which employs them. The very people who are best educated, most cosmopolitan in outlook, and best prepared for leadership are often not willing to occupy their time with local affairs, when their economic and social rewards are controlled from elsewhere and when they are likely to move to a new location within a relatively short time.

Those residents who do maintain a strong commitment to the local area are often traditional and provincial and have the least understanding of the larger societal changes to which their community must adjust. The "leaders" are often local business people, professional people, or farmers who feel that the answers to their dilemma rest somehow in reversing the

Figure 2-6 The country store. The country store serves an important function in many rural communities, as a social center as well as a source of daily food and household needs. However, the income provided to the proprietor is usually so marginal that buildings tend to deteriorate and become a blemish on the landscape. The closed-up store is a common scene in many rural regions. (*Photos by W. R. Lassey.*)

trends or turning back the clock to some former ideal era when people seemed committed to the neighborly community.

The very idea of planning is often unacceptable to longtime small town residents because it smacks of "socialism" or threatens outside government control over local freedom of decision. The profound and dissonance-producing changes that may be necessary for local community survival, and which may involve new forms of community collaboration, restructuring of local government, and radical changes in marketing and service approaches, are regularly dismissed by local decision makers as impossible dreaming.

However, newer residents (and less traditional longtimers) often grasp at planning as a means to improve the physical and social facilities of the towns, while controlling—or at least modifying—the negative influences from nonlocal businesses, landowners, or higher levels of government. There seems to be an increasing number of rural residents, particularly new migrants, who seek escape from the even more unsatisfactory environment of the city and who recognize the possibilities for innovation and adaptation of business and institutional approaches. However, these progressive types often find that professional help and organizational resources are not available to do the necessary planning and feasibility testing—and they have a particularly hard time gaining the collaboration of local governments in using existing legal tools which might make a planned approach productive (Williams & Lassey, 1973).

Inadequacies of Local Government

Local government responsibility in rural areas, particularly at the county level, has been limited until recent years largely to construction and maintenance of physical facilities for the benefit of citizens. The county courthouse (Figure 2-7) serves as the center of government in most rural communities, and the decision-making bodies are usually elected county commissioners or supervisors. Part of the tradition includes the assumption that the elected local officials should be "amateurs"; that is, they should be public-spirited citizens, serving in a part-time capacity, and should respond to clear preferences expressed by a majority of citizens with whom they come in contact. Their pay should be low so that the primary reason for service in elected capacities is dedication to public well-being, rather than financial remuneration. Employees in local government offices are often appointed as part of a patronage system and are not always skilled in the assigned tasks. They are often paid less than the average wage in the community or county and learn their role through a process of on-the-job training.

In earlier times, when government at all levels was much less complex and was largely made up of well-intentioned and dedicated amateurs, this

Figure 2-7 The county courthouse, center of rural government. The county courthouse is the center of government for rural areas in most states. It is the usual headquarters for planning departments associated with county government. In some instances counties have adopted advanced planning methods, but more often the norm is minimal local government initiative in planning. (*Photos by W. R. Lassey.*)

approach functioned reasonably well. However, national and state governments are increasingly inhabited by officials who must be college-educated and who are reasonably well compensated; state and federal civil servants tend to be highly specialized professionals when compared with their local government counterparts. State governments have in many instances been slow to adjust and adapt, but pay scales and professionalization are increasing, although with wide variation between states.

Because small town and county governments have been in the backwater, so to speak, local officials find themselves at a severe disadvantage in attempting to collaborate, and on occasion compete, with the modernized structures of professionalized private enterprise; there is often a high degree of frustration and even strong feelings of helplessness among unprepared local politicians and officials (Williams & Lassey, 1973). The local reaction is often to resist changes recommended by higher level government officials out of fear that local "autonomy" will be lost; the consequence of such resistance is often abrogation of former local responsibilities to state, regional, or federal government, which further decreases local autonomy.

The mechanisms of local government are often not prepared to deal with the complexities of an urbanizing rural society. Management systems (such as record keeping) are often archaic and inefficient; because of low pay scales and demanding time requirements, well-qualified people will not usually contest for local elective offices.

Although notable exceptions are on occasion evident, the inadequacies of local government are in major part responsible for failures of attempts at locally initiated rural planning. The small town and rural constituency does not generally have sufficient confidence in elected and appointed officials to place planning responsibilities in their hands. Moreover, local officials often try very hard to guard against encroachments on their power by higher levels of government; the consequence is often a standoff in which no significant planning occurs and obsolescence abounds. Since local government pay scales, taxing power, and legal responsibilities are usually defined by state legislation, the difficulties of local government often rest on the doorstep of shortsighted state legislatures.

Positive adjustment is certainly occurring in many localities, but the basic characteristics of rural government as described above remain largely intact throughout most of the United States. Yet this level of government maintains primary decision responsibility for planning in rural regions. Because these responsibilities are so often abrogated, state and federal government have assumed the initiative for many former local government functions, including the more advanced approaches to planning.

Local government inadequacies are partially overcome, in some instances, by the formation of "area" or "regional" councils of government or development organizations which can combine resources, or secure state or

federal grants, to hire full-time professional staff with assigned responsibility for planning and development functions (Williams & Lassey, 1973).
Recent legislation in a few states has increased the funding capability and
power of local governments and widened their sanctioned responsibilities.
The changes are nevertheless extremely slow when compared to the rapidity
of change and the pressure of urban impacts on rural territory. At the
present pace, it is uncertain whether increasing federal and state assumption of planning responsibilities should be avoided if the problems are to be
dealt with prior to further irrevocable damage to rural environments.

Obsolescence of Rural Institutions

Apart from local government, many other rural institutions have been very
slow to adapt. Health services have modernized very slowly, while population shifts have altered the location of client groups; this has often meant
extreme difficulty in securing qualified medical personnel who are willing
to practice medicine in rural areas away from highly developed medical
technology (McBroom, 1971).

As briefly noted earlier, provisions for reasonable and adequate attention to the needs of aging citizens, who are an increasing proportion of the
population in most rural areas, have been very slow to evolve. The county
"old folks home" or privately operated nursing homes are a pathetic and
disgraceful institution in many American communities; but these are often
the only alternative for elderly citizens, who have been somewhat abandoned as a consequence of changing traditions in family structure, particularly if they do not have the income to provide for themselves in more
modern nursing homes or retirement communities.

Although it is increasingly evident and endlessly documented that lifelong and individualized education is essential for effective adaptation to a
rapidly changing occupational structure, local communities in rural areas
are generally making only meager efforts to provide new educational opportunities. The cooperative extensive service and community colleges are
responding to some of the needs. But in many states the extension service is
staffed largely with agriculturists and home economists whose training has
prepared them primarily for servicing the increasingly smaller proportion of
the population actually engaged in agriculture or the more affluent rural
population. Community colleges often do not have adequate resources to
serve the rural (and particularly, the low-income) populations. Local high
schools occasionally provide evening courses, usually oriented to hobbies or
leisure pursuits.

Community colleges, vocational-technical schools, and universities offer evening and continuing education courses on an occasional and unsystematic basis. These efforts usually reach only a very small proportion of

the rural population, most of whom are in the least serious need of advanced approaches to educational opportunity; that is, it is most often the middle- and upper-income individuals who take advantage of the opportunities offered, while the least-prepared citizens cannot afford the fees or transportation and are not attracted by the classroom-lecture approach to learning. Exceptions to these generalizations can readily be noted, but only in a limited number of innovative examples.

Natural Resource Depletion

Despoliation of rural areas through mineral or timber extraction has been a recurring theme in many parts of the world as zealous and wasteful methods deplete the supply. In most instances, measures have not been taken to restore the physical and biological system to a state of attractive balance. The consequences are profoundly visible and depressing to anyone who has visited strip-mining areas of Appalachia or Montana, or a clear-cut and eroded mountainside. Erosion and stream pollution (Figure 2-8) are direct results of the unplanned use of natural resources. Although environmental impact regulations are evolving, there is little reason to believe that depletions will end unless further strong measures are taken to alleviate the situation in affected rural areas.

Since it is usually possible to predict some years in advance that a transition from production to depletion will take place, adequate foresight might achieve the systematic redirection of resources, including possible alternate work activities, new uses for physical structures involved, maintenance of important social and other service functions for communities, and restoration of landscape. The investment in such preparation could in many cases avoid substantial waste of physical and human resources, while finding worthwhile new uses for rural territory, such as recreation or alternate resource-based industries.

Social and Economic Costs of Space

It is somehow assumed in much federal and state legislation that per capita costs of services ought to be uniform, regardless of the territory in which these services are to be delivered. Yet studies of service costs in urban and sparsely populated areas suggest strongly that there is wide disparity in per capita expenditure requirements for equivalent levels and quality of service. The major issues include: Do people in circumstances of sparse population deserve less or lower-quality service? Do they deserve to pay higher costs or be deprived of service? Should they be encouraged to migrate to locations where service quality and availability is more complete? Or should the public assume some responsibility for subsidizing more remote population groups to assure availability of resources in rural areas? The pattern of migration from rural to urban regions and from urban core areas to suburbs

Figure 2-8 Erosion and stream pollution. Erosion results both in removal of valuable top soil and in stream pollution but has been very difficult to control. Recent national legislation designed to control nonpoint water pollution may provide considerable incentive to control erosion, but will in all likelihood require major efforts to reward or chastise farmers as encouragement for using appropriate methods of control. Preservation of agricultural land, through avoidance of urban infringement or soil preservation, is one of the most significant rural planning issues of our time. (*Photos by W. R. Lassey.*)

suggests that more steps of this nature may be necessary if a more satisfactory level of population distribution is to be achieved (Dillman & Dobash, 1972).

Apart from the economic issues involved, studies have also revealed that substantial social-psychological "costs" of both population sparsity and density may occur. The incidence of mental illness, social disorganization, and general social or individual pathology seems to be higher than average, under both extremely sparse *or* extremely dense circumstances (Kraenzel, 1971). At the same time the availability and quality of services to inhabitants of these areas, and the inclination to use them, seems to be relatively lower (McBroom, 1971). Systematic planning to deal with some of these issues is well under way in urban areas but very slow to develop in rural regions (Sennet, 1972).

Leisure and Recreation

Reference has been made at several points in this discussion to the increasing relevance of leisure and recreational activities for rural regions. Many of the more picturesque parts of rural America (and the world) are becoming playgrounds for increasingly affluent populations. The workweek is shortening in many employment categories, and there is an increased capability to travel long distances for leisure activity. For example, it is now common for individuals and families to fly or drive a thousand or more miles for an annual week of skiing in the less crowded areas of the Rocky Mountain West. Another increasingly popular pastime is camping (see Figure 2-9).

A decline in the "work ethic," with replacement by a "recreation ethic," has been suggested by some observers (Toffler, 1970). This has made it acceptable to spend a higher proportion of income for recreation, while feeling less compelled to spend free time working around the house or expanding income through overtime work.

These converging forces make it clear that the demand for rural leisure and recreation space is growing at an increasing rate. Heavy pressure on facilities and severe damage to the environment are notable in many locations. Increased recreation in rural areas creates the problem of overuse of local, state, and national public and private natural resources (Figure 2-10). However, major attempts to avoid damage within particular developments are also evident, particularly in those instances where development of property is controlled by a single corporation or individual. But, there is often little or no provision for planning the protection of surrounding areas because organized means do not exist to deal with the problems involved (Williams & Gilchrist, 1973).

The potentially negative aspects of recreation development are often overemphasized, however; such developments represent a significant opportunity for well-ordered development of rural areas. Redesign and development could substantially improve the ecology and aesthetic quality of areas now devoted to marginal agriculture, lumbering, or mineral resource extraction. Recreational use could well be more productive and less damaging than a variety of alternative uses. Similarly, the removal of marginal mineral deposits might be much less profitable than long-term recreation development.

Some of the difficulties with seasonality of recreation can be overcome by greater attention to potential year-round activities. Innovations in this respect are notable in recent recreational developments (i.e., Big Sky of Montana; see Chapter XI). The pay scales in recreation enterprises have often tended to be low because of seasonality and easy availability of students in summer and winter to staff many resorts, and because the skills required are often minimal and easily learned; however, four-season recreation in which a variety of skills are required is changing this pattern (Blann, 1975).

A basic conflict between resource-extractive uses of land and recreational uses exists in many rural places. There is often a local resentment toward encroachment by outsiders, or recreation is not deemed a productive use of land if *any* other kind of production is possible. This conflict has by no means ended, but careful planning in some locations has done much to minimize the threat to existing rural interests and furthermore provides for the satisfactory wedding of existing and new recreational uses, to the great advantage of all concerned (see Chapter XI).

Transportation Systems

Inadequate transportation arteries are often a major impediment to rural development, while new forms of transportation often have profound development impact when citizens may prefer otherwise. The railroad, once the lifeline of transportation in America, has declined in status as other modes of transportation have come into use (see Figure 2-11). In the more remote and sparsely settled areas, costs of transport from producer to market often consume an inordinately high proportion of the total retail value of products, to the comparative disadvantage of natural resource–based agricultural and extractive producers. Likewise, the costs and efficiency of imports to such regions are high, thus raising costs of production. The continuing decline in rail service to many low-population regions is apparently necessary for the economic viability of railroads, but often causes significant decreases in competitiveness. Passenger traffic on railroads has declined steadily, in part because of increasing air and automobile travel, but also in significant degree because of absurdly poor service quality (particularly when American railways are compared to European systems).

Declining population in many rural regions tends to make bus, air passenger, and freight transportation systems marginal profit producers;

Figure 2-9 Camping in public forests and parks. National forests and state parks have become increasingly popular for camping and other outdoor recreation. Although modern motorized recreational vehicles are in vogue, tent camping remains highly popular with the hardier souls who like to be a bit closer to nature or who cannot afford the luxury of more modern equipment. Recreational planning is becoming of much greater significance, usually as part of comprehensive land-use plans by the U.S. Forest Service, Bureau of Land Management, other federal land management units, and state resource management agencies. (*Photo by W. R. Lassey.*)

Figure 2-10 Recreation in rural areas. Recreation in rural areas is an increasing source of both employment and problems. Local, state, and national parks in most locations are crowded during the heavy summer season and often do not have adequate facilities for control of waste disposal or management of visitors. Nonetheless, public use of recreation opportunities is likely to increase. Adequate planning may be essential if recreational uses of land and other resources are to preserve the amenities on which they are based, while being integrated with other economic and social activities in the communities impacted by recreation development. (*Photos by W. R. Lassey.*)

hence the remaining systems tend to be of low quality, be irregular, and charge high rates per passenger. For most types of industries—and for public institutions of all kinds where staff mobility is a key element of institutional service—regular, dependable, and relatively low-cost air transportation is considered essential. This factor alone militates against many kinds of development in rural areas and in fact often causes existing industries to close shop and move elsewhere.

Provision of public services is strongly influenced by transportation accessibility to specialized services in larger population centers. Professionals in medicine, education, law, social services, and many other fields hesitate to move to areas of low transportation quality because their work is made more difficult, while access to cultural and social amenities is limited.

Transportation is therefore a key part of the matrix in which many rural areas find themselves; communities are unable to secure good transportation systems because of low population and poor services and, because of poor transportation, are unable to improve services and increase jobs which would attract more population.

From the urban perspective, improved highways and high-speed public transportation have created new opportunities to enjoy the countryside. As noted earlier, this has placed tremendous pressure on accessible and attractive rural areas, while significant new rural development opportunities are provided. However, without careful forethought and systematic preparation, this contribution of transportation systems to rural opportunity could obviously be destructive over the long term.

Another issue receiving increasing attention is the tendency for planners and designers of transportation systems to cause the destruction of important elements of human, biological, and physical systems. Farms and towns are cut up by limited-access highways; systems of secondary roads that formerly facilitated local commerce and social life suddenly distort such activities in the interest of safety requirements imposed on new interstate or intercity highways. The tendency has been to leave planning of highways to engineers and highway department officials, who often have little comprehension of the havoc they may create in the process of producing high-speed throughways with minimal local access. Such control over the future of rural life, in the interest of a particular form of transportation, is of uncertain value to the long-term best interests of society. Airports and air transportation planning, based on the "needs" of airplanes rather than human values or the physical-biological environment, often provoke comparable criticisms.

Transportation facilities are using up increasing amounts of land and energy formerly allocated to other purposes. Thorough consideration of these and other issues could well lead to major restructuring of the patterns of rural and regional transportation systems.

Functional Specialization of Activities and Towns in Rural Areas

One of the major trends of our time is the increasing specialization of activities and roles at all levels of society. Knowledge has proliferated to such complexity that it is difficult to achieve excellence in professions or service without carving out a small segment of the whole (in the medical sciences, for example) and learning all the intricate details of that subspeciality. Service agencies of government have found it necessary to proliferate and specialize so as to deal at some depth (and, it is hoped, excellence) with specialized needs of population subgroups.

New types of population are entering rural areas for specialized purposes. The specialized company town (Figure 2-12) is typical, with its growth centered around the industry which provides its economic base. Functional specialization of communities is not new, but current manifestations are unique to the present era: towns based on recreation (often for all seasons of the year), "bedroom" residential towns from which commuting takes the family to other locations for work and education, and temporary

Figure 2-11 Rail transportation decline. Railroads served as the lifeblood transportation system for the early development of the United States but have fallen into a lesser role in serving the transportation needs of rural regions. Withdrawal of rail service has often been highly destructive to local economies, even though provision of the service was not economically profitable for the railroads. Public and private transportation planning for rural regions now must encompass airports, highways, helicopters, boats, and even animal transportation, as well as railroads. Energy shortages are likely to require increasing emphasis on public transportation, after years of increasing dependence on autos and trucks as the principal connectors to rural places. (*Photos by W. R. Lassey.*)

towns for resource extraction or construction. Mobile homes and modular public facilities make it possible to create the physical structure of a town with relative ease and at modest cost—*but* the creation of a social, political, and economic structure to fit this level of temporariness is much more difficult and is often largely neglected.

The functional specialization of communities in rural areas should logically be part of a larger scheme for population distribution and preservation or renewal of the ecological processes necessary to maintain and sustain improved life-support systems. This suggests that new towns located in presently rural environments must be planned and constructed on the basis of much more complex considerations than has usually been the case. The

knowledge and skill of the architect, engineer, and contractor must be inter-related with specialized wisdom from physical, biological, and social science professionals, as well as other related knowledge and skill areas (see Figure 3-1 and Tables 3-2 to 3-15).

Studies of new town development in Europe and the United States suggest that planning procedures for new or expanded communities in rural areas are still in their infancy in most locations (Strong, 1971; Clapp, 1971; Constandse, 1973). Nevertheless, many countries are creating new towns or totally transforming existing places, as a deliberate policy to slow the growth of urban centers, to disperse industry, or simply as a means of making more adequate use of land (as in the case of land reclaimed from the sea in the Netherlands). Whatever the basis for growth of new towns or the expansion of older places, it is increasingly clear that designing the physical environment without adequate and systematic attention to ecologi-cal-social-political-cultural-economic factors has been less than satisfacto-ry, particularly in terms of impact on the surrounding or remaining rural environment. The lumber industry (Figure 2-13) and the U.S. Forest Ser-vice have discovered that adequate planning is necessary to provide stabili-ty to communities based around this natural resource. The planning tradi-tion has been oriented primarily to redoing or supplementing existing systems and has not until recently given particular attention to the impact

Figure 2-12 Specialized company town. The specialized town is a continuing phenomenon, particularly when extractive industries such as lumbering or mining provide the principal economic base. In these circumstances most of the social and physical planning revolves around the requirements of the supporting industry, often with minimal involvement of higher levels of government and without benefit of contributions from professional planners. (*Photos by W. R. Lassey.*)

of implanting towns on rural territories. Small wonder that the rural people and governments have often reacted and resisted with alarm.

"New towns" provide a rare opportunity to apply knowledge derived from research and experience. New or expanded rural towns could have a high potential for producing more ideal human, biological, and physical conditions.

Legislative and Legal Inadequacies

It is in the development of a legislative and legal framework for rural planning that many European countries are well ahead of the United States. For example, in both the United Kingdom and the Netherlands, laws have been passed which require planning for *all* rural subdivisions. If a crisis or an opportunity arises which threatens the ecology or social well-being of an area, it is possible to move with due haste to correct the situation—without waiting for enactment of special legislative provisions—as is now often necessary in most states of the United States. The tendency in European coun-

Figure 2-13 The lumber industry. Lumbering is a major industry in many parts of rural America, particularly in the more remote and sparsely populated mountain areas. Timber harvesting and processing has often been environmentally and socially suspect. Logging has tended to seriously mar the landscape and has led to serious erosion and stream pollution. It has often contributed to instability of communities, because of changing demands for lumber and varying locations for lumbering operations. More recently the U.S. Forest Service and large lumbering companies have indicated increasing consciousness of the need to plan carefully for maintenance of the resource and thoroughly consider the future of the communities on which it depends. The development of regional plans for forested areas is now common practice for both public and private land. However, substantial improvements in the substance and process of planning may be essential to the assurance of an adequate future supply of the resource while improving the communities which are dependent on the industry for survival. (*Photos by W. R. Lassey.*)

tries is to establish a national pattern or framework, which must them be implemented by lower subdivisions of government so as to adjust the national guidelines to local uniqueness.

Since the consequences of planning are in most instances controversial, it is important to create legal mechanisms through which the offended individuals can be heard and their claims arbitrated; the possibility then exists for the public interest to finally predominate, rather than the occasionally narrow, sometimes selfish, and usually profit-motivated private interest. Because of the weakness of local government in many rural places, any issue which is likely to arouse significant controversy is often avoided, in part because effective tools are not available to resolve controversy, but also because the special interest groups which oppose formalized planning are often highly influential and can directly threaten the future of local politicians.

It therefore seems evident that legislative actions to increase the effectiveness of planning may be essential at three levels: federal statutes for issues that are clearly national in scope; state-level laws relating to issues that are primarily of concern to individual states; and local legislation for issues which are strictly local.

Incentives are needed to supplement existing control devices, such as zoning. More positive tools might include public compensation for significant damage to property values caused by new rules which result from sound planning. It may be necessary to assure compensation for noneconomic damage, such as conversion of a highly valued private hunting reserve to public use requiring open passage to reach a public recreation area. If reasonably just compensation for damages were assured, opposition to planning would probably diminish substantially.

The key requirement is that the legislative and legal base for planning result in effective action, so that planning studies which define the most appropriate uses of land or requirements for social well-being (or other elements which comprehensive planning should incorporate) have a high probability of implementation.

Financing

Since rural planning has been very much an occasional and unsystematic activity, few funding sources—the federal government, state legislatures, county governments, or others—have seen fit to provide continuous and adequate support. Were it not for support by the U.S. Department of Housing and Urban Development (HUD) through the comprehensive planning and assistance program (section 701), there would be very little financial support for planning of nonpublic rural areas. This lack of explicit financial underpinning is a clear signal that appreciation of the appropriate role of planning is limited, among citizens, leaders, and policymakers.

Various sources of support exist for rural development in selected areas, through the "Resource, Conservation, and Development Projects" funded through the Soil Conservation Service of the U.S. Department of Agriculture (USDA); other USDA agencies, such as the Cooperative Extension Service and the Farmers Home Administration, provide educational support or studies of housing and community facility needs. But each of these is a federal source, and local governments have shown relatively little interest in providing funds apart from modest cost-sharing for federally supported activities. When funds become short, planning activity is often one of the first programs to be cut, which again illustrates its relative lack of relevance for both citizens and public officials.

The Economic Development Administration (U.S. Department of Commerce) and the Office of Economic Opportunity have each provided planning funds for rural areas of high unemployment and low income, but with relatively little permanent participation or visible commitment from local or state sources. In both instances the "planning" is relatively short-range and is intended primarily to produce improved job capability and new employment opportunities, or the programs serve a "welfare" function for individuals marginally capable of moving into the job market. These two relatively major federal programs are only two among a large number of often shortsighted efforts, which appear to have contributed only marginally to the solution of endemic problems.

If rural planning is to proceed as a mechanism for dealing intelligently with a balanced approach to rural people and territory, a new or radically revised system of funding seems essential. This new scheme will require consideration of rural planning as an investment in the future, much like we are learning to think of education. Although education is much more visible to most of the population, it seems no more relevant to the future fulfillment of human potential and environmental enhancement than does careful attention to the rural environment in its role as the primary life-support system.

Thorough planning studies are expensive; however, shortcutting the completeness of investigation in the interest of cost savings can only lower the quality and utility of the planning process. Although federal sources of funds may well be necessary to support these costs, through revenue sharing or otherwise, it is quite clearly important for local levels of government to participate if they are to develop commitment and appreciation. Total reliance on local financing is likely to be inappropriate because of tax revenue constraints in areas of limited population, low per capita income, and low tax ideology, particularly in areas where planning is more crucial to avoidance of severe environmental despoliation. The need for rural planning is heavily a state and national concern in any case, particularly in the more urban states, and the more urbanized areas within states, which will receive major benefit over the long term.

Some combination of federal, state, and local financing—as is currently the case with many urban planning programs—may be the most workable formula, but this must clearly involve an educational process at each level so as to increase the appreciation and perspective about problems and limitations at each level. If planning as an approach is to be effective, it will surely require professionalization and continuity as well as money, if competent individuals are to be attracted, trained, and respected by citizens at all levels. This is not likely to happen if funding is sporadic and generally insufficient to achieve a high level of excellence.

Education for Rural Planning

Most individuals engaged in rural planning have had little or no specific professional preparation for work in rural regions. They enter the arena from a great variety of fields, often assuming that theirs is the most appropriate background for "managing" the rural planning process. Likewise, as noted earlier, there has been relatively little attention in most rural regions to educating the citizen public on the issues, procedures, and increasing relevance of rural planning for the future well-being of the planet.

First, it seems entirely clear that education for planning requires a strong focus on operationalization of a planning process and public participation model; numerous efforts to develop an appropriate generalized model have been produced (Chadwick, 1971; McLoughlin, 1969; Branch, 1966). Progress in theoretical development is evident. Secondly, rural planners need thorough exposure to theory and methods of ecological and social scientific research, as well as substantial preparation in environmental design. Because of the proliferation of knowledge in these areas, it becomes increasingly clear that the most effective and complete planning processes must involve a team of individuals with subspecializations that enable them to deal collaboratively with the intricacies of each major factor in the planning process. They must also have a broad capability to understand the larger dimensions of the process, and must know how to function as members of a team—often consisting of divergent and difficult personalities—which must collectively do the planning and implement action.

Very few academic programs now exist which approach this conception of rural planning education, although urban and regional planning schools in a few universities are making significant progress. Major effort and substantial resources will be required to implement effective programs.

A second kind of educational effort must effectively reach the nonprofessional officials and the citizen public. An American tendency is to assume that somehow the mass media and the general educational process will adequately accomplish this task. It seems quite clear to this writer that such an ad hoc process is not adequate. Rather, a carefully designed adult education program is needed to supplement what goes on in the formal academic environment and in the public media. Many efforts are now under way to provide "environmental" education programs to the public; these are often sponsored by universities or other educational institutions, and occasionally are organized by citizen groups of various complexions. Rural planning concepts ought to be incorporated in programs which attempt to increase internalized and action-oriented understanding of the total environment.

Citizens and public officials must understand the need for legislation to implement effective planning; they must understand the level of funding required and the investment-in-the-future nature of such funding; they must understand the implementation processes necessary to assure that worthy plans do not collect dust on musty shelves; and they must understand that professional planning knowledge and skills are necessary.

Obviously, much remains to be done in developing professional and citizen competencies for planning. A later chapter will attempt to explicate a more detailed design for both professional education and public education for planning.

Chapter III

Planning Elements
and Contributing Sciences

Effective planning must rest upon a firm knowledge foundation arising from science and experience. The encompassing ecological system approach to planning suggested in Chapter I becomes an initial basis for defining those substantive elements of knowledge which offer important contributions. The critical categories and conceptual relationships are outlined in Figure 3-1.

Tables 3-1 through 3-14 summarize both the range of subject matter areas or topics about which scientific or experience-generated information will usually be necessary and the interrelating, projecting, decision-making, and implementing categories usually required for adequate planning. Physical and biological factors are discussed first, followed by institutional, design, and development issues; the priorities suggested here assume the need for understanding of ecological systems, and social-cultural-political-legal-economic institutions, as a basis for environmental or institutional design and development. Figure 3-2 depicts natural areas whose unspoiled beauty can be preserved if their qualities and characteristics are defined as essential for human and ecological values.

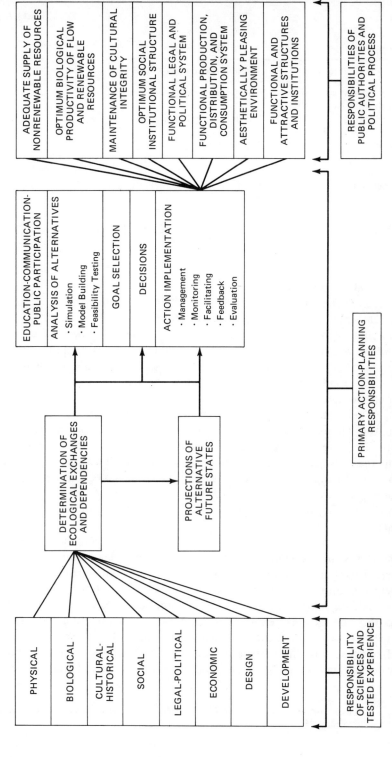

Figure 3-1 Conceptual relationships among planning elements and processes.

Table 3-1

Physical factors	Relevant knowledge/skills
Surface and subsurface earth formations	Geology and subdisciplines
Land forms	Physical geography, geomorphology
Soils	Soil sciences
Water	Hydrology
Climate	Climatology
Precipitation, air	Meteorology, microbiology
Solar energy	Physics
Fossil energy	Engineering, chemistry
Nuclear energy	Nuclear physics, engineering

Physical Factors (Table 3-1)

The character of the foundation on which the visible landscape rests is fundamental to understanding the appropriate uses of land. If structures are built, canals dug, roads constructed, or vegetation grown, the *subsurface geology* will have a profound effect on the results of human activity. If greater attention had been paid to the subsurface conditions where many cities are built, the cost of construction and environmental deterioration might be significantly less.[1]

The earth's visible surface is misleading as a factor in deciding about appropriate uses; building houses on mountainsides is often possible, but can also be extraordinarily dangerous if the mountainside happens to be a moving rock glacier, to use an extreme example. There is usually much more to the earth's surface than is readily visible; geological science has the tools and a store of knowledge which can help to assure that errors are minimized in tampering with the substances beneath and above that surface.

The form and shape of the earth's surface, apart from the nature of the physical structure which underlies it, are basic to land utility and human use. This is the usual realm of physical geography, knowledge of which can help substantially in defining the potential and limitations of *landforms*.

Although *water* is obviously basic to the ecological scheme of things, its sources and impacts below the surface of the earth are not always appreciated. Yet water permeates the geological foundations and is powerfully affected by how the surface is altered. The "hydrology" of underground water systems must be understood if we are to avoid negative effects

---

[1] A useful reference for this discussion is Ian McHarg's *Design with nature.* Garden City, N.Y.: Doubleday, 1969.

through surface alteration, by pumping or discharge; each such activity will have a long-term effect that can later substantially limit availability and quality of water at the surface.

As the demands on water supply increase, the historical acceptance of water as essentially a free good is altering drastically. The quantity and quality of water, as well as its intricate internal characteristics, must be understood and incorporated in any calculations of present or future organic activity.

The content, chemistry, texture, and nutritive richness of *soils* determine its utility for all forms of plant life and establish certain limits for use. Soils vary widely in their ability to provide firm foundations for structures such as highways, homes, and business establishments. Permeability and texture establish the difficulty and costs of sewage or waste absorption and surface water diffusion. A clear understanding of soil characteristics, based on detailed scientific investigation, is central to any decision about future land use.

Each of the factors noted above is a consequence, in part, of the kind of *climate* which characterizes a land area. Variations in temperature, wind persistence and velocity, quantity and distribution of rainfall, incidence of sunshine and clouds, as well as numerous other climatic factors, heavily influence the reactions of physical and biological objects, particularly the activities of people. A subset in the science of climate, *weather*, is an increasingly important subject of study and alteration through weather-modification schemes. Climate and weather variations prescribe the limits of plant and animal life and regulate many of the activities of people.

Regardless of the potential for controlling or modifying the effects of climate, which are costly activities, it must be thoroughly appreciated as part of any thoughtful preparation for the future. Understanding of air content and movement becomes particularly critical as the incidence of air pollution increases and affects the health of plant and animal life; the potential destructiveness of air pollution must be a central consideration in decisions about location of industry, outdoor recreation areas, urban areas, transportation, and a host of other activities which contribute to alteration of air content.

Solar, fossil, and nuclear *energy* supplies have become exceedingly important ingredients in planning—as shortages of nonrenewable fossil fuels become evident. The issue of energy supply and production will have a profound effect on decisions about future resource allocations. Thorough understanding of energy supplies and characteristics is therefore basic to realistic planning.

Biological Factors (Table 3-2)

In combination with physical factors, *vegetation* determines the forms, densities, and variety of animal life which can survive in a given territory. Until

Figure 3-2 Natural areas. Unspoiled natural areas are available for public enjoyment in many parts of the United States, but particularly in the mountainous areas of the West. Environmental impact statements are now required before any changes can occur in publicly owned areas, often resulting in considerable controversy and conflict between conservationist groups and extractive industries that want access to such areas. The conflict becomes increasingly vigorous as nonrenewable resources become less available and demand for timber increases. (*Photos by W. R. Lassey.*)

the advent of agriculture, the limiting power of physical factors and vegetation was much more profound; the impact of cultivated alterations of the vegetative environment has not only expanded the density of animal life but has fundamentally both altered the face of the earth and increased the

Table 3-2

Biological	Relevant knowledge/skills
Vegetation	Botany, forestry, agronomy, horticulture, etc.
Animals (land) Herbivores—decomposers Carnivores	Zoology, animal husbandry, wildlife
Aquatic animals	Fish culture
Land microbes	Microbiology
Water microbes	Limnology
Processes in nature	Nature conservation, ecology

freedom of people to pursue intellectually expanding and specialized tasks (such as formalized planning!).

In the planning context, vegetation—in its manifold forms within agriculture, forestry, nature-at-large, and as a part of the ecological process—is the most basic unit of the living environment and must therefore be considered as a key variable and central focus of planning.

Animal life plays a central role in whichever vegetative environment it occupies, whether domesticated for food production or as a part of untamed nature. Provision must be made for adequate space and vegetative environment for whatever animal species we expect to survive, increasingly as much for aesthetic and recreational purposes as for sources of food and maintenance of ecological balance.

Aquatic life, in the form of fish and infinite varieties of other water-dependent creatures, can be considered in the same general context as other forms of animal life, except for the details of environment. However, because water serves a huge variety of functions other than support of aquatic life, the relevance of water shortages, or alterations in water content and quality, on aquatic life is becoming decidedly more crucial in measuring pollution impact and as a variable in planning.

Understanding of the quality of air, water, land, and the associated natural and built environment depends heavily on the invisible living and nonliving objects which generally fall within the province of *microbiological sciences*. It is ever more clear that the tendency of the human population to ignore the effects of pollution is in part a function of the fact that we were not aware it was going on because of its "invisibility." For purposes of planning, information about largely invisible conditions becomes crucial, because small changes in the behavior and complexity of microbes give us our principal early clues about alterations in environmental and ecological circumstances. Therefore, we must rely on this information for the kind of farsighted direction that is needed to restore or preserve the ecological balance (Jezeski et al., 1973; see especially Roemhild).

Cultural-Historical Experience (Table 3-3)
The cultural and historical experience of a territory and a people has profound influence on the physical-biological environment and the socioeconomic condition of the inhabitants. Historical sites can be enjoyed to the advantage of both visitors and residents (Figure 3-3) when their care and maintenance are part of an overall planning scheme. It is therefore of prime importance to understand this experience as one crucial input to any discussion of the future. If the physical or biological environment has been severely damaged, this will obviously constrain the potential for creation of a satisfying future environment and implies a need for improved understanding by the human inhabitants who have misused the territory; like-

Table 3-3

Cultural-historical	Relevant knowledge/skills
Existing culture artifacts	Anthropology
Cultural experience	History, cultural anthropology
Political, social, economic, and technological experience	History

wise, a wisely treated environment may suggest a much more perceptive cultural experience, as well as greater openness and preparation for incorporation of ecological concepts in planning.

An understanding of the cultural experience of a people, in terms of political and institutional structure, decision-making processes, incorporation of and dependence on technology, and other cultural factors, will suggest limitations on implementation of planning processes and will modify the analysis of existing social and economic realities. Planning implies processes of highly systematized and organized change; if this is foreign to the experience of a people, the time frame of planning may be substantially altered; learning to incorporate required changes in institutional structures and attitudes will quite clearly be necessary. Or, if strong rigidities exist in cultural patterns, political systems, and social organization, it may not be immediately possible to proceed with the kind of scientifically based approach under discussion here; rather, mandatory changes imposed from higher levels of government may be required, to allow for planned adaptation of human institutions in the interest of preserving the life-support system.

Government-Political-Legal Factors (Table 3-4)

Formalized planning is essentially ineffective without political and legal sanction. If planning is to have impact, it must be tied directly to the public

Table 3-4

Government-Legal-Political	Relevant knowledge/skills
Political ideologies related to planning	Political science, planning
Planning laws and statutes	Law, legislative process
Structure of government	Political science
Operation of government	Political science
Ordinance and zoning regulation	Local government, law
Federal and state agencies with planning responsibilities	Government sciences, public administration

Figure 3-3 History-based recreation. History often serves as the basis for establishment of recreation-based industries, particularly if the designation of historical sites is part of a larger plan for serving visitors and residents while enhancing the environment for the enjoyment of both. (*Photos by W. R. Lassey.*)

decision processes which establish the guidelines for action. Otherwise, planning is likely to serve as only one kind of lobbying effort in the decision arena and will not secure the formal and informal support and attention required if it is to be an effective mechanism in designing and implementing a more desirable future.

Likewise, the planning process must be undergirded by a set of policies enacted into law and which define the responsibilities of elected and appointed officials for planning; such policies must indicate the organizational structures and incentives to be used. Unless these legal tools exist, there can be no means for financing the preparation of plans, implementation, and evaluation; and there can be no effective mechanisms for enforcing compliance to plans, either by citizens or by public officials responsible for implementation.

The political and governmental processes can therefore be considered the foundation upon which effective planning must rest. If there is support and understanding at the political level, it should be possible to create the needed legal mechanisms and governmental structures within which planning can proceed.

Social-Psychological Factors (Table 3-5)

Social organization in rural regions is in a rapid state of transition, as noted in the previous chapter. This is heavily a function of urbanizing impacts but is indigenously generated as well. However, any effort to formally plan for the use of the land or human well-being runs headlong into the accumulated rigidities of social organization, institutions, and the social psychology of populations. Clear understanding of and respect for existing social systems is highly important if unnecessary damage to inhabitants and institutions is to be avoided.

Social analysis should include a careful delineation of those social issues which will be affected by physical and biological changes and accommodations that must be made as a consequence of change. "Social planning" will require definitions of existing social inadequacies and consequent desirable social goals.

Table 3-5

Social-psychological	Relevant knowledge/skills
Social organization	Sociology
Social institutions	Sociology
Recreation activity	Sociology, recreation
Family life	Family life sciences
Values, beliefs, attitudes, goals	Social psychology
Unique rural characteristics	Rural sociology

Social-scientific input to planning will require analysis of existing and potential population characteristics in terms that are substantially more detailed than might be of general concern. Cultural uniqueness, values, belief systems, attitudes, behavioral patterns of individuals, groups, and organizations, and preferences for community structure will each be relevant points of inquiry. The ideologies and participation patterns will be important issues in the definition of acceptable planning goals and in the implementation processes for achieving those goals.

The human occupations in the process of decline (such as natural resource extraction in some locations) or increasing (such as recreation) must be considered as impacts on the physical-biological and social environment; the impacts should be described or projected with sufficient clarity to note the potential negative and positive effects. Measures might then be taken to design or redesign social organization to minimize negative effects and enhance the physical and social environment. If a high value is placed on particular forms of family life, as in Holland and many other countries, the family life sciences (i.e., home economics, sociology, etc.) will need to help define what kind of community design is necessary to allow and encourage family activity in conformance with the preferred values.

Rural society contains a variety of human "casualties" resulting from inadequate governmental and social structures or as a consequence of external change. Social service delivery systems have not kept pace with the rapid pace of change. Social-psychological analysis should be helpful in defining the human problems of rural regions and should contribute to the design of new institutional forms to maximize the potential for rural citizens to realize an improved future.

Economic Factors (Table 3-6)
Description and analysis of economic issues is of critical importance to adequate planning. Land tenure systems, land prices, and price trends, as well as other issues related to land use must be thoroughly understood. The changes under way in each dimension of land use—particularly as a conse-

Table 3-6

Economic	Relevant knowledge/skills
Land tenure	Land economics
Land price and exchange	Finance, real estate
Employment	Demography
Business and industry	Business administration, organizational science
Transportation	Transportation economics
Economic growth	Development economics
Public investment	Public finance

quence of urbanizing impacts on the countryside—must be described. A clear understanding, description, and analysis of the economic issues surrounding land use is exceedingly important to intelligent decisions on planning policy and programs.

Past, present, and projected employment patterns are one of the bases on which future population characteristics and distributions are derived. This must arise from changes in industrial and business development, changes in the service structure of the economy, and related factors. Each of these factors will weigh heavily in any scheme to prepare for future development of physical and human resources; understanding of changes in employment, population density, and population distribution provides major inputs to decisions about public investment in facilities or inputs to policy decisions which might deliberately redirect employment and population distribution.

As noted earlier, economic growth may be inappropriate when instances of resource depletion or environmental despoliation are highly probable. It is within the province of economics to help determine when plans should constrain as well as promote growth (Barkley & Seckler, 1972).

The analytical and quantitative tools developed in the fields of economics can be of substantial help not only in economic planning but also in supporting knowledge systematization in fields less quantitatively oriented. Similarly, economic analysis can be improved by inclusion of the social and ecological factors which affect economic issues.

Design Factors (Table 3-7)

Systematized planning has been central to the process of creating the built environment; architects and engineers have long been conscious of the need for organized preparation of designs for physical systems. The design of landscape by landscape architects and structural systems by architects

Table 3-7

Design	Relevant knowledge/skills
Landscape	Landscape architecture
Buildings	Architecture, civil engineering
Transportation	Civil engineering
Sanitation systems	Sanitary engineering, microbiology
Communication systems	Electrical engineering, communication
Activity spaces	Geography, planning
Mapping, graphics	Cartography, graphics, audiovisual
Aesthetics	Landscape architecture, architecture

and engineers was the foundation for urban planning and provides much of the conceptual base for systems of rural planning.

The interrelationships between various components of the "adapted" environment—buildings, highways, communication linkages, and other implacements on the landscape—has not always been clearly perceived by the various design professions. Nor has the relevance of human behavior to the design of such adaptations been consistently recognized. However, a convergence of appreciation is now emerging among designers of the physical environment and designers for the needs and preferences of individuals, groups, and organized society. The designers of the physical systems are increasingly conscious of the inadequacy of planning which fails to achieve a positive response from the population which must inhabit their creation. Students of social behavior are meanwhile becoming increasingly conscious of the relationships between the physical-biological environment and social dependencies. As this convergence blossoms, it becomes evident that the design of physical structures and systems must attend not only to human need but, more fundamentally, to ecological criteria. The design of landscape, buildings, communities, transportation, sanitation, communications, human activity spaces, and human organizational systems must become increasingly informed by understanding of ecological systems.

Maps and graphic representations of the interrelationships are helpful; but those who perform the cartographic and other graphic representations must themselves understand the processes and interrelationships if their work is to be illuminating rather than misleading. Visual clarification of physical, biological, and social elements is crucial to the educational functions discussed below, as well as to the decision-making processes to which the documents and graphics are usually directed.

Development of Environment and Institutions (Table 3-8)
The final product of physical planning is either preservation of physical features or some form of physical adaptation or construction. The products of social or human resource planning on the other hand are principally new forms of social patterning which alter (or possibly preserve) the organizational structure or network through which human goals are accomplished.

However, systematized planning has usually focused on guiding the physical development of communities and regions, without specific attention to the patterns of social organization. Both forms of activity are critical if the planning process is to be complete and effective over the long term. Buildings, highways, waste-treatment facilities, and a variety of other physical structures will be improved by effective planning. Similarly, the human institutions through which goals and values are realized must also be reconstructed or developed to fit the new physical and social circumstances.

The physical construction process will probably remain largely within

Table 3-8a

Development of the built environment	Relevant knowledge/skills
Buildings	Architects, builders
Roads, highways, railways, airports	Civil engineers, builders
Parks and landscape	Landscape architecture, landscapers
Utilities	Electrical and mechanical engineers, contractors
Interior spaces	Interior design, interior decorators
Agricultural and forest systems	Agricultural engineers, foresters, other agricultural professionals

Table 3-8b

Development of organizations and institutions	Relevant knowledge/skills
Government institutions	Political development specialists
Public organizations and agencies	Organizational development specialists
Educational institutions	Educational development specialists
Economic institutions Public enterprise Private enterprise	Economic development specialists
Public participation processes	Participation process facilitators

the province of private enterprise or government agencies, but responsibility for social organizational construction or development is less clear. A wide variety of private firms and public agencies is engaged in group development, community development, or other forms of organizational development. But these individuals or units are not clearly identified with implementation of planning processes. Rather, they tend to be ad hoc contributors who are employed, assigned, or initiate activity outside the context of guidance systems—in much the same manner that physical construction takes place when no plan exists.

The assumption here is that both physical *and* social construction and development will proceed more productively if guidance is provided by an informed planning process.

RELATIONSHIP ANALYSIS

The process of determining the interaction and connections between the factors relevant to planning process requires analytical thinking and unique skills. Ecologists and planners are quite often specialists within their general fields, or within one of the substantive fields responsible for the inputs to planning; hence, the composite of skills required for adequate *integration of information* are rare indeed, particularly in rural planning.

This task requires sufficient understanding of physical, biological, political, cultural, social, economic, design, and construction systems to predict how variations in each general set or subset of variables affect the entire system. If these relationships are not well understood, it is most difficult to undertake the planning process with confidence.

The interrelationships should be quantified whenever possible and appropriate. But unless such quantification is undertaken with full consciousness of those variables to which valid and reliable numerical values cannot be attached, the results of quantitative studies can be profoundly misleading. It is crucial that quantification be conducted with the more qualitative or numerically neutral factors in full view. Precision is less possible under such circumstances, but substantially more realism about implications of the interrelationships is likely.

With this qualification in mind, it is entirely evident that information-processing technology, as exemplified by the computer, has added substantially to the capability for understanding interrelationships and achieving greater precision in estimates of past, present, and future cause-and-effect relationships. If we can discover adequate methods to quantify additional factors in valid and reliable form, the capability to produce realistic predictions of potential future states, and viable alternatives for action, will obviously increase.

Increased understanding of probable cause-and-effect relationships has led to greater appreciation of the threat to ecosystems caused by pollu-

Table 3-9   Relationship Analysis

Interrelationships among factors	Relevant knowledge skills
Physical, biological	Ecology: physical, biological, chemical
Human interrelationships	Social sciences
Quantitative interactions	Statistics, computer sciences
Nonquantitative relationships	Conceptual sciences
Implications of interrelations	Planning sciences

tion and natural resource depletion. The publicizing of these dangers has arisen from a great variety of sources, but it is the articulate ecologists, planners, and interdisciplinary thinkers who have given substance to the concern (Commoner, 1971; Meadows et al., 1972; Catton, 1976). Further empirical elaboration of interrelationships and causal-effect dimensions are essential to planned action in correcting the destructive tendencies of human activity.

Projections of the Future

Goal setting, design, and implementation must rest upon realistic conceptions of what is likely to transpire in the future under varying conditions. Linear programming and other techniques can be used to generate "neutral" projections of future population numbers, distribution in geographic space, age structures, and other demographic details. Projections of urbanization, migration, and dispersion of population settlement will help indicate the likely environmental impact of people and their artifacts. It will be exceedingly important to understand potential new or probable forms and locations of social organizations, business organizations, government organizations, technology, and other large systems which will have significant impact on use of land and other resources.

Experiences with social and technological changes of recent decades suggest the need for careful attention to potential new combinations of, or innovations in, technical, social, organizational, and general systems, which will entirely alter our present conception of the possible future. The controversies over recent widely varying population projections, resource depletion projections, energy requirement projections, and pollution projections suggest a need for a substantial increase in the precision of projections and concomitant implications for future ecological balance (Steinhart & Steinhart, 1974).

General systems analysis can help account for major variables of central importance and large numbers of less critical but relevant factors. Computer models of physical, biological, political, social, and economic systems may not be accurate in every detail, but offer firm impressions about probabilities of future events; opportunities for planning to avoid destructive

Table 3-10

Projections of the future	Relevant knowledge/skills
Population projections	Demography
Employment projections	Economics
Urbanization projections	Urban studies, urban planning
General land-use projections	Land economics
Societal projections	General systems
Technology	Technological forecasting

tendencies and enhance constructive alternatives will thus be improved (Meadows et al., 1972; McGloughlin, 1970).

KEY PROCESSES

Educational, Communication, and Public Involvement
Processes (Table 3-11)

If planning is to be successful, a major reordering of public education, involvement, and communication processes may be necessary. Existing communication technology, scientific knowledge about effective communication processes, and knowledge about human learning provide vastly increased potential for public understanding, appreciation, and involvement in significant societal decisions. Formal educational methods for diffusing information and internalizing knowledge are archaic compared with the potential learning capability of the human population. It is increasingly clear that lifelong educational processes are essential for adequate human adjustment to changing job requirements and life-styles, but effective communication of knowledge crucial to public decision making is equally important if the planet is to survive (Toffler, 1970).

An expansion and reorganization of adult-level extension and continuing education programs might provide one of the mechanisms to inform and affect the behavior of citizens. Educational design that achieves greater stimulation from learning about central societal issues is required. We have so far used the electronic and printed media with reasonable effectiveness as advertising and entertainment devices but have only marginally tapped their potential for education. There is substantial evidence that it is the better-informed and higher-educated citizens who tend to participate more in public activities and decisions. If the information-, knowledge-, and experienced-based learning levels (Table 3-11) can be further advanced, the

Table 3-11

Educational and communication processes	Relevant knowledge/skills
Elementary, secondary and higher educational systems	Educational development, communication process
Adult education	Adult and continuing education and extension education process
Community education	Community development, group process, community educators
Mass media education	TV, radio, news media specialists

probabilities of more effective participation by large numbers of citizens should certainly be increased as well.

Educational and communication processes must be directly tied to the planning system and its output, if planning is to serve the kind of "societal guidance" function envisioned by Friedmann and others (Friedmann, 1973). Effective public education must be complex if it is to be meaningful. The output from the planning sciences is prolific indeed, and even selected crucial elements of that output will fill substantial time blocks in the education and communication channels potentially available to the public.

Citizens and public officials must not only understand the nature of the issues facing society, but must gain more adequate skills in methods for adapting, adjusting, and reorganizing public and private institutions which can implement the decision outcomes. Public knowledge of alternatives for social and institutional reorganization is much less complete and widespread than physical and biological knowledge; hence, the obvious frustration and apathy of many citizens who recognize the problems but do not have access to knowledge and educational programming that leads to understanding or problem solving.

Alternatives for Decision and Action (Table 3-12)
Ideally, the delineation of alternatives and decisions based on the most viable possibilities ought to await certainty of information; however, it is forever obvious that many unknowns or imprecisions will remain. Decisions will entail a certain degree of risk regardless of the care with which the planning process is undertaken. However, the minimization of risk and uncertainty through informed examination of alternatives should increase reliability of decisions.

The delineation of alternatives is increasingly a scientific enterprise. Mathematical systems and simulation tools facilitate advanced consider-

Table 3-12

Alternatives for action	Relevant knowledge/skills
Land and resource use	Physical, biological sciences
Human activity systems	Social sciences
Social services	Public administration, sociology, social welfare
Economic growth	Economics, political economy, regional science
Optimum organization forms	Organizational sciences, political science

ation of the consequences of various choices and can allow the pretesting of many combinations of variables to predict logical consequences. These tools are limited, however, when factors not readily subject to quantification must be injected, which is unexceptionally the case in planning. Consideration of complex alternatives can be achieved more adequately by use of advanced modeling, simulation, and visualization techniques; but these techniques must be accompanied by full consideration of qualitative and aesthetic variables, which may not be fully quantifiable but which are nevertheless necessary inputs to consideration of alternatives.

Goals (Table 3-13)

General goals for a "desirable" future already exist in a variety of public documents. But once we understand the existing facts about the present, and implication of these facts for the future, it is essential to make societal goals explicit and detailed. The process of goal setting is clearly a complex process if one attempts to use the variety of data generated by the systems heretofore described. If goal decisions are to be socially and ecologically sound, they must be based on a high level of public understanding about the consequences of various possible alternatives and the value conflicts arising therefrom. Elected officials, policymakers, and administrators will need a much more detailed and precise knowledge of alternative goals if they are to legislate and implement appropriate and specific action which will satisfy ecological and social values.

One of the more serious mistakes in current planning efforts has been the assumption that only the "experts" (scientists, planners, policymakers, and officials) need to understand the goals arising from the planning-related sciences; unless the public has a large measure of understanding, they will fail to insist upon, and vote for, the well-informed representatives who will be responsible for the formal decisions and resource allocations associated with preferred goals.

Implementation: Management, Monitoring, Feedback, Evaluation (Table 3-14)

It is in the crucial and ultimately conclusive implementation arena that most knowledge development is needed; however, vigorous application of

Table 3-13

Goals and objectives	Relevant knowledge/skills
General public preferences	Social scientists
General alternatives	Scientists, policymakers
Specific goals arising from the planning-related sciences	Planner-ecologist, action-planner, legislators, citizens

Table 3-14

Decision implementation	Relevant knowledge/skills
Government organization	Political science
Planning organization	Public administration, organizational science
Legislative and legal tools	Political science, law
Management information systems	Communication, management
Citizen involvement process	Community organization, community action, involvement process facilitation
Evaluation	Social sciences, ecology
Systems management	Management, management engineering

existing knowledge can vastly improve the implementation of planning. If the complex array of factors noted above is to be adequately considered, carefully coordinated teamwork will be required—based on sound knowledge about social organization process. Planning information systems need to facilitate effective monitoring, feedback, and management, while serving as a basis for evaluation and adjustment of the planning and action process.

Functional political and administrative processes are necessary to assure that planning is undertaken under the informed control of elected policymakers and administrators. This conception of planning process assumes that an informed citizen public and their elected representatives will want to make intelligent preparation for the future and will want to realize societal goals based on realism about the consequences of various alternatives before us.

An intelligent planning process will facilitate the reform and redesign of the many existing government structures which are now geared primarily to maintenance of existing, and often inadequate, social and physical systems. Although resistance will certainly be encountered, it is essential that the effectiveness of local and higher levels of government be improved; well-conceived planning that helps improve management, monitoring, accurate information, and evaluation is a tool which can assist with that process (Kulp, 1970).

Chapter IV

Regional Planning
and Regional Collaboration

"Region" is an attractive concept for comprehensive inclusion of human activities which extend beyond the confines of communities, towns, or counties. As population mobility increases and the scale of economic and public enterprise expands, the activities which can productively be considered on a regional basis become more evident.

Alternative planning activities may be most effectively and efficiently undertaken with varying territorial boundaries. For example, it is unlikely that the distribution pattern for medical services will coincide with desirable or existing administrative boundaries for educational services. Nevertheless, there is likely to be sufficient relationship with natural environmental systems boundaries (such as river valleys) which contain at least some of the major human activity systems extending beyond existing jurisdictional boundaries.

The focal points for more specialized environmental planning or social service functions will usually be located in major service centers—"regional" cities which support, and are supported by, activity in a definable space. In more sparsely settled areas, there are often two or more cities which might share the service center function within a larger region. Several levels of "regions" may be delineated: subdivisions of a country encompassing several states; subdivisions of states including two or more counties; and countywide or subcounty regions. Agreement on boundaries of regions which satisfy many kinds of public activities is essentially impossible; the formal designation of regions for administrative planning purposes must therefore be somewhat arbitrary.

Within any defined region (and often between regions) interdependencies will exist. That is, smaller cities may depend on larger cities for specialized medical services, while larger cities may depend on smaller cities as customers for wholesale distributors. Manufacturing industries in larger cities will depend on rural areas for inputs to the production process, while rural areas depend on the cities as sales outlets for production and as sources of supply for production inputs. Basically, cities depend on rural areas for their source of fresh water, clean air, and food, while the amenities desired by the rural dweller are often available only because the larger cities serve enough population to make the production and distribution of those amenities possible. The key issue for the purposes of this discussion arises from the need to understand the interrelationships, interactions, and interdependencies of human and ecological activity on a scale large enough so that critical factors are considered; this can often be achieved only in regional spatial divisions, since confining "plans" to existing localities or administrative boundaries limits adequate consideration of critical environmental factors.

The regional approach to analysis, planning, and implementation of adaptive or developmental programs allows for the kind of comprehensive and complex consideration of issues which would not often be possible within the constraints of existing political or population subdivisions. Within the context of "region," various kinds of subsystems can be defined for specific consideration. For example, the subsystem of water supply and demand can be isolated and examined based on its natural and constructed characteristics. Water systems usually defy traditional jurisdictional boundaries. Availability of specialized nursing and diagnostic services or accessibility of medical care for elderly residents may be more adequately considered on a regional basis than in a more local setting. The size of the region for adequate consideration of health services might differ markedly from the regional dimensions for other amenities, such as entertainment, recreation, or food marketing.

Rural and Regional Distinctions

The principal basis for emphasizing "rural" planning apart from "regional" planning is the historical tendency to consider regional planning from an essentially urban viewpoint, in which rural territorial uses are considered as a function of urban needs or requirements, with only modest consideration of rural social, economic, and political integrity or the essential and unique rural environmental role in maintaining the ecological balance. Regional planning has usually concentrated attention on the needs of the urban centers, while treating the rural periphery as a dependent entity. The result has often been inattention to the fundamentally rural requirements and contributions to the regional system.

One consequence of such biases is the tendency to conclude that urban centers subsidize rural areas in the provision of roads, social services, inputs to agricultural productivity, and tax-generated expenditures (Green, 1971, p. 59). The fact that rural areas have tended to export an educated work force whose income and taxpaying potential is then lost to rural areas is not always considered; nor is the essential requirement that the managers of the rural landscape have responsibility for maintenance of the basic physical and biological life-support system (water, air, food, raw materials, etc.) on which the urban region depends.

Much of the literature on regional planning assumes the need for a center-periphery dichotomy, with the center serving as the generator of "development" which then spreads to the periphery. If the maximization of "economic" development is the primary goal, this assumption may very well be appropriate, but ecological balance, rural integrity, and long-term optimization of the life-support system require modification of the center-periphery assumptions (Hilhorst, 1971). This is not to deny the historical tendency of urban centers to dominate and in some sense subvert the rural regions to urban needs, but rather suggests that such tendencies may need to be countered by more deliberate attention to the rural parts of regions.

Delineating Boundaries for Planning Regions

Urban and regional planners, economists, and geographers have usually emphasized boundary definitions on the basis of service areas surrounding central places. These are often referred to as polar regions—that is, poles of influences are defined from objective measures of service peripheries for economic or social activities as they penetrate the surrounding smaller cities, towns, and rural areas.

There are several difficulties with this approach. As noted earlier, each kind of major service is likely to have a somewhat different degree and depth of penetration, so that boundaries drawn for banking services might differ substantially from boundaries drawn for medical services. In addition, boundaries of influence poles (major regional centers) are likely to change significantly over time, because of changes in competitive or service advantage. Such changes occur for a variety of reasons:

1 If one center is better equipped with respect to economic potential, social services, governmental services, or political power, it will tend to expand at the expense of surrounding centers.

2 If new development takes place within the region influenced by a major center, regional service boundaries relating to the new development are likely to expand.

3 New transportation or communication channels or routes may positively affect one sphere of influence, while negatively affecting another.

4 One area may decline simply because of resource exhaustion, changes in technology, or lack of economic, social, or political dynamism.

Such alterations in existing conditions will tend to make boundaries or defined regions obsolete in a relatively limited time period, *if* boundaries were defined on the basis of polar influence criteria. Whether or not this occurs, boundaries are likely to be fuzzy for residents or agencies within a region, particularly if located on the outer periphery. Diverse personal service preferences and ease of mobility in going to (or drawing on) services wherever they might be located will result in unique definitions of "region" by each person (Hilhorst, 1971, pp. 56–57).

The difficulties with boundary delineation can be alleviated somewhat by analysis of present and potential factors which contribute to reasonably permanent boundaries—somewhat regardless of alterations in major trade center influence—and with the understanding that boundaries must remain flexible for most purposes. Regions may best be defined for planning and administrative purposes by combinations of existing jurisdictions, *but* with provisions for deliberately generating interregional communication, interaction, and collaboration among planning and administrative bodies appropriate to changing circumstances.

Effective planning will require subdividing of territory on bases other than existing boundaries if manageable segments for analysis and action are to be differentiated. In most instances the following levels must be considered, depending on the issues under consideration (Hilhorst, 1971, p. 28):

1 *Macrolevel*: For planning issues with broad implications for an entire nation or even among nations, when planning by any one nation or part of a nation would be inappropriate or inadequate. Water resource planning is often of this nature.

2 *Sector segments*: The economy and society can be viewed on the basis of sectors of activity which cut across all boundaries, and deserve attention on a general basis. Within the rural planning context, agriculture, recreation, forestry, minerals, medical care, education and other subdivisions are usually defined for specific attention across any kind of jurisdictional delineation.

3 *Interregional*: In some instances planning issues are relevant to several potential regions, but not necessarily the whole nation. Water resources such as large lakes and rivers again illustrate this circumstance.

4   *Regional*: A territory defined by whatever criteria considered appropriate for specific planning or administrative purposes and which encompasses several existing political territories or homogeneous areas (such as river valleys, or combinations of contiguous river valleys and surrounding drainage areas).

5   *Local*: Existing communities, towns, cities, counties, or subdivisions thereof, usually predefined on the basis of governmental service areas.

6   *Project*: The level at which action on a specific problem or opportunity might occur, and which is the ultimate outcome of planning and administration. A project may intersect with all of the other levels, or with only one, depending on its nature and complexity. For example, a project to institute comprehensive health care for the aged may have international, national, regional, interregional, and local dimensions within the health planning sector.

Coordination as the Key Regional Function

A planning region can often serve as the major coordinating point, between higher levels of government, other regions, and subdivisions of territory or sectors within the region. The unique potential of the regional concept arises from the coordination requirements between state or federal levels and local jurisdictions; local governments often do not have the experience, understanding, or skill to manage planning programs from a perspective which includes all essential considerations, while higher administrative levels are often too far removed from the scene to gain a full grasp of unique local and regional idiosyncracies or problems.

Operational agencies of government often exhibit a high level of competence within their own sector of activity, but are not easily able to understand nor coordinate with other agencies at local, state, or national levels; the regional unit may have the best potential for establishing an effective formal communication and exchange network among these agencies, while providing for coordination and collaboration with local units. This could hinder the maximization of efficiency within any one sector of activity, but may increase the potential for maximizing efficiency of planning and programming for broader environmental or social priorities.

If such a regional mechanism is to be effective, sufficient commitment from subunits within the region is required to enable communication and exchange, while mediating potential disputes or disagreements between levels of government and between sectors in the conduct of specific projects. The regional mechanism may facilitate mutually agreeable new or redefined program areas for operational agencies.

Regional coordination will usually be helpful at several points in the planning and action process:

1   In policy setting and goal selection
2   In the interpretation of executive action initiated at the national or state level, but with joint implications for several jurisdictions

3   Among major programs within sectors (i.e., agriculture, recreation, etc.) having at least subregional (area) and regional impacts

4   Between programs initiated by state and national executive agencies which overlap local jurisdictions and/or sectors (i.e., water resource, air quality)

Coordination will require a well-designed formal communication system, connecting the knowledge production and analysis units (i.e., universities), various technical planning subdivisions (i.e., the Soil Conservation Service), administrators and officials of local government responsible for decisions (i.e., county and city commission members), and action agencies at each of the defined jurisdictional levels. Understanding of the communication and exchange requirements is needed continuously in regional activities and interactions; initial understanding should be supplemented by continued study, to assure adaptation and adjustment of any regional communication/exchange system (Hilhorst, 1971, pp. 148–150).

Basis for Regional Collaboration

An important issue in any revised conception of rural planning and development is the changed matrix in which development can occur. The individual and the community have been the traditional focal points for inputs intended to produce change. Farm programs have supported individual or firm efforts to increase income through price supports, conservation payments, and loan programs. Rural development programs have tended to support measures that would produce "community" development through broadly based citizen problem-solving groups, improved organization, or specific programs to alleviate sewer, water, or other local problems.

These programs have certainly helped some individuals and selected communities, but they have not achieved a sufficiently broad conception of social organization nor taken account of the critical role that complex organizations play in generating or obstructing change (Warner, 1971). Individuals and communities are caught up in an organizational matrix which is the source of an increasing number of decisions and action—and which often influences individual behavior and opportunity to a greater degree than the community of residence.

An increasing proportion of private firms have a regional, statewide or national network of locations. Employees of these firms are often only temporary residents of any one community and owe their primary allegiance to the goals of the larger firm and society, rather than to any one geographical location (Warren, 1972). Similarly, many public agencies have regional, state, or national structures. Public and private organizations often have a deliberate policy of regular employee transfers (or promotions) which effectively serves to curtail commitment to any single location, while increasing the dependence on the organization for reward and sustenance.

Of equal or greater importance is the tendency of individuals to join associations which transcend localities, thus linking them to regional, state, national, or even international networks. Labor unions, professional societies, commodity groups, and business associations illustrate the point.

Another dimension of personal or group identity with the larger society is the rising influence which complex transcommunity organizations have on local decisions. It is persistently frustrating for local officials and citizens to discover that they cannot control either the resources or the destiny of their jurisdictions. They may have influence, but many of the decisions which affect them are made by firms, individuals, agencies, or organizations outside the local area who fail to understand or appreciate the particular characteristics or environment of any single community. Local community institutions have gradually given up many of the functions which they formerly performed, because the specialized public and private agencies are more efficient in providing single services. Local leadership skills for solving specialized problems have been lost to highly mobile professionals who feel relatively little allegiance or responsibility to any single locality or community (Bennis, 1969). The professionals often have difficulty in perceiving rural problems in any holistic sense, and fail to understand how the program for which they are responsible relates to the programs of other agencies and the larger concerns of the region.

Research, development, and experience have multiplied what we know about the world which surrounds us. This achievement has led to knowledge specialization directly related to the inadequacies of rural planning and development; formal mechanisms to provide for integration at the local level are either weak or do not exist. In many rural regions, and among many agencies, four forms of isolation and alienation have resulted, each forming an impediment to comprehensive and effective rural planning and development (adapted from Moe, 1973):

1 Separation and isolation of agencies and organizations from each other
2 Separation and isolation of agencies and organizations from local communities
3 Estrangement of agencies and organizations from the people they are designed to serve
4 Separation, isolation, and estrangement of professionals employed by agencies and organizations from each other and from citizens at the local level

These forms of alienation often lead to weak and inadequate efforts toward comprehensive planning and development programs in rural areas. At least two potentially damaging by-products are evident. First, the potential for increasing development through productive interaction between complementary programs is lost. Second, adverse effects are generated, both within a rural region or outside of it, because of uncoordinated or competing program activity. That is, a single program may appear to be successful, but in reality may create a larger problem which is even more difficult to resolve (Ditwiler, 1974). What appear to be positive changes may therefore be temporary; the changes generate little or no commitment because they do not fit into a larger whole that can be directly related to the value systems and priorities of those affected.

Decisions by higher levels of government often constrain the local decision-making process. At the same time the role of local elected officials is becoming more important as they are required to adapt to new laws, regulations, and guidelines for a variety of new public programs—particularly, the various forms of revenue sharing (Gessaman, 1974; *Revenue Sharing and the Planning Process,* 1974).

In sum, community leaders and citizens are unable to effectively achieve their preferences because of organizational complexities they encounter; they have difficulty understanding how specialized organizations or agencies can be most useful to them. The jargon and bureaucratic orientation of agency professionals often make it difficult for effective dialogue to occur. Rural citizens lack many of the skills and resources to solve regional or community problems or to capitalize on existing opportunities; they may also be short of confidence and knowledge to deal effectively with agencies designed to help them. Meanwhile, professionals within the agencies often lack sufficient inclination and skill to achieve effective collaboration and comprehensiveness of programs.

Major Obstacles to Effective Collaboration and Integration

It is presumptuous to suggest that coordinated regional planning can be undertaken without significant constraints. Research and experience have revealed a series of factors which may in some circumstances seriously challenge the achievement of the program objectives (adapted from Moe, 1973):

1 The climate of competition, conflict, distrust, and suspicion which often characterizes relationships within and between many public and private organizations at local, state, and national levels

2 Continuing competition for funds, clientele, and status among and between organizations and local jurisdictions

3 Concern about the survival or loss of organizational or jurisdictional identity, which tends to generate high commitment to one's own organization or community, while excluding recognition of the appropriate role of other units or regional collaboration

4 Lack of clarity about the utility and payoff from collaborative regional efforts, with consequent confusion about how organizational or jurisdictional goals can better be served through collaboration

5 Concern over who is to have the major authority or control over key decisions affecting organizational or jurisdictional personnel and resources, or who controls whatever joint resources might be generated through collaboration

6 Concern over whether collaboration will generate greater benefits to individual organizations or jurisdictions, or whether the costs in time and resources might outweigh any benefits generated

7 Unwillingness to share risks in a venture in which success is not certain even though potential payoff may be substantial if success does occur

8 Anticipation of substantial time demands for discussion, education, communication, and learning to collaborate, when this time must be taken from ongoing organizational or jurisdictional efforts to achieve pre-defined goals

9 Fear that new "umbrella" organizations may take over some of the functions of existing organizations or jurisdictions

10 Prior experience with efforts to "force" collaboration through executive mandates or pressure from other organizations or jurisdictions

This imposing list of constraints will quite clearly require vigorous and sustained effort over a substantial period of time if they are to be overcome. Despite the growing body of evidence that regional collaboration increases overall effectiveness of rural planning, many individuals within organizations and local jurisdictions will feel strongly that single organizations or single community actions are more satisfying and productive than collaboration (Finley, 1970).

Chapter V

Changing Conceptions of Land-Use Planning

Americans are in the process of altering many of their basic attitudes and values toward the use of the land. We have become increasingly conscious of our dependence on the land resource (as well as air and water) for basic sustenance, maintenance of a high standard of living, and environmental amenity; highly visible land pollution, desecration of high-quality natural areas, and blighted urban and suburban conditions are forcing us to realize that changes in management and control of land may be necessary if we are not to lose many of the utilitarian and aesthetic attributes of the countryside.

However, the potential for enlightened change in land-use decision patterns is impaired by certain enduring attributes of the American value system. The social and value system surrounding private land ownership is at the core of the resistance to new land-use possibilities. Those who control much of our privately owned land place extremely high value on individual freedom in doing with and to the land what the owner chooses, often without regard to effects on the ecological system, neighbors, or the general public. Many citizens (particularly landholders) lack confidence in the abil-

Figure 5-1 Land subdivision. Breaking up of valuable agricultural land and other rural property into "farmettes" or "ranchettes" has led to urbanization of the countryside, while removing land from other productive uses. Large blocks of land have been sold for future development but remain out of any productive use for long periods while the new owners acquire the resources to develop the land or until the development "climate" is right. Comprehensive efforts to determine and plan for land according to some kind of intrinsic suitability criteria remain to be achieved in most rural regions. (*Photos by W. R. Lassey.*)

ity of local and higher officials of government, whether elected or appointed, to make adequate decisions about uses of private land; there is a widespread belief that the aggregate of private decisions will be more beneficial for the public good than centralized decisions, particularly with respect to land use. This lack of confidence has been sustained regularly; our public institutions are only beginning to attain the capability to make informed and effective land-use decisions (Reilly, 1973, pp. 7–12; Clawson, 1971, pp. 74–75).

The land market has a high potential profit to landowners, realtors, lawyers, accountants, assessors, appraisers, financiers, bankers, speculators, and a variety of other "specialists" who make up the present social system surrounding land use; the social structure of the land market serves as a major obstacle to improvement in the decision process about how land is used. Figure 5-1 illustrates land subdivision, which involves dividing the rural countryside into blocks for future development. However, ill-prepared plans often leave the land unproductive while resource funds for development are being obtained. Many members of the existing system depend on land-use exchange and decision patterns for their livelihood, status, and fulfillment. Change in the system threatens their economic survival, which can only cause them to resist, regardless of the potential for improved public well-being. Obviously some members of the existing land market system recognize its inadequacies, and on occasion serve as leaders in the quest for improvement. But in rural and urban fringe areas, evidence of enlightenment is not highly visible in most parts of the United States.

Nevertheless, a new mood toward use of the land exists among an increasing number of Americans in both rural and urban areas; the new value position questions traditional assumptions about the desirability of uncontrolled urban and economic development. We may be entering a period of extensive change and intensive conflict over who controls land use—particularly prime development land near urban centers and recreational areas or open space in rural locations.

The conflict is already evident between (1) the private decision-oriented land market system noted above, which wants to sustain private control, and (2) the public rights groups who insist that land is a basic resource requiring development largely under public control (Jezeskie et al., 1973, p. 34). Change in who controls the land will result in major alterations in local power structures, involving a shift from the current land market system, which now often has dominant influence over local government land-use decisions, toward increased power for land planners and local, state, and federal government decision makers. This kind of power shift has occurred in the United Kingdom, the Netherlands, and other European countries where physical and land-use planning are pervasive (Clawson & Hall, 1973, pp. 160–167). However, there is little evidence that democratic process has been damaged in these countries. Rather, the shift in power has placed control of land development clearly in the public debate and decision arena and has removed much of the speculation from land transactions. Careful land-use planning has become a highly developed and respected tradition in many of these countries, and the resulting countryside attractiveness, preservation of agricultural land, and controlled urban development are impressive (Lassey, 1973).

Although land-use planning systems which appear to work reasonably well in other countries can be helpful as examples, it is clearly inappropriate to assume that the same systems will work in the United States. Many of our basic values, experiences, and social-organizational systems are unique to this country and would not absorb approaches or models from other countries without careful adaptation.

Emerging Concept of Land[1]

"Land" means something different to the present generation than it did to our grandfathers. Population growth and the mobility afforded by modern transportation services have resulted in more intensive settlement patterns and a whole new set of demands upon land.

The economic or social value of land derives from the services it provides to people. It may be used to grow food or fiber, to contain housing units, to support transportation arteries, to provide a clean watershed, to offer attractive scenery, to allow recreational use, or to serve as a diluent for pollution. Each of these uses is characterized by a specific public demand, which, unfortunately, cannot be specified with the same precision for each use. To further complicate the issue, many of these demand relationships are interdependent.

Among the current demands for uses of land are those related to recreation, aesthetics, and environmental quality. The demands for these uses cannot be adequately met through normal market processes; some public action is normally required.[2] The possibility of conflict is present because the characteristics of the resource user group (those who seek recreation, aesthetics, and improved environments) are generally different from the resource owners (farmers, railroads, timber companies, speculators, etc.). Part of the conflict over the meaning of land and the relative values to be

---

[1] Much of the material in this section is adapted from James C. Barron, William R. Lassey, & C. Dirck Ditwiler. *A search for new approaches to planning in Washington.* Pullman, Washington: Washington State University, 1976. (Agricultural Research Center Circular No. 595)

[2] The technical economic reason for the failure of market processes is the existence of public goods. A public good is involved when consumption of the good does not diminish the quantity available to consume. Clean air, a pretty view, or a highway are equally available to all regardless of one individual's consumption. Thus there is no private market incentive to provide such goods if self-selected consumers cannot be excluded.

placed on alternative services of land stems from this separation of resource users from resource owners.

A growing awareness of possible resource scarcity also contributes to the emerging concept of land. In the aggregate land may not be scarce in the United States, but in certain areas there are problems of congestion, conflicts among uses, and actual shortages for some uses. As cities have swelled into the suburbs, land has been used less intensively for commercial and residential uses, thus contributing to real or perceived scarcity.

An important issue in the land-use debate concerns agricultural use. One of the most visible effects of urban growth is the conversion of farmland and other open space in the urban fringe to intensively developed uses. Worldwide food shortages have made people more aware of food production, but the primary reason cited for controlling urban fringe development has to do with aesthetics. For most people, it is far more pleasant to drive out of town into a cluster of farms than into a cluster of neon signs. Consequently, there is a growing debate in nearly all areas of the United States over how land use can be influenced in such a way that the loss of agricultural land will be minimized.[3]

Redefinition of Property Rights

As noted earlier, the institution of property rights is critically important in regulating land use, tenure, and distribution of returns from land.[4] Property may be defined as the right to control an economic good or service subject to the limitations established by laws and regulations. Each society or culture determines its particular set of property rules in accordance with its values; a major role of the state is to enforce these rules for the protection of property. Not only may the rules differ among societies but they may also change within a given society in response to changing goals or constraints imposed by new conditions. "Such changes are necessary because the concept, the social purpose of property rights, changes over time. The structure, the legal body of property rights, must be adapted accordingly" (Ciriacy-Wantrup, 1963, p. 146).

The public does hold certain rights in all private land which it may exercise at any time:[5] eminent domain, police power, and taxation. Emi-

---

[3] For a more complete discussion of this issue and the means of implementing control strategies see William H. Gray. *Agricultural land use in Washington: Conversion or preservation.* Washington State University, April 1975 (Extension Monograph 3935, Cooperation Extension Service); and William H. Gray. *Methods of agricultural land preservation.* Washington State University, February 1975 (Extension Monograph 3906, Cooperative Extension Service).

[4] Institution is defined here as a well-established social structure that sets the rules within which people behave with respect to some fundamental interest in life.

[5] A more complete discussion of public and private property rights is available in M. M. Kelso, "Management and use of land as a public good," and David Allee, "Public and Private Property Rights," in *Increasing understanding of public problems and policies,* Chicago, Ill.: Farm Foundation, 1972.

nent domain is the right to condemn a piece of property and acquire it for public use. The constitutional guarantee of due process requires that it truly be for a public purpose and that just compensation be paid to the owner. The police power is the right of the public to restrain or prevent certain uses of land which may be detrimental to health, safety, or welfare. No compensation is required for any rights of private owners which are enjoined. The normal exercise of the police power is negative in character—thou shalt not do this or that—but it may also be positive by requiring that specific actions be taken. The right of taxation is in effect a public right to a share of the product from land through ad valorem and severance taxes. It is a sort of "public rent" paid by landowners to the public for the right to manage the land for their private gain and for the public's protection of their property interest.

There is virtually no dispute over the actual legal existence of these three public rights in private land, but there is disagreement over their application. Eminent domain is accepted for acquiring land for schools, courthouses, streets, and fire stations. But is it appropriate for public parks, a scenic area, preserving vanishing ocean front, or assuring access to lakes and streams? The question of what constitutes a legitimate public purpose is crucial and subject to changing values and social goals. Similarly with police power: all will agree that a recalcitrant suburbanite should be forced to use the public sewer system rather than polluting a common watercourse. It is also pretty obvious that industrial development "should" be located outside residential neighborhoods. Again, however, there is a vast gray area where solutions are less certain and subject to legal dispute. Requiring a farmer to continue producing cabbage (because it is a pleasant pastoral land use) rather than permitting the farmer to build a shopping center is open to question unless a compelling public effect is shown.[6] Property taxation has corresponding characteristics. The controversy is over equity, administration, and relation to other tax bases rather than over whether property should be taxed in the first place.

Extensive land-use regulation, primarily through the police power (zoning), dates from the 1920s in the United States.[7] Regulation was not used to conserve land for certain purposes but rather to prevent its use in ways that would lower the value of neighboring property. In other words, regulation was a means of protecting or maximizing land values. Where development would not harm property values it went unregulated. The last decade, however, has brought increasing recognition that the purpose of

[6] A detailed analysis of legal issues in the exercise of the police power is contained in Fred Bosselman, David Callies, & John Banta. *The taking issue*. Washington, D.C.: Council on Environmental Policy, U.S. Government Printing Office, 1973.

[7] There were many earlier exercises of zoning for various reasons, but the major issues confronted in the 1970s began to develop in the 1920s.

land regulation should go beyond merely protecting the commodity value of land. Social, economic, and environmental goals require more specific controls on land to meet a wider variety of public uses.

A major question involved in the exercise of the police power is the economic impact of regulation and how those benefits or costs should be distributed. Virtually all the opposition to land-use planning or to a restructuring of the planning process is based on the fear that some rights will be lost or reduced in value with no compensation to the holder now or in the future. Such fears are not unfounded. There are precious few instances where economic changes do not create losers as well as gainers. If the two problems of separation of property rights and compensation can be solved, much of the controversy will be removed. In other words, if the public purchases the development rights from a farmer, they will not have to be purchased again from the farmer's heirs or the next owner.[8]

While a redefinition of property rights in society may be under way, it is by no means a simple proposition. The issues raised here barely scratch the surface. Extensive public debate and an evolution of changing values and social goals must precede "final" solutions.

Role of the States

Changes in land use within a state often have major ramifications far beyond the immediate vicinity.[9] Local governments have traditionally had the responsibility for land-use planning but do not usually have economic or political incentives to take into account the effects of their decisions on neighboring government jurisdictions.

State goals are not necessarily a simple summation of the goals of subunits within the state. State policymakers must consider trade-offs among different regions and interests. When conflicts arise, the statewide perspective seeks to modify the impacts of decisions so as to represent a true statewide interest. The wider public may be better served if the state has a role in the decision process for major impacts. The problem is to identify a process whereby each successively higher level of government deals only with those problems or decisions that transcend the boundaries of the next lower level of government.

In seeking to define a process for land-use planning that provides a role for each level of government, several considerations seem important. As Boulding perceptively notes:

[8] Property rights are separable, even though they are normally held or exchanged in bundles. Use rights (present use) and development rights (future developed uses) are usually kept together, but more attention is being given to their separation. Control of the development rights naturally confers significant influence over future land use.

[9] For a more detailed treatment of this issue see *Land: State alternatives for planning and management*. Lexington, Ky.: Council for State Government, 1975.

The world moves into the future as a result of decisions, not as a result of plans. Plans are significant only insofar as they affect decisions. Planning may be defined in such a way that it is part of the total decision making process; but if it is not part of a decision making process, it is a bag of wind, a piece of paper, and worthless diagrams (Boulding, 1974, p. 8).

The land-use planning process must be comprehensive in the sense that it includes all relevant decision makers and jurisdictional areas involved, while relating to the kinds of decisions for which each is responsible. It is of no use, for example, to plan for agricultural development in a region if there is not a supply of water or if some decision maker(s) outside the process can effectively prevent the delivery of water.

A new role for the state must be developed in such a way that existing planning is not disrupted. Shoreline management, water planning, environmental policies, and other programs are ongoing under a different set of processes than land-use planning. Coordination is essential to avoid the chaos which results when many programs affecting the same region function independently of each other.[10]

Some observers suggest there is a revolution under way with respect to the processes of land-use planning (Bosselman & Callies, 1971). Realignments of decision-making power are emerging which increase the role of state government relative to local governments. As the debate continues it will demand a high level of competence on the part of citizens, elected public officials, and professional staff to ensure that land-use planning and decision making is carried out in the best interest of citizens, while enhancing the physical-biological environment.

Alternative Forms of Social Organization for Land-Use Guidance

There appear to be at least four major possibilities for land-use policy formation and planning, varying from the historic ad hoc reliance on the marketplace to outright public ownership of greater quantities of the land resource. The following general alternatives essentially represent a continuum, rather than distinct and exhaustive categories:

1 *Reliance on the marketplace and private land-use decisions*: This alternative predominates in most rural parts of the United States. It results in maximization of the individual right to use land creatively or destructively without constraint and has led to some impressively worthwhile uses of land. However, it often leads to disregard for the intrinsic capabilities of the land; urban blight, rural slums, and serious despoliation of the land resource are evident.

---

[10] For a discussion of state issues in land-use planning see James Dolliver. Land use issues at the state level. In James C. Barron (Ed.). *Land use policy*. Pullman: Cooperative Extension Service, Washington State University, 1974, pp. 3–8.

2 *Private ownership and decision, with public constraint through zoning, regulation of some kinds of development, and land-use limitations based on health standards*: This pattern predominates in most urban areas and in rural counties of some states which have enacted the appropriate legislation. It results in maintaining the predominance of private land-use decisions, while controlling some of the most extreme misuses of the land. It has generally not resulted in long-term land-use policies and planning systems designed to optimize the use of land for maintenance of the resource, environmental improvement, and long-term human welfare.

3 *Private ownership with stringent permit or planning permission requirements for new development*: This approach predominates in only a few urban areas and some states, and has become the norm in the United Kingdom, the Netherlands, and to some degree in other European countries. It results in firm limitation of individual decisions about land use unless public permission is granted; increased government involvement in establishing and implementing land-use goals and policies is required, and public planning units within local, regional, state, and federal levels of government attain increasing responsibility for determining the best uses for all land parcels.

4 *Public ownership of land, or public control of all development rights, requiring formal decisions on all land uses*: This alternative predominates in most socialist countries, and occurs in the United States with respect to all publicly owned land. It results in the requirement that private uses of land occur only with public permission—usually through government agencies staffed by professional land planners or managers, under the general supervision of elected public officials. Standardization of land-use decision patterns becomes the rule, and the quality of those decisions depends heavily on political factors as well as the quality of personnel within the land-use control agencies.

Social and Organizational Implications of the Alternatives

As noted above, each of the alternatives can occur within the democratic governmental framework. However, as the variation ranges from alternative 1 to 2, 3, and 4, there is an obvious and profound shift in power from ad hoc systems of local land-use decision makers to public appointed and elected officials. If the ad hoc systems are enlightened, and appear to be making decisions which optimize land use in terms of the best intrinsic capabilities of the land, this might be better than an alternative which places reliance on public land use decisions—particularly if the public officials are ill-equipped to understand, organize, and develop quality land-use policies and planning processes.

However, alternative 1 is heavily dependent on enlightened individual decision makers and has thus far been unsatisfactory in avoiding gross misuses of land; private "enlightenment" has been sporadic, and no control exists over occasional spoilers who cause severe damage to their own land and infringe on the rights of their neighbors or the general public by the destruction or nuisance they create. Private development often leads to the obligation of public funds to accommodate uses in locations that are inappropriate because of land characteristics or other development limitations. The basic question must then be faced: Is the value of the individual freedom of land-use decision sufficiently important to risk the destruction or deterioration which may ultimately lead to decreased quality of environment and human welfare for the larger society? Or, is it better to allow greater public responsibility for land-use decisions, even though the quality of these decisions may often be inferior because local, state, or federal officials are also incapable of optimum guidance of land use?

The most obvious conclusion would be to work systematically at increasing the quality of both private and public decisions—so that public decisions are required only when private decisions could result in severe misuse, *and* high-quality public decisions are probable. However, it is an uncertain question whether such a compromise would result in policies and planning procedures which will optimize the long-term best uses of land, in relationship to other resources and with respect to human welfare optimization. Without serious attention to improving public institutional capability, ad hoc land-use policies and planning procedures at the local level may be no more productive over the long term than unrestricted, private land-use decisions (Clawson & Hall, 1973, pp. 270–271).

If the public mood is, in fact, shifting toward a greater concern for systematic methods for preserving and enhancing land resources, increasing public responsibility for land-use policies and planning may be demanded, even at the expense of income potential, status, and influence of individual landholders and the prevailing land market system. Under this assumption, a shift toward alternative 2, and eventually toward alternative 3, may be demanded. To a considerable degree, the nation is shifting partially toward alternative 4—public ownership of substantial additional land areas which have special characteristics. Between fiscal years 1966 and 1970, the National Park Service, the U.S. Forest Service, and the Bureau of Sports Fisheries and Wildlife purchased more than 820,000 acres at a cost of over $240 million. A number of states are substantially increasing purchases of open-space land, often through voter-approved bond issues. State expenditures for parkland purchase increased more than four times between 1960 and 1970 (Reilly, 1973, pp. 107–111).

The Basis for Greater Public Control of Land

The basis for public acquisition or strict regulation of land use has developed through a long series of court proceedings, arising in part from the "takings clause" in the Fifth Amendment of the U.S. Constitution: "nor shall private property be taken for public use without just compensation"; regulations restricting use have been challenged if they appear to decrease the potential development value of land. The conclusions of the courts have not been entirely consistent, but have generally supported the public right to regulate land use. We seem to be moving toward the justifications used by the British for strict planning controls (Reilly, 1973, p. 170):

1 The potential development value of land is essentially uncertain or speculative. Therefore, property restricted to current use is not considered reduced in value, and the "potential" development value of the land cannot be considered as a basis for compensation through public purchase or otherwise.

2 Land values are largely considered to be created by public actions, such as construction of highways or facilities, and the private right to profit from public action is not considered universally appropriate or acceptable.

On the basis of these justifications the British now require "planning permission" for essentially any significant land development by private landholders or public agencies. The planning permission requirement is potentially comparable to some elements of the National Environmental Policy Act (NEPA) of 1969 for environmental and social impact analysis. However, the NEPA requirements are presently limited to actions of federal government agencies, while state and private actions are not universally subject to environmental impact statements—except in a few states. Although the statements are required, they do not generally have the power to stop development that may be judged inappropriate—as in the British "planning permission" system. If environmental impact statements were extended to include greater attention to social impact, and were treated as direct requirements on decisions by government officials, they would have much greater influence on land use. A higher standard of performance by public land–influencing agencies would generally be encouraged (and appears to be in process), since citizen groups are permitted to bring suit if the agency decisions appear questionable.

A required environmental and social review process, prior to approval of specific developments, could be considerably streamlined by rigorous comprehensive planning. Exploring development policies and alternatives in advance could lead to a much sounder data base for impact analysis of individual developments.

However, the adequate development of policies and alternatives, as well as specific planning processes and implementation procedures, depends heavily on a well-designed and efficient planning organization. Piecemeal and ad hoc organizations will usually lead to intermittent and ineffective long-range planning *and* to public fear of inappropriate encroachment by planning departments and local governments on individual property rights.

Planning for Human Services in Rural Regions

Formalized planning for the complex of human services in rural regions is in the process of evolution. Much of the current activity within state and local levels of government focuses on specific program areas, such as comprehensive health, law, and justice, services to the aged, or other subsets of human service. There is little common understanding or agreement about what "human services planning" should include. This chapter attempts to summarize definitions and dimensions of the topic.

Although the terminology and content are comparable to "social planning" in many respects, "human services" seems to be both more acceptable as a descriptive term and more comprehensive in scope, when compared to the traditional welfare-oriented activity encompassed by much of social planning. In any case, the expanding emphasis on formalized planning for human services requires a more adequate conception of content, organization, method, and process, as well as clarification of relationships with other planning activity.

City, county, and regional planning departments have been assuming (by assignment or request) increased responsibility for human services planning as an adjunct to their more traditional physical and land-use planning activities. In most instances, planning directors and existing staff have had relatively little experience or preparation for rural human services planning. As Figure 6-1 illustrates, the services available are often makeshift or minimal compared with urban areas. However, planning directors and local officials have become sharply conscious of the need for better understanding of human resource issues.[1]

Definitions

In its most elementary form, human resource planning can be defined as a focused effort to guide public and private institutions in improving individual capability to meet basic needs: physical comfort, social security, and psychological fulfillment. The underlying goal of human services planning is to improve institutions and organizations which contribute to more ideal conditions.

The human services planning process therefore involves at least these stages:

1 Identifying the basic problems of major social categories of the population
2 Measuring the existing human service provisions for each subcategory
3 Establishing "ideal" conditions in the form of general goals to be achieved
4 Measuring the gap between "existing" conditions and the "ideal" conditions, to develop specific operational objectives or targets
5 Designing procedures or programs, and locating sources of funding, by which objectives can be met in some order of priority
6 Helping to monitor and guide the programs toward reaching the objectives
7 Measuring results, progress, or failure

As part of this process, human services planning becomes the guiding mechanism for a stronger and more effective linkage between (1) defined goals or policies for meeting human needs and (2) the programs which attempt to alleviate or fulfill those needs, by:

1 Coordinating the activities of social institutions or agencies to provide improved service delivery across a single functional field (i.e., health

[1] William R. Lassey (Ed.). *Human resource planning*. Pullman: Washington State University, Cooperative Extension Service, 1974. Much of the material in this chapter is adapted from papers presented by local government officials, human services planners, and social scientists, as part of a seminar in March of 1974. The contributions of Kathy Utz, Maurice Bender, William Mahan, Hazel Burnett, Pauline Loveless, and Victor Thompson were particularly helpful.

Figure 6-1 Human services in rural areas. Social services in rural areas are often inferi-
or, in part because population sparcity makes provision of services very expensive per
capita but also because little effort has been undertaken to plan for institutions that
uniquely fit the needs of the people who inhabit rural communities. Transplant of service
concepts from urban circumstances to rural regions often results in a lack of fit and
inadequate use of the services provided. (*Photos by W. R. Lassey.*)

care) and to provide for the delivery of integrated and comprehensive services

2   Coordinating with (*a*) physical planning, which has traditionally been concerned with providing the "facilities" for meeting human needs; (*b*) land-use planning, which is concerned with locating those facilities in appropriate or ideal land spaces

3   Redistributing wealth; i.e., planning provides guidance for relocating goods and services outside the market system to individuals and groups with special needs

4   Examining and redirecting social institutions toward a future orientation, in accord with technological, social, economic, and political changes which dramatically affect individual and collective well-being

The basic assumption is that fulfillment of group and individual needs can be achieved through specific and coordinated programs, undertaken by public and private agencies, and under the general coordination and guidance of legislative and administrative bodies.

State government has historically been responsible for provision of human services not performed by private groups in local communities, while local governments have concentrated their resources on the provision of capital facilities, i.e., sewer, water, and road systems. State governments deliver human services at the local level, but often operate separately from local government through independent planning and administrative systems.

A most important problem facing local human services planning is the multiplicity of agencies containing information systems on various aspects of the human condition, arising from whatever data-classification techniques were current at the time they were established.

Information and referral services are proliferating almost as fast as computers themselves. Obviously, data bases are necessary tools for planning; coordinated human services planning can provide the mechanism to publicly share information without requiring a massive retooling of information systems. The answer certainly is not a giant "bank" which all individuals and agencies can tap as needed. Cooperation between agencies, and frequent communications between and among local planning jurisdictions, is needed. The population generally moves about freely to seek services without respect to political or agency boundaries. Planning for human needs must somehow be reconciled with territorial delineations. If not, planning by city, county, regional, and state bodies tends to become a professional exercise, often marginally useful to governmental units.

Constraints and Conflicts in the Role of State and Local Government

Although elected and appointed officials in local jurisdictions (towns, cities, and counties) should be directly involved in human services planning, they are finding this task difficult. The new responsibility for setting social goals and priorities is both more complex and not entirely comparable to traditional planning. County and city functions are now broadened to include social activities not previously administered on the local level; therefore, local governments have little experience with developing policies and plans. Yet this shift of responsibility is considered increasingly necessary, because the pattern of human needs is unique to particular geographic areas; an agency headquartered in Washington, D.C., or the state capital cannot effectively deal with the distinct requirements of each rural region.

Laws establish local responsibility for physical problems related to growth, but few requirements exist with regard to human problems. Meanwhile, the elected official is faced with an increased range of demands for uses of the tax dollar. Even those public officials who do want to plan for future eventualities have trouble measuring the value of social programs, since it is more difficult to count illnesses cured and impaired social conditions improved, compared with new buildings constructed, new roads built, or other physical changes.

Among elected officials there is usually an orientation to respond to needs expressed by significant numbers of voters. Although numbers of people affected by social problems are significant, severe problems usually impact only a small portion of the community, whose discomfort is not in public view as often as those physical issues that affect larger segments of the population.

It is apparent that local elected officials will have to deal with a twofold role: (1) assuming greater responsibilities for social problems and (2) endeavoring to interrelate programs for maximum effectiveness. The local official's coordination and management job is not easy, because of the segmented approach used by many federal and state agencies.

Interactions with Physical and Land-Use Planning

As noted above, physical planning has traditionally been primarily concerned with providing the "facilities" for meeting human needs, while land-use planning is concerned with locating those facilities in appropriate or ideal spaces. Until recently most planning departments have not clearly understood the specific needs of population groupings; this has limited their ability to design facilities and locate them for the benefit of population subgroups. Rather, facilities and location have often been planned for relatively ill-defined "average" populations. Figure 6-2 pointedly depicts inadequate housing as a serious problem of rural communities, whose average resident age is usually above the national average. The consequence has been detrimental to population subgroups which do not have the ability or the visibility to make their needs known. Human services planning has the task of demonstrating the relationships among social needs, programs, physical facilities, and land use.

Figure 6-2 Inadequate housing, particularly for older people. Adequate housing is a perennial problem in most rural communities. There is almost invariably a substantial number of older, deteriorating homes, often occupied by older people who cannot afford anything better. The average age of the population in most small towns is much higher than the national average. Very little specific planning is under way in most rural areas that can effectively alleviate the housing and maintenance problems of older people. (*Photos by W. R. Lassey.*)

In primarily rural counties, several additional issues obstruct effective planning:

1 County commissioners are often disillusioned because expensive planning studies are gathering dust, while there are too few resources to achieve planned programs.

2 The lack of revenue is severe; many rural counties have large geographic areas with low population density; rural areas often have a high percentage of nontaxable lands—state, federal, and Indian land generates little tax base. There is often a high proportion of low-wage earners and often high unemployment. County officials feel forced to operate on a crisis basis in making resource allocation decisions.

3 Rural counties are often unprepared to add professional staff for increasing demands in human service.

4 Constraints are imposed by categorical grants; federal and state

Figure 6-3 Health services. Medical services are a particularly difficult and expensive problem in many rural regions. Hospitals (if they are available) are often not able to afford the modern equipment and services which well-trained and specialized physicians expect. This means that doctors are difficult to attract or retain. Ambulance services to transport patients to local hospitals or larger urban centers are expensive to maintain and must often be headquartered at major distances from much of the rural population. Health services planning on a regional basis may be essential if adequate medical care is to be available, particularly in sparsely settled rural areas. (*Photos by W. R. Lassey.*)

guidelines often do not fit local conditions, and the rural areas often cannot compete for small grants funded on the basis of population numbers.

5 There are few mechanisms for integrated human resource planning: (*a*) the transportation problem in rural areas hampers development and delivery of services; (*b*) most rural social programs have limited staffs and budgets to deal effectively with large geographic areas; (*c*) there is a lack of coordination between social agencies, which often creates a duplication of services or leaves gaps due to lack of information about other programs; (*d*) there is often marked "turf" protection and professional jealousies between agencies, which interferes with effective delivery of services; and (*e*) human service programs do not have the staff capability for treating generic problems. The lack of adequate health services (see Figure 6-3) in most rural areas indicates the need for effective health services planning.

Citizens and local officials tend to be interested primarily in relatively specialized sets of priority activities—and cannot effectively engage in or understand the complexities of the total planning effort. Formation of citizens and local officials into advisory or policy groups for the various subcategories of planning activity can allow specialized study and input to planning and programming. However, if this is to avoid segmented and uncoordinated activity, a formal structure is needed to assure that planning subunits, and their advisory groupings, are integrated.

Elected local officials must assume responsibility for assuring the integration, by (1) hiring professional administrators who can oversee the total process, (2) maintaining sufficient involvement to provide the coordination, or (3) forming citizen planning commissions which have the mandate and the power to direct and supervise the planning process. In many multijurisdictional regions this could result in consolidation of local services and integration of programs, as well as more coordinated planning.

Chapter VII

Planning Dimensions
and Illustrative
Analytical Procedures

Broadly conceived planning requires a range of methodological skills which go well beyond the data collection and analysis processes discussed in earlier chapters. Planning methods might best be derived from a mix of scientific rigor and practical experience blended with the realism and political pragmatism of elected local officials and appointed professionals. Communication, education, and public involvement methods might best be undertaken collaboratively with professional educators, volunteer leaders, and public officials; the skills associated with translating plans into action have often been the missing link in public planning and are discussed in considerable detail in Chapter VIII.

This chapter describes selected procedures which illustrate planning methodologies particularly applicable to rural regions. No attempt is made to comprehensively examine the full range of methods and procedures appropriate to the larger discipline of planning. Several useful texts describe these methods, as noted in the references at the end of the book.

Alternative Approaches to Planning[1]

Four distinct approaches to planning can be identified which elicit quite different consequences and priorities:[2]

1 Crisis intervention
2 Regulatory control
3 Entrepreneurial innovation
4 Systems analysis

Crisis intervention responds only to issues that obviously demand action and focuses more on "problem-solving" than on "planning" as defined here. This approach was largely followed by all levels of government up to about World War I and remains the norm in many local jurisdictions. It is consistent with the philosophy that decisions, actions, and change are a matter of free choices and interactions of individuals within a society in which there is seldom any need for collective action. It focuses on present concerns and reacts to past problems. In the short run some solution is devised, but little thought is given to the future impacts of the solution.

Regulatory planning goes beyond crisis intervention by trying to guide or influence actions and trends to avoid problems in the future. It seeks to anticipate the future by determining trends—then adapting planning to fit those trends so that decisions are in accord with future expectations. There is no major attempt to influence the future but rather to balance out conflicts or avoid problems. This approach is basically conservative since it seeks to maintain existing values. Examples of regulatory planning include: building codes to maintain sound and healthful buildings; subdivision regulations to ensure orderly and pleasing site design; and zoning ordinances which establish separate areas of differing economic activities to protect property values, public safety, etc. Much of land-use planning up to the present is of this order.

Entrepreneurial planning is common for private firms because their planning horizon is longer (perhaps by a generation) than that of most public agencies. Entrepreneurial planning looks for new opportunities in the future. Instead of adopting regulations simply to preserve the status quo, entrepreneurial planning seeks speculative options that will actually change the direction of the future. For example, real estate investors in the late 1940s observed the trend toward suburban living. They devised the

[1] Adapted from Barron, Lassey, & Ditwiler, 1976. A new book on rural planning methods is in preparation by the American Society of Planning Officials; it will offer detailed treatments of methods and procedures for land-use analysis and control.

[2] See Brian J. L. Berry. The question of policy alternatives. In *The good earth of America: Planning our land use,* copyright © 1974 The American Assembly, Columbia University, pp. 158–160. Adapted by permission of Prentice-Hall, Inc., Englewood Cliffs, New Jersey.

planned shopping center as a means of actually directing the future. This not only transformed retail marketing in America but also drastically changed land-use patterns. Public planning agencies have generally not adopted entrepreneurial planning or have had insufficient vision and resources to incorporate this approach.

Systems planning requires that future goals be established. The physical-biological-social system is analyzed to determine the tools needed to steer it toward those goals. Progress is constantly monitored, and adjustments are made to keep it on course. If this style of planning is to be effective, it requires more centralized control than we have normally been willing to grant to public authorities. The choice may hinge on whether or not the present system is capable of achieving the goals set by the public.

In sum, crisis intervention is past-oriented; regulatory planning tries to adapt to the future; entrepreneurial planning seeks to shape the future in limited ways; and systems planning works backward from a desired future and devises policies to get there. Ideally, planning should incorporate each approach while emphasizing the more comprehensive and long-term systems perspective.

Comprehensiveness

Comprehensiveness implies taking into account those factors most relevant to preparation for the future, assuming from the very outset that resources and understanding will not allow for the detail, completeness, and interrelating of factors that might ultimately be desirable. The "comprehensive" plan becomes a best effort to include all factors relevant to policy and action decisions.

As noted in Chapter I (Figures 1-2 and 1-3), the planning process should be the central element of the ongoing input to critical decisions about the future condition of a jurisdiction or region. The chief clients are publicly chosen decision makers, although the social-biological-physical environment is obviously the ultimate beneficiary and "client." Comprehensive planning in this framework attempts to productively structure the formal communication and interaction mechanism between policy makers, professionals who implement policy decisions about the future, and the citizen public. The planner's role is to serve as a continuing adviser and consultant to public officials and citizens, with particular responsibility for optimizing application of existing knowledge to decisions and actions. The comprehensive planning process can also serve as "in-service" training for legislators, public officials, and citizens. It should increase understanding of the region or jurisdiction and the external forces and influences which affect it.

Various levels of comprehensiveness are enumerated in Table 7-1. Current or operational plans focus on issues of greatest immediate priority. As

Table 7-1   Levels of Comprehensiveness and Scope in Regional Planning

1   Current or operational planning:
   a   Attempts to describe, integrate, and coordinate current and continuing short-range action programs
   b   Incorporates only sufficient efforts at projection into the future to facilitate immediate decisions about action
   c   Should be derived from intermediate and long-range plans, as an increment of progress, insofar as longer-range plans exist
   d   Specifies immediate quantities, schedules of activity, materials, skills, energy, costs, methods of implementation, etc., for a period of a few months or 1 year
2   Medium-range or intermediate planning:
   a   Extends dates, probabilities, and desirable states over a fixed time span, such as 3 or 5 years
   b   Provides a conceptual, analytical, procedural, and action "bridge" between the present and the more distant future
   c   Specifies clear-cut goals and actions for completion at the termination of a fixed time span
   d   Includes but usually supplements and expands upon factors considered in current planning
3   Long-range planning:
   a   Specifies general goals and desirable future actions based on most advanced current knowledge and projections about the future
   b   Specifies long-term plans on the basis of available resource expectations and ecological constraints
   c   Is designed to be flexible so that periodic modification can be incorporated
   d   Usually includes a range of possible and potentially desirable alternatives rather than specific utopian expectations
   e   Attempts to collect, assimilate, interrelate, and incorporate all information relevant to selected comprehensive goals

Source: Adapted from M. C. Branch, *Planning: Aspects and applications.* Adapted by permission of John Wiley & Sons, Inc.

current plans are initiated, based on the best existing knowledge about desirable intermediate and long-range goals, more emphasis can be given to longer-range planning, with adaptations applied to current plans as new and better information about the future is generated. This emphasizes the importance of "flexibility"—so that changes can be made in current- or intermediate-range plans as more is learned that has relevance to the immediate action effort (Branch, 1966, p. 304).

Designing with Nature
McHarg (1969) and Lewis (1968) propose methods of long-range and systematized planning based on "physiographic" regions. McHarg emphasizes the need to secure sufficiently detailed information to define "intrinsic suitabilities" of the landscape. These suitabilities are based on analysis of the most scientifically reasonable locations for the various classes of human activity and natural process. Intrinsic suitabilities are selected on the basis

of "social" value attached to land uses. Relative social value of an area or location is assigned a rank from one to five, based on potential contribution to maintenance of ecological integrity and realization of social needs. Social value implies a very long time perspective; "high value" assumes the designated land use will lead toward enhancement of the environment. Values are assigned to land capability for each of several major categories, such as agriculture, natural resource extraction, forestry, recreation, residential habitation, industry, and conservation.

Important natural characteristics noted by McHarg:[3]

- Bedrock foundation
- Soil foundation or surficial geology
- Climate
- Hydrology
- Slope
- Soil drainage
- Surface drainage
- Susceptibility to erosion
- Plant ecology (including forest and woodland)
- Animal ecology (particularly wildlife)

Human-use considerations include:

- Historic landmarks
- Scenic locations
- Recreation locations
- Water courses and impoundments
- Residential areas
- Social-industrial locations
- Business and industry
- Public utilities
- Agriculture
- Natural resource extraction
- Forestry

The *natural processes* which must be preserved because of the crucial work which they perform include:

- Natural water storage and purification
- Atmospheric pollution dispersal
- Climatic amelioration or moderation
- Flood, drought, and erosion control

[3] From *Design with nature*, copyright © 1969 by Ian McHarg. Reprinted by permission of Doubleday & Co., Inc.

- Topsoil accumulation
- Animal and plant reproduction
- Protection from incursions by ocean or sea (beach sand dunes)

Figure 7-1 illustrates ocean beaches, which are increasingly becoming an ecological concern as we try to maintain their recreational appeal while making use of them for industrial and life-support functions.

McHarg insists the natural process factors must be given primary consideration because of their essential input to the sustenance of the region. Human use of certain areas must be severely constrained because of potential damage to natural processes which might eventually be destructive to human survival. Such areas include surface water, marshes, flood plains, aquifer recharge areas, aquifers, steep slopes, forests, and prime agriculture areas.

Special attention should be given to:

- High-quality forests

Figure 7-1 Ocean beaches. Beaches are both fragile and delightful as locations for recreation. Uncontrolled development often leads to crowding and serious destruction of ecological systems adjacent to salt water or fresh water. A variety of actions have been taken to alleviate such problems, such as the National Coastal Zone Program, but much remains to be achieved if ocean beaches are to be maintained or enhanced as locales for essential life-support processes as well as recreation and ocean-related industries such as fishing. (*Photos by W. R. Lassey.*)

- High-quality marshes
- Bay beaches
- Flowing streams
- Dry land wildlife habitats
- Water-associated wildlife habitats
- Intertidal wildlife habitats
- Unique geological features
- Unique physiographic features
- Scenic land features
- Scenic water features
- Scarce ecological associations
- Historic sites or locations

In attempting to understand the nature of physiographic regions, McHarg and Lewis recommend studies proceeding from the basic factors to more dependent factors. This means that the first order of examination should be historic geology and climate, which have created the basic landform. Current morphology is then examined to determine the pattern of rivers and streams and distribution of groundwater, including quantities and properties thereof. The movement of sediments reveals the pattern, distribution, and properties of soils, which provide the basis for incidence of plant types and communities; these in turn provide sustenance for and determine animal species and distribution. Data from each type of study can be displayed on transparent maps, which collectively begin to reveal relationships among characteristics of the landscape.

Analysis reveals the fundamental nonhuman ecology on which the human systems have been implanted. Study of the human elements begins with demographic determination of characteristics and distribution of the population in relationship to the existing ecological system. Human institutions are examined in terms of their ability to meet changing human needs, while avoiding despoliation of the nonhuman ecological system. The existence of social pathologies is examined as indicators of malfunctioning of social institutions or environmental health inadequacies (McHarg, 1969).

Preservation and enhancement of the basic community functions are also critical for helping individuals to function as part of society within the natural environment (socialization); managing the human tendencies to disrupt, disorganize, or destroy the social system (social control); caring for those individuals who are dependent for reasons of age or infirmity (mutual support); providing opportunities for individuals and groups to meet their needs for contact and communication with other individuals (social participation); and the basic production, distribution, and consumption (economic) activities for meeting individual needs (Warren, 1972).

Table 7-2 summarizes the central concepts, elements, and methods in the McHarg regional analysis method, but adds the social-institutional pro-

Table 7-2 Designing with Nature: Key Concepts, Methods, Factors, and Processes

Basic concepts	Basic natural factors	Human value factors
Physiographic regions	Bedrock foundations	Historic landmarks
Intrinsic suitabilities	Soil foundation	Scenic locations
Social value	Climate	Recreation locations
Ecological integrity	Hydrology	Water courses and impoundments
	Slope	Residential areas
	Soil drainage	Social institution locations
	Surface drainage	Business and industry locations
	Erosion susceptibility	Public utilities
	Plant life	Agriculture
	Animal life	Natural resource extraction
		Forestry
		Transportation

Basic methodological requirements	Natural processes to be preserved	Human processes to be preserved
Understanding of natural and social factors	Natural water storage and purification	Socialization
Establishing interactions between factors and processes	Atmospheric pollution dispersal	Social control
Mapping physiographic locations	Climatic amelioration or moderation	Mutual support
Assigning social values and ecological requirements	Flood, drought, and erosion control	Social participation
Locating intrinsic suitability areas for human activity	Topsoil accumulation	Production, distribution, and consumption
	Animal and plant reproduction	
	Protection from incursions by ocean and sea	

cesses emphasized by Warren. The major innovations of the McHarg planning system include (1) the production of overlay maps to visually illustrate and display the interrelationships between landscape and human elements, (2) the commitment to consider physiographic regions, beginning with foundation material and proceeding to the increasingly dependent factors, and (3) the attempt to base the study and design process entirely on ecologically sound principles so as to preserve and enhance the life-support system.

Construction of Conceptual or Mathematical Models

If comprehensive rural or regional planning is to be useful, it must be reasonably successful at conceptualizing probable future conditions. Simulation and modeling can be useful tools for this purpose. Quantifiable information must be distilled to the essential elements or it becomes enormously expensive to manage, even if computers are used to manipulate data.

Variables that cannot be fully quantified must be included as part of conceptual models—the usual predecessors of mathematical models. Important variables should be treated analytically at the conceptual level, rather than ignored, if they have a high probability of partially explaining relationships among factors in a regional system.

If simulation and modeling are to be supported by policymakers, their use and output must be comprehensible. This suggests that pictorial and graphic presentation of model components is essential, so that the nonmathematician can perceive the issues and activities encompassed by planning procedures. Obviously, the validity of such models must be regularly tested and revised as new information is acquired and as action occurs which is inadequately predicted by the models.

The McHarg framework can help to organize and interrelate a wide variety of data. In those instances where the physical and biological factors clearly indicate constraints and desirabilities with respect to location of human activity, the method can be considered reasonably complete. However, in most instances such data will not provide an adequate basis for delineation of alternatives and decision making unless supplemented by detailed economic, social, and political analysis.

Several applications of quantitative analysis have been illustrated in a volume by Isard (and others) dealing with economic-ecological models for regional planning (Isard et al., 1972). Analytical models are suggested, illustrated, and applied to a case study.

In each instance an economic model is extended to ecological analysis; economic and ecological variables are interrelated in conceptual, or occasionally mathematical, form. The work is intended to be exploratory but provides a basis for interrelating significant factors in a productive and illuminating manner.

Comparative cost analysis is used to evaluate the cost of various alternative developments, or comparative locations for a single development; direct costs of development are compared with estimates of indirect costs resulting from ecological damage. The final "solution" encompasses detailed consideration of potential environmental impact.

Input-output analysis is used to delineate the total inputs required for planned changes in land use as well as the total expected outputs, again with respect to both economic and ecological factors; quantitative methods are used, unless it is clearly inappropriate or impossible to ascribe numerical values to ecological factors. In these instances, descriptive analysis is used to estimate the relevance and impact of the nonquantified factors.

Spatial interaction analysis is used to evaluate the relative advantages and disadvantages of alternative locations for developments, based on measurments of tendency for potential uses to occur at each location. Estimated impact of users on ecological systems is included, as well as quantities of potential uses. These estimates are based on existing capacity of transportation arteries, estimated increased automobile pollution, and other potential direct impacts of human use on elements of the ecosystem.

Activity complex analysis attempts to combine various kinds of activities associated with the potential development and assess interrelationships of costs, inputs, outputs, and spatial interaction. It is an integrative process and again attempts to take broad account of both ecological and economic impacts (Isard et al., 1972, pp. 6–48).

Isard also develops a *natural resource classification* system to assist in decisions about the use of such resources. The major categories include:

1 Nonrenewable resources which are largely lost once used, such as minerals
2 Flow resources with constant supply, such as water and solar radiation, which may be damaged or polluted but are not destroyed by use
3 Naturally renewable resources, such as plants and animals

The method then outlines the components of ecosystems and the necessary conditions to avoid depletion of nonrenewable resources, maintenance of flow resources without despoilation, and support of naturally renewable resources to assure their continuing supply—all considerations which must enter directly into regional planning analysis (Isard et al., 1972, pp. 50–53).

Socioeconomic-Political Considerations

The Isard analytical and mathematical planning models are an attempt to integrate ecological and economic variables within a single framework. Sismondo and Eberts have made a similar attempt using sociological, economic, and political variables. The basis for the model is an underlying theory that planned socioeconomic change results from certain fundamental orga-

Table 7-3   Model of the Relation among Four Sets of Variables in Planned Socioeconomic Change

Advocacy and strategy	Lag →	Policy and programs	Lag →	Community or regional system changes	Lag →	Desires, wants, goals of individuals

nizational characteristics of regions and communities (Sismondo, 1972 and 1973; Eberts, 1971). The Eberts-Sismondo model further rests on an assumption that political pressure from constituents is a prerequisite if policymakers are to implement planned programs to achieve the basic goals of the population (such as greater income, better housing, good health, better jobs, and prevention of such disrupting factors as crime, delinquency, and mental illness). These human desires can be achieved through a deliberate strategy, beginning with the advocacy of needs through political programs, pressure groups, power holders at various levels, public relations, and planning-oriented research; however, a carefully designed planning strategy and method is necessary to bring the needed changes to the attention of decision makers in a manner that is comprehensible to them.

If the need is clearly perceived and the pressures of advocacy sufficient, policies will be formulated in special legislation intended to achieve the desired goals; these may take the form of programs for housing, welfare, education, industrialization, or other direct efforts to facilitate change through use of public taxation or subsidization of private enterprise. The new policies can then lead to changes in the organization and structure of regions or communities by tying the area more directly to outside influences, which provide inputs (linkages) to individuals and organizations in the given territory. The new inputs tend to upset the existing, and often ineffective, status quo, leading to greater openness (fluidity) to change and greater equality of opportunity and participation. New opportunities for business, employment, and services arise (differentiation) which then contribute to the desires, goals, and basic needs of the population. The conceptual models are summarized in Tables 7-3 and 7-4 (Sismondo, 1973, pp. 40 and 43).

Table 7-4   General Model of Community or Regional System Change

Time stage:	I II	III	IV	V
Linkages —————————→ Differentiation —→ Equality				↘ New linkages
Equality —→ Fluidity			Fluidity ↗	
Quality of life			Quality of life	

The concept of "linkages," which is considered the principal and initial causal force in these formulations, is derived from research traditions in cultural anthropology, economic geography, and human ecology. It is based on the fundamental importance of the intensity and form of communication channels as a causal force in socioeconomic-cultural change (Sismondo, 1973, p. 44; Lassey, 1968).

The conceptual model can then be quantified with specific measurements of linkages as well as each of the other variables in the model, followed by mathematical measurements of the interrelationships among variables or factors as posited. Sismondo and Eberts have used Guttman scaling, factor analysis, linear regression, time-lagged correlation matrices, and path analysis to initially test the models (Sismondo, 1973, pp. 211–280). The mathematical application of the model in Table 7-4 is illustrated in Figure 7-2 (Sismondo, 1973, p. 289).

It is important to note that this model is in the process of testing, and therefore both conceptual formulations and mathematical results are considered preliminary and tentative. But the illustrative use of simulation, conceptual, and relational models, with mathematical applications, is useful in illustrating the potential utility of advanced analytical tools in planning.

As noted earlier, this discussion of approaches to method and practice in regional planning is intended to be illustrative rather than comprehensive. The emphasis on "regional" boundaries, rather than towns, cities, or rural areas, arises from the recognition that each such unit is part of a larger regional system, which must be treated comprehensively if planning is to effectively deal with the interdependencies which clearly exist. No attempt

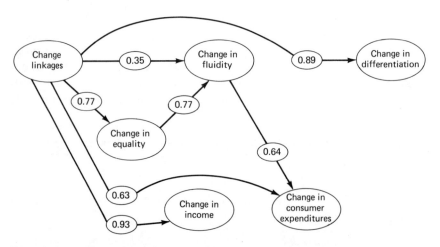

Figure 7-2 Mathematical relationships (R^2) between major variables.

is made to specifically define the nature of a "region," since any region is essentially an arbitrary subdivision of a larger regional system; the crucial issue is to assure that regional boundaries are so defined that provision is made for interrelating data from among jurisdictions. The total ecosystem is eventually considered and actions are initiated which take the interdependencies of the total system into account.

The Lewis-McHarg regional planning method offers a useful conceptual framework for dealing with physiographic regions, while specifying methods for studying, analyzing, and interrelating the relevant factors which must be included in ecologically sound planned action. The Isard economic-ecological method of study and analysis illustrates one of the more advanced attempts to use social, economic, political, and psychological research to deliberately plan and measure change.

Chapter VIII

Increasing the Payoff from Planning: Implementation and Involvement Processes

Effective planning can be considered essentially a sociopolitical process; in the longer perspective, it is likely to require major adjustment in social, economic, and political structures. If planning is considered the primary tool which links knowledge with action, it can also be considered the principal vehicle through which analysis and evaluation of basic institutional structures of society are undertaken. If these structures do not function adequately in solving problems and realizing opportunities, unstabilizing changes must be proposed and implemented. If fundamental changes are to occur, without imposition by higher authority, locally elected political figures must inevitably be involved and held responsible for decisions.

Individuals representing interest groups and organizations threatened by changes can be expected to initiate vigorous opposition to protect their economic, political, or social status. The consequences of informed planning will almost inevitably involve decisions which oppose valued patterns of behavior solidly wedded to the status quo.

Both the difficulties and the possibilities for increasing the utility of planning suggest the need to understand and affect the political context in which planning occurs, regardless of the specific locale. The conceptual framework for planning was described in Chapter III, but further elaboration is needed to identify individuals, groups, and organizations who may participate in each planning phase, apart from public officials, professional planners, and scientists. Likewise, it is important to understand how potential participants in planning implementation might be involved at each phase of the process. The outcome of decisions will reflect the values, goals, and interests of those participants who occupy key positions in the decision-making arena, or who have the sharpest skills in negotiating, or who have the most effective skill in the tactics of influencing the behavior of individuals, groups, and organizations.

Potential participant activities or roles are noted in Table 8-1.

During the preparation phase, advocates of planning will help establish the climate for initiators of specific activity. Technical experts, scientists, data analysts, integrators, educators, and the news media can help provide the information base for decisions. During the goal setting and decision phases, opinion leaders for various special interest groups, respected community figures (legitimizers), critics of planning, financial controllers or power brokers, political officeholders, managers of the planning process, and individuals with skill in the integration or mediation of value or belief differences can each play key roles. Once decisions are made, the implementation strategists, organizers of action programs, mediators between individuals and groups affected by the action, enforcers of rules, and evaluators of planning become prominent. Although these roles are discussed here in terms of planning phases, in reality they will each have a continuing function in an ongoing process.

Rural planning consists of a highly complex system (depending somewhat on the region under consideration) of individual attitudes, small group

Table 8-1 Key Participant Roles in Planning Process

Preparation phases	Goal-setting and decision phases	Action-implementation
Planning manager	Political office-	Strategist
Advocate	holder	Organizer
Initiator	Opinion leader	Mediator
Technical expert	Legitimizer	Enforcer
Scientist	Critic	Evaluator
Data analyst	Social-emotional	Educator
Integrator	integrator	
Educator		
Newsperson		

Source: Adapted from R. S. Bolan, Community decision behavior: The culture of planning, *Journal of the American Institute of Planners,* vol. 35, no. 5, September 1969. Adapted by permission of the *Journal of the American Institute of Planners.*

and organizational special interests, governmental structures, physical environmental conditions, and sociopolitical experience. The formal political decision structure may be highly focused and centralized, or it may be dispersed through a range of less prominent but autonomous decision centers; ordinarily the more focused the structure, the more likely it will be to produce action on a planning proposal which it supports. A highly competent and stable local government bureaucracy is more likely to produce positive decisions and action on proposed plans than a political environment lacking stability and competence. The major difficulty in most rural planning environments is the decided lack of either high planning competence or stability of planning functions (Bolan, 1969).

The informal structures within the sociopolitical environment are also of central importance. The existence of strong interest groups usually provides a more viable context for realistic consideration of planning issues than an environment in which private interests are apathetic or dispersed. In other words, rural communities or planning regions with relatively strong integrative mechanisms for reconciling diverging viewpoints will tend to have a greater capacity for purposeful decision making (Clarke, 1968, chap. 2).

The Action-planning Concept[1]

Formalized planning processes at national, state, regional, and local levels have generally assumed that professionals draw up plans based on careful processes of problem identification, collection of needed data, analysis of needs, setting of appropriate objectives, and outlining of a detailed physical, economic, or social plan. The product then goes to a decision-making body for acceptance, modification, or rejection. This approach assumes that "planning" and "implementation" are two separate and distinctive activities, the first of which is undertaken with minimum involvement of citizens or policymakers.

Failure to achieve systematic implementation is blamed on a variety of obstacles, primarily the failure of local politicians and decision makers to appreciate the virtues of the plans or inadequate communication between the planners and their clients (Friedmann, 1973). The traditional approach generally assumes that professionals have the ability to offer proposals and devise efficient plans which are technically and operationally superior to what might be produced with the involvement and assistance of lay citizens and/or local officials.

---

[1] This section draws heavily from John Friedmann. Notes on societal action. *Journal of the American Institute of Planners*, vol. 35, no. 5, September 1969. Adapted by permission of the *Journal of the American Institute of Planners*.

Friedmann (1969) proposes an alternative conception:[2]

There is a good deal of evidence for the hypothesis that planning in its most generalized form is an ubiquitous activity, that all deliberate actions consider the value implications of choice, imply a knowledge of alternatives foregone, attempt to relate means to ends efficiently and correct on-going actions on the basis of information about their results. This may not always be done well, but it is done. A superabundance of plans is conceivable, but deliberate action without some kind of planning is not.

Action planning fuses planning and implementation into a single operation so that the usual "stages" of planning are integrated into a cyclical process that is ongoing and is directly related to action steps; planning becomes an integral part of a decision-making and managerial process. If this is to occur, several subcategorizations of action planning are helpful. Efforts to improve on an existing system can be either *adaptive* or *developmental*; "adaptive" activity attempts to maintain the system in response to the outside pressures for change or when the system might become nonfunctional if certain adjustments were not made. Responsive planning is usually preferred by communities in which citizens or leaders do not recognize the need for radical departure from convention.

"Developmental" activity operates to promote changes which will result in some greater level of activity, or seeks realization of new goals. The social system may be substantially modified but does not necessarily take any radical new form. If rural societies are to adjust to the changes under way in the larger society, developmental planning activity will be necessary.

Two further subcategories help to clarify the kinds of activity called for. *Allocative activity* is concerned with the distribution of existing or potential resources among competing uses. This is the usual expectation among local planners, public officials, and agency professionals. *Innovative activity* is much more demanding: it seeks new approaches to problem solutions or searches for new goals which may require restructuring resource allocations.

The action-planning process cannot become the exclusive responsibility of a centralized government agency; rather, many individuals and groups must be involved. Neither do all participants have to operate under a single set of objectives nor be deliberately supervised in any pervasive sense. However, a mechanism is required for linking the activities together in a formal coordinating system. In rural areas this linking function might be provided most appropriately by elected officials or their appointees, since they have responsibility for some degree of societal guidance.

---

[2] John Friedmann. Notes on societal action. Reprinted by permission of the *Journal of the American Institute of Planners*, vol. 35, no. 5, September 1969.

Innovative planning may introduce new roles, such as professional local administrators (city or county managers, for example) and highly trained specialists in subjects where special skills are needed. One of the most critical tasks for innovative action planning is to effectively evaluate current performance of existing community institutions, leading to an objective assessment of successes, inadequacies, and failures. Evaluation processes are not well understood or appreciated by most professionals in local or larger planning systems and may often be threatening to politicians and administrators. However, if effective action planning is to be instituted, reasonably accurate understanding of existing levels of performance is crucial. The selection of objective evaluation procedures and competent personnel is difficult, but increasingly possible as the sophistication of evaluation procedures increases.

The action-planning conception can radically change the role of professional planners. Instead of technical analysts who provide the background information for someone else's decision, action planners may become directly involved in designing and administering the action process. Their advocacy role is legitimized by a high level of technical competence, but their interactive and communication skills must be highly developed as well if they are to effectively relate with politicians, other administrators, and influential citizens who are responsible for parts of the planning, decision, and action processes.

The Formal Decision Process

The decision process with respect to specific proposals will usually take a form similar to the steps listed in Table 8-2. (This chart expands the "decision" element noted in Figure 3-1.) The initial step clarifies the issues about which a decision is to be made. This is profitably followed by a simulation of alternative decision consequences to determine the potential supporting and opposing forces and to determine whether sufficient support exists to enable effective action. Such activity often involves intensive efforts at persuasion and bargaining, with supporting and opposing forces each attempting to secure additional strength for their position.

It is at the point of formal decision that the full forces of existing values, beliefs, prejudices, political preferences, and special interests come into full expression, particularly if there is a high likelihood of major social or physical changes resulting from the decision; the adequacy of organization for planning and effectiveness of communication and education processes are often under severe test. There is likely to be a high level of misinformation generated by individuals who resist change and who will try to protect their values and self-interest at all costs. If the forces in support of planning proposals are not well organized and prepared to counter misinformation quickly and expertly, the opposing forces can often gener-

Table 8-2 General Steps in the Planning Decision Process

Step 1 *Structuring and defining the issues for decision*
   a Recognition of a discrepancy between desirable and existing conditions
   b Recognition that the issue can be resolved through appropriate action
   c Formulation of possible alternative feasible solutions

Step 2 *Simulation testing of the alternatives*
   a Merits of alternative solutions as evaluated by experts
   b Value orientations of influentials responsible for implementing each alternative
   c Anticipated resource requirements for each alternative, and the effects of resource allocation on influentials and the total social unit involved
   d Potential effect on the position and status of influentials in the various positions within the social unit
   e Potential aggregate or total support from the social subunits for each alternative

Step 3 *Clarifying the nature of forces affecting the decision*
   a Identification of potential supporting and opposing groups and individuals
   b Initial seeking of support from all relevant groups and individuals
   c Initial negotiations to suggest needed information sharing or exchanges to secure support from marginal individuals and subgroups
   d Designing a strategy for the formal decision
   e Organizing people and other resources

Step 4 *The formal decision*
   a Public acknowledgement of commitment, opposition, and allocating responsibilities for marshaling positive and negative support
   b Engaging the relevant groups and individuals in consideration of the issues
   c Discussion and exchanges of support (bargaining, trading for support on other issues, etc.)
   d Final negotiation prior to decision
   e Decision and commitment
   f Initiation of legalization process

Step 5 *Implementing the decision*
   a Designation of persons responsible for segments of the action
   b Consummation of bargains and trading
   c Appraisal of effects on influential leaders, other directly affected individuals, and the larger power or status groupings
   d Projection of action consequences in the form of specific objectives
   e Design of systematic evaluation procedures to measure decision achievements
   f Final review of the process and necessary action resulting from the designation of responsibilities, bargains and trades, appraisals, specific objectives, and evaluation

Source: Adapted from R. S. Bolan, Community decision behavior: The culture of planning, *Journal of the American Institute of Planners*, vol. 35, no. 5, September 1969. Adapted by permission of the *Journal of the American Institute of Planners.*

ate sufficient fear of change and doubt about the utility of a planned approach to overturn "rational" decisions (Williams et al., 1973).

FORMS OF IMPLEMENTATION STRATEGY

Within any planning situation, action strategies are likely to take at least three forms: (1) efforts to reallocate or constrain the distribution of financial and physical resources, when it is determined that inappropriate uses exist; (2) efforts to change individual, community, or larger social unit behavior, when it is determined that present behavior is antagonistic to long-term goals; and (3) efforts to change institutions and organizations within society, when they are determined to be nonfunctional or partially ineffective in dealing with defined problems or opportunities. Yet it will clearly be easier to get new goals accepted if action efforts do not appear to drastically threaten the status quo. The strategies proposed in the following pages are designed to assist effective action, while minimizing conflict with existing values. Educational and involvement processes are the key inputs. Nevertheless, it must be assumed that if the planning process is democratically based, there will be resistance and conflict over goals which threaten the status of existing individuals or influence groups.

The cost factor will always be relevant. The total cost of any action proposal, and the benefits to be achieved, will be subjects for detailed debate and influence. Whether the issue is cost or some other relevant factor, an action proposal will ordinarily have greater probability of success if there is opportunity for negotiation and alteration to satisfy some of the objections. This is the fundamental basis for developing action plans with a series of alternatives, rather than a single firm recommendation, which may appear to be the best alternative to the initiator but less than the best to critics.

Apart from the characteristics of the action proposals, further contextual issues should be noted. Action proposals resulting from planning will usually be processed through at least three levels: (1) formal public announcements, hearings, and sessions of legally constituted bodies; (2) informal group activities, such as meetings of groups interested in the issue who may decide to either support or oppose the action; and (3) independent activities of individuals or organizations who adopt the issue as a cause to be supported or opposed (Lassey & Navratil, 1972).

The processes are further complicated by the usual requirement that two or more levels of government are involved, or more than one local unit of government must participate in decisions. Most federal and state grant-in-aid programs for action projects contain coordination and joint decision requirements. Since each government unit, and each level of government, is likely to have unique functions, traditions, and styles of operation, the potential for misunderstanding and conflict is substantial (Bolan, 1969; Lassey & Ditwiler, 1975).

In addition to governmental units, a wide variety of other groups external to the immediate decision environment can become involved in complex issues, particularly (of late) if decisions involve some potential threat to the environment. In these instances, environmental impact statements and litigation can add a substantial time extension of the decision process.

As a general rule, the authority and responsibility for rural planning remains fragmented and dispersed. This means that the proponents of action plans are required to work through informal influence processes for achieving decisions. A coalition of divergent groups and individuals, with mutual interest generated only for resolution of specific common interests, will often be the rule in early stages of the planning enterprise. This can be a frustrating task, as any participant or observer will testify (Lassey & Williams, 1972).

The specific approach to implementation can take several forms—each widely used in contemporary action programs. Probably the most generally accepted strategy attempts to inform and educate citizens and decision makers, based on the underlying assumption that people are rational and will make correct decisions if they have sufficient understanding of the issues involved (Chin & Benne, 1969, p. 34). A second general strategy attempts to involve individuals (citizens and/or decision makers) as participants in a systematic effort to alter values and behavior patterns from less appropriate to more appropriate orientations. A third approach is based on application of power to change behavior without necessarily bothering to inform, educate, or involve individuals in decisions. The influence process forces individuals and groups with less power to abide by the plans or decisions originated by those with greater power.

The first strategy, *information-education*, assumes the chief obstacles to progress are ignorance and ideology. Scientific investigation and research are accepted as the primary mechanisms for increasing the supply of reliable information as a basis for education. Whenever a problem is encountered or an opportunity defined, it is assumed that methods of careful investigation can produce satisfactory findings, which will then be disseminated through public or private educational channels. If individuals in positions of responsibility do not act on the knowledge, the appropriate action might be to replace them with someone more fit and knowledgeable, rather than attempting to systematically change the position occupant's ability to act. Another kind of action taken under this strategy might be to hire consultants who have the requisite knowledge and skill, rather than encouraging high involvement by local citizens, local leaders, and locally employed planners.

Within the planning framework, the typical approach under this strategy would be to assemble the existing information and prepare a plan which contains the alternatives and recommended actions; the results are then publicized for the citizen and decision maker to examine and act upon as they wish. If the plan did not prove adequate, those responsible for preparing it might be replaced by a more "competent" group, or the planning approach would be redesigned for greater efficiency. The research, education, and extension approach of the United States land-grant universities typifies this strategy. There is a high commitment to basic and applied research, the results of which are then disseminated through formal education of students and through cooperative extension programs to adults or youths.

The key characteristic of this strategy is the assumption that the recipient of the new information is free to be relatively passive, rather than feeling compelled to engage directly in examination of values, knowledge, and behavioral alternatives.

The second strategy, *active learning*, assumes that human beings are more likely to change if existing knowledge, values, habits, and behaviors are directly challenged; an opportunity is provided to examine and experience alternative forms of behavior and organization. It assumes that people must *participate* if their behavior and actions are to be significantly affected. The approach relies heavily on direct involvement of affected individuals and groups in the total planning process, from collection of basic information through implementation of decisions. It is assumed that the "problem" or reason for failure to plan rests at least partially in attitudes, values, norms, and inadequate relationships among individuals, groups, or organizations. Intervention by trained individuals may be necessary to facilitate participation of individuals and groups involved in examining the functioning of the total system. Knowledge from the behavioral sciences about individuals and larger systems is applied, as is knowledge about the social, political, economic, and ecological characteristics of the planning region.

This strategy centers on the notion that "people" are the fundamental units which must change, just as forms of technology must change to achieve desirable biological and physical systems. The action focus may therefore attempt to directly increase the skills with which individuals and groups can solve problems, as well as increasing the information available about the nature of the problems and alternative solutions. This assumes that planning problems are not typically social or technical only, but rather sociotechnical. The individuals involved in planning must *learn* to function collaboratively, and institutional structures may need to be redesigned for maintaining and improving the planning process.

The emphasis is on experience-based individual learning as an essential ingredient in effective long-range change processes. Openness of communication, trust between persons involved, lowering of status barriers, and constant reeducation as new knowledge or skills become known are each required to solve new planning problems or realize new opportunities.

The third strategy is characterized by the use of *coercion to achieve compliance*, as opposed to the voluntary action assumed under the prior approaches. Sanctions are invoked against those who fail to act according to formal rules. Fines and even incarceration for disobedience of zoning ordinances or other planning rules are the more extreme forms of potential coercion. But force can be more subtle than outright actions; economic pressure can be brought against citizens or public officials who attempt to initiate planning efforts which might be antagonistic to entrenched private interests. Strategies which invoke force often generate counterforce, resulting in confrontation and vigorous efforts to resist the actions of officials or professionals who attempt to secure compliance with planning goals which go against the values or understanding of citizen groups.

Federal and state laws establishing minimum pollution standards constitute a form of forced compliance, which are often not understood and as a consequence are strongly resisted by individuals and business organizations whose interests are adversely affected. Much of the current effort to institute planning regions within states was begun by administrative declaration from state governors; in those states where strong educative efforts have been in process or were instituted prior to attempts at forced compliance, such decrees have worked reasonably well. In other instances, where understanding and appreciation of the area planning concept was minimal, compliance has been very slow or was strongly resisted (Lassey & Williams, 1973). (Table 8-3 summarizes the characterizing features of the three strategies.)

Research findings generally suggest that the "active-learning" approach is likely to be the most successful if democratic values are to be upheld while respecting individualism; on the other hand, some individuals will resist all efforts at learning through such a process and some form of forced compliance or police power is usually necessary regardless of the undesirabilities of coercion (Kelman, 1969; Chin & Benne, 1969).

Types of Influence Associated with Each Strategy
Each strategy is associated with specific types of influence processes as summarized in column 2 of Table 8-3. The effectiveness of each strategy will depend on the process used to secure positive response (Kelman, 1969, p. 224).

Under the "information-education" strategy, individuals would tend to identify with planning because they understand the importance of the defined goals or they respect an individual or group which supports the goals. They are subject to social or individual influence from sources which they value. They may recognize certain internal conflicts with value systems but subvert these in the interest of sustaining the relationship with the individu-

Table 8-3 Change Strategies, Public Reactions, and Influence Processes

Basic strategies	Principal influence processes	Probable public reactions
Information-education	Mass media communication Meetings Speeches Preparation and publication of written and audiovisual presentations	Identification Increased knowledge Conformity behavior
Active learning	Citizen and leader involvement Intensive experience-based learning Interpersonal communication	Internalization Changed values Changed behavior
Force or coercion	Laws, rules, ordinances Police action Economic sanction	Compliance Resentment Dissonance

Source: Adapted from Herbert C. Kelman, "The process of opinion change," in Bennis, Benne, and Chin, *The planning of change.* New York: Holt, Rinehart and Winston, 1969, p. 223; and Chin and Benne, "General strategies for effecting change in human systems," same volume, pp. 32–57.

al or group with whom they identify. Achievement of conformance in this instance would result from exercise of influence or education initiated by an individual or a respected organization.

Under the "active-learning" type of influence, "internalization" involves acceptance and support of planning goals on their intrinsic merit because the goals conform to the changed (or existing) value and action inclinations or preferences of the individual or his or her reference groups. This level of acceptance can be considered the most desirable, and probably the most permanent. It would require minimum policing of planning implementation, since there is little basis for failure to conform to any rules or regulations arising from efforts to achieve goals. Individuals would tend to accept the norms established to achieve the defined ends.

"Coercive" influence is based on authority or police power, as in the case of zoning regulations or ordinances. Under these conditions there is often considerable resentment and antagonism toward the source of authority, which forces individuals to conform when they may not understand or appreciate the rationale for rules and requirements; or conformance with planning goals may be antagonistic to their basic value systems. In this context, antagonists to planning are likely to fight imposition of planning controls and avoid conformance if they can also avoid the sanctions associated with nonconformance.

The three forms of influence are associated with different degrees of commitment to participative planning strategies. In the third form, the goals of planning are often defined by experts or political leaders, who also define the processes and rules required to achieve goals, without benefit of significant involvement by the affected public. Compliance is imposed and expected because of the "rightness" of the ends to be pursued. Little attention is paid to educational or communication processes which would help to increase understanding, identification, and internalization of the goals and means to achieve them.

As part of "information-education," an effort is made to inform public bodies, organizations, and influential individuals about possible goals and the design of the planning process to implement goals. Since the presumed opinion leaders and influential groups are directly involved, they would tend to support the goals and means; the citizen public would then be expected to identify with the influential individuals or groups and support goals and means out of respect for and desire for approval of the influentials, *not* necessarily because they fully understand or appreciate the rationale for goals or means to achieve them.

In the context of "internalization" a much more fundamental process of education, communication, systematic public involvement, and value confrontation may be necessary. Rather than relying on involvement of only opinion leaders and high-status groups, a strategy is devised to assist the general public to understand and internalize the underlying premises on which planning goals must be based. This could take the form of educational meetings, mass media coverage, and widespread individual contacts. Once the issues are reasonably clear, a similar process is used to secure widespread public involvement in defining desirable goals and means to achieve those goals. The participating individuals will presumably recognize challenges to their basic value systems, and must decide whether the proposed goals can be accepted as part of an existing value structure; *or* values must be adapted as a result of new information and involvement in decision making; or individuals decide they cannot "internalize" the goals and associated values and must therefore reject the goals. Internalization could therefore take the form of either acceptance or rejection, but in either case the issues have been thoroughly considered on their own merits, as opposed to more superficial acceptance because of subjection to authority or identification with influential individuals or groups.

"Internalization" as a form of influence would generate support only for those goals which are acceptable to an informed, educated, and involved public. *But* the strategy is also difficult and time-consuming at least in the short run; it will require substantial costs for communication and involvement processes and will demand strong professional skills in social organization, education, communication, and group dynamics.

If the concept of public planning is new to a community or region, mass media information is usually necessary to encourage awareness of planning. The evidence from studies of communication, diffusion, and innovation suggest forcefully that education and mass communication are not sufficient conditions to secure widespread acceptance and support.

Rather, interpersonal influence and group or organizational involvement are critical and necessary to secure commitment of more than a few of the most innovative individuals. An intense process of education, communication, *and* direct personal contact at the individual, group, and organization levels would be important to maximizing the potential for successful implementation (Rogers & Shoemaker, 1971).

An alternative to the intense "active-learning" approach would emphasize alteration of the structural or institutional conditions associated with planning. Rather than attempting to educate, inform, or otherwise influence individuals, the strategy would attempt to create new institutions or conditions which would cause planning to occur. This is essentially the approach operative in many national, state, and local programs when planning programs are installed through special funding from federal and/or state program; funds are provided from outside to conduct planning studies, *without* securing widespread local approval or legitimization. In some cases this approach is close to the form of influence labeled above as "coercive." In other instances individuals comply with the new program because it is supported by individuals or groups whom they respect, although they do not understand its relevance (Becker, 1969, p. 255).

A related structural or institutional change involves creation of new legal enactments and agencies to protect the environment. Polluters are located and subjected to the new rules and regulations, although they may not understand or appreciate the relevance of new requirements for preservation of the life-support system. Many individuals will comply simply because of the sanctions involved. Others may identify with the ideas of the environmental movement, and support the new requirements without internalizing the knowledge and the values on which the new rules are based. Finally, the new rules may represent the fulfillment of values that were internalized at some prior point in time, so that conforming to the regulations may represent fulfillment of opinions, values, and behavioral endeavors.

RESISTANCE TO CHANGE

Resistance to changes that are so "obviously" needed, from the point of view of sponsors, is always a frustrating experience to planners, educators, and local officials. The frustration arises in part because we do not adequately understand why individuals and social groups tend to resist alterations in organizations or changes in the "technology" by which tasks are achieved. However, there has been sufficient research on "resistance" factors to clarify the basis for such behavior.

It is quite clear that individuals tend to prefer reasonable stability of circumstances in preference to dissonance or tension resulting from alteration of behavior patterns (Festinger, 1957). If this were not true, it would be difficult to develop and maintain the highly organized systems which lead to economic production, public services, and other forms of complex organization which we label "civilization" and "culture." The individual whose reaction to proposed changes tends to be "show me its value and I'll consider it" serves a most important function in the avoidance of destructive errors (Watson, 1969).

The resister has become particularly relevant as we discover that adoption of certain technology is leading to overexploitation of resources and apparent mistreatment of human beings subjected to advanced technology (Reich, 1970; Commoner, 1971). Likewise, resistance to the well-intentioned but potentially erroneous decisions of professional planners is an important mechanism for sorting out the weaknesses and strengths of plans. The difficulty arises in attempting to isolate the essentially irrational resisters from those who have important points of view or criticism that could point plans in a more informed direction. A number of characteristics of individual personality and social systems have been isolated which provide the basis for resistance to planning goals or implementation processes. These are summarized in Table 8-4.

Table 8-4   Factors Associated with Resistance to Change

Individual factors	Social factors
1 Need for internal balance	1 Need to maintain social relationships and cultural coherence
2 Habit	2 Social norms or rules for accomplishing desired goals
3 Previous experience	3 Institutional or organizational historical experience
4 Limited ability to understand	4 Institutional or organizational blockage of threatening new information
5 Tendency to depend on traditional values and beliefs	5 Tendency to distrust nontraditional patterns of activity and responsibility
6 Tendency to prefer individual over group decisions: independence	6 Tendency of groups with a high stake in the status quo to prefer existing methods and priorities
7 Distrust of self-judgment in the face of group pressure	7 Distrust of outsider influence and behavior contradictory to existing patterns
8 Insecurity and anxiety about the unknown	8 Group intolerance for untested or unexperienced patterns of action

Source: Adapted from Watson, 1967, *Concepts for social change.*

The human species has a strong need to maintain internal consistency; if new ideas conflict with existing conceptions of what is valued, individuals tend to reject the new possibility in favor of the old. It is easier to maintain old habits than to learn new behavior. In some sense all of us are captives of our previous experience and prefer to rely on that experience, unless there is a clear-cut reward or incentive for changing. In much of Western society a high value is placed on the right of individuals to decide what is good for them; a similar high value is placed on the right of individuals to do what they wish with their own property or possessions. Many of us lack sufficient confidence in our own judgements to take actions which are clearly contrary to established means of achieving our needs. We tend to be insecure and anxious when facing new experiences or uncertain effects of present action.

Each of these factors operates to some degree in all of us, but there tends to be wide variation in the individual tendency to be creative or innovative, or otherwise step beyond tradition toward new patterns of behavior. Or, individuals may tend to resist some kinds of change, while strongly promoting other changes. A notable example is the tendency to criticize the industrial polluters of the air, while driving an automobile with little regard for its sizable contribution to both air pollution and destruction of nonrenewable petroleum products. We might support plans to control industrial pollution, while resisting plans which would restrict the use or pollution output of our automobile.

The central point is that individuals have certain psychological characteristics or tendencies which somewhat involuntarily support resistance to any kinds of changes threatening our security and integrity as individuals. If it were not so, we would have difficulty maintaining mental balance in the face of a rapidly changing social environment. In fact, many social statistics in the United States and in other rapidly changing industrialized countries suggest forcefully that an increasing proportion of individuals are not able to adequately cope with change, leading to alienation, delinquency, mental illness, crime, and assorted other individual behaviors associated with failure to find a satisfactory role in society.

But resistance to change is not only characteristic of individuals; it is clearly noticeable in social groupings, organizations, and institutions. The consequences of group tendencies to resist change were noted in Chapter II (key issues in rural society). Although groups are obviously collectivities of "individuals," it is a basic tenet of social science that groups, organizations, and institutions have an identity and behavior that leads to actions which would not necessarily occur on the basis of individual action alone. Some of the major factors involved are outlined in column 2 of Table 8-4.

Any group must provide a satisfying social environment for individuals, if they are to maintain their allegiance to the group and its goals. In the larger sense this social environment becomes the "culture" of the group or community, with an intricate set of expected behaviors from which individuals dare not significantly deviate if they expect to remain accepted within the group. The culture and rules (norms) arise from experience over time as the group (organization, institution) attempts to achieve valued goals. Any change which threatens the integrity of the developed "system" of activities tends to be resisted. Those individuals with a high stake or investment in maintaining existing patterns of land use would tend to lead the resistance to land-use planning, particularly if their status were threatened.

Changes proposed by individuals from outside an existing social group are often rejected primarily because "insiders" feel that "outsiders" will disrupt their comfortable patterns; the assumption that "outsiders" do not understand the local system is a common (and often correct) response by local residents. Unless the group has had some prior experience with land-use planning (for example) and can identify it as potentially useful, they will often resist the change regardless of its possible merit.

There is obviously wide variation among groups, organizations, and institutions in rural regions. If there is a norm or established pattern for examining and experimenting with new technology or organizational procedures, this may provide a "built-in" legitimizing procedure for introducing tested new alternatives. However, such deliberate mechanisms for testing new procedures or technology are rare indeed within public and private organizations and institutions, particularly in rural localities. Organized and innovative planning procedures can serve this function, but only if such procedures are accepted as legitimate activity.

Overcoming Resistance

Resistance to change serves an important function in maintaining the stability and continuity of individuals, groups, organizations, institutions, and communities. However, maintenance of stability in the short run could be detrimental or restrictive of human or ecological welfare in the long run; if so, measures can be taken to reduce the resistance. Such methods have been tried and tested in a variety of circumstances but may not apply in every situation. The underlying assumption is that people will tend to offer less resistance to any change which they understand and have internalized (Lippitt, 1967).

Resistance to change will generally be less if the individuals involved (particularly leaders or higher status persons) feel the idea, goal, or set of plans is their own, rather than something devised by outsiders for imposition. If resistance is to be avoided, or minimized, a high proportion of leaders, officials, or other legitimizers of change must ultimately learn to support the basic intentions and procedures of the plan or proposed action.

Furthermore, resistance will tend to be less if individuals affected in some manner by the change recognize positive values for them as a result of the planned change. They must feel there is some reward or lessening of difficulties for them as individuals and as groups, even if this is only a vague hope of "a better place to live." Related to this is the tendency to offer less resistance to plans or actions which do not threaten basic values or ideal forms of achieving individual or group satisfaction. If the plans or action suggest the possibility for new experience or new opportunities which could be interesting or stimulating to individuals, the likelihood of support and decreased resistance will increase. Serious threats to the independence or autonomy of individuals must be minimized if resistance is to be overcome.

Within this context, the very essence of effective planning becomes an involving and educational process which helps people to grow in understanding and appreciation of the factors which can lead to a more satisfying *or* more limited future. Resistance to change will be lessened if affected individuals have helped to diagnose the nature of existing problems and opportunities and have developed an appreciation for those opportunities with high potential for improving their individual and collective welfare.

If outsiders must be involved, which often is necessary when local people are ill-prepared to develop their own plans, the "visitors" are less likely to be resisted if they exhibit a genuine appreciation for the people involved and understand the "meaning" of existing value and behavior patterns. The outsiders must recognize valid objections to proposals and must be prepared to make appropriate adaptations. The outsider can often help substantially to alleviate unjustified fear about the consequences of a proposed change.

It is essential to recognize that innovations are *likely* to be misunderstood and misinterpreted initially, if they are substantially different from conventional procedures. Provision must be made for clear feedback about the nature of the misunderstandings and misinterpretations so that specific clarification can be provided.

It is likewise important to maintain an atmosphere in which affected individuals experience acceptance of their ideas and value as persons and are supported and trusted in expressing their misgivings. They must remain confident or gain confidence in their relationships with one another and with the outsiders who might be associated with introduction of proposed changes. An openness by the outsider to alteration or revision of goals, plans, and procedures is crucial to full acceptance and support by leaders or citizens.

These "principles" associated with resistance to change assume a basic respect for the integrity and value of the individual and the larger social groupings of a community or region. Overcoming resistance while respecting the individual is contrary to an authoritarian or legalistic approach which attempts to impose plans devised by experts who somehow "know better" than local people. The experts may very well know better, in some respects, but if they are to democratically implement that which is better, it must be accepted and approved by at least a majority of the persons affected (Watson, 1969).

Helpful Roles of the Resister in Planning

Defensive actions have probably done much to preserve the rural landscape from greater destruction than has so far occurred. Such actions often take the form of organized planning *against* changes (i.e., activities of the Sierra Club) which might irredeemably alter the position or status of individuals and social groups, as well as irrevocably damage land and other physical structures (Klein, 1967).

Maintenance of individual and community integrity is usually a highly valued goal, despite its possible opposition to the reality of changing trends. The defender of the status quo can serve a useful function in educating or informing the local population, outside planners, and government officials about the central social values and systems of social, physical, and economic organization which would be affected by change; these central issues are then much more likely to be understood and incorporated into any planned changes that do occur.

In the contemporary bureaucratized complexity of most industrialized countries, individuals and their social groups are regularly and severely assaulted by the impersonal organization and abstract goals which underlie public attempts to serve human needs. The defensive resister can help to articulate and emphasize the potential inadequacies. Planners are often located in positions which essentially isolate them from their clients; this tends to alienate those who are not able to approach the planner and do not understand the products of planning. The kind of collaboration between planner and citizen which might successfully overcome this breach, and increase the realism and potential utility of plans, is costly, time-consuming, irritating, frustrating, and often risky to the planners and their official sponsors. The outsider who does not appreciate the value of the resister role is often also defensive, which can obviously lead to failure of effective communication—even though both parties may very well have similar final goals.

The planner who is willing to pay attention to the resister can often respond with more adequate proposals as a consequence of criticisms and thereby in some sense co-opt the resisters by helping them to realize their personal goals as well as the larger planning goals. This simply reemphasizes the need for interaction, exchange, and communication between the *planner* and the *planned for*—in which the resister or critic can help to maintain the integrity of the culture, the social system, the ecology, and other components of the community or area in question by forcing planners to plan with individuals and environments.

PUBLIC INVOLVEMENT IN PLANNING[3]

If both the supportive and defensive roles of the citizen are to be productively facilitated, the professionals managing the planning-action process can promote involvement by helping structure the participation environment. However, a clear distinction must be made between *informing* and *involving* the public. It is often assumed that "allowing" citizens to review and criticize draft proposals or results of surveys constitutes involvement. If participation is thus limited, the lay citizen is put in the role of critic and resister rather than engaging in the more positive stance of direct contributor to the ideas from which goals, policies, and proposals are generated. In the first instance the consequence is often frustration and acrimony between citizens and officials, while in the more involving circumstances the public, including elected and employed representatives, may forge a partnership which is highly productive and satisfying to all parties. This will require time and energy of both citizens and officials, but such costs may be basic to the effective functioning of democracy in preparing for and designing the future.

The Rationale for Public Involvement

Public participation may be viewed as a desirable phenomenon from several perspectives:

1 Much of the fear and uncertainty about the negative impact of planning on personal freedom and property rights is a consequence of misunderstanding, which arises directly from lack of involvement, and therefore leads to minimal appreciation of the positive consequences which can result.

2 Citizens are likely to be much more familiar than technically competent planners with the specific circumstances in the localities where they live and can therefore make a positive contribution to the knowledge base on which plans are formulated.

3 Citizens are likely to be sensitive to the practical possibilities for implementing plans and can therefore contribute to the formulation of both feasible alternatives and workable procedures for implementation in a particular locality.

4 Since the resources and competencies of planning departments are likely to remain relatively limited, citizens with professional competencies

---

[3] Much of the material in this section is adapted from William R. Lassey & C. Dirck Ditwiler. Public involvement in federal land-use planning. *Environmental Law*, 5 Env. L. 643, June 1975, pp. 650–659, copyright © 1975 by *Environmental Law*.

related to planning may contribute valuable talent to the technical procedures of planning.

5 If planning is to be effective in the long run, it must be politically and publicly supported; public involvement in all phases and components is likely to increase political acceptance and public support.

Other bases for citizen involvement could readily be cited, but these five points serve to illustrate its utility. The issue then becomes: How can public input be effectively achieved? Can we expect a high proportion of citizens to participate, and if so, how can their input be incorporated into the planning process?

Public Participation Alternatives

A variety of legitimate participation alternatives is available:

1 Reading, hearing, or viewing presentations related to planning, via the mass media in some form, without any required individual initiative

2 Membership in organizations with programs which include a focus on planning; individual initiative may be limited, but regular opportunities are available to become informed

3 Responding to systematic public opinion surveys focused on preference or attitudes regarding the elements or goals of planning, via personal interview, mail questionnaires, telephone surveys, or other public opinion sampling techniques

4 Volunteer input to planning activity, in the form of "letters to the editor," deliberate attendance at meetings where planning is a featured topic, or other demonstration of active interest or concern

5 Participation in public hearings or other formalized methods for securing public input to planning policy, procedures, or plan review

6 Serving on appointed committees or commissions or in professional capacities with some form of planning activity as a specific task requiring deliberate allocation of time and energy

7 Actively campaigning for public office or leadership in voluntary organizations in which planning is one of the central responsibilities

8 Serving in elected or appointed public office with planning responsibilities

This list of alternatives is not intended to be exhaustive but rather represents a range of participation, from the passive receiving of information to highly active participation in the political decision-making processes associated with planning. Although a relatively small proportion of the population will participate beyond alternative 2, a much larger proportion can be "engaged" through the first two forms if the quality and intensity of presentations through the media and existing organizations is sufficiently high.

Public participation does not necessarily require active involvement of large numbers of citizens in the roles called for in alternatives 3 through 8. The survey process noted in alternative 3 can be a means of measuring the representativeness of participation under any of the remaining alternatives.

PHASES OF PLANNING PROCESS AND PARTICIPATION ALTERNATIVES

The nature, intensity, and extensiveness of useful public participation can vary widely depending on the phase of planning activity. Although the elements of the planning process are divided variously, the following general phases are usually considered essential in land-use planning:

1 Goal setting
2 Policy formation
3 Information or data collection
4 Identification of intrinsic suitabilities or limitations on uses of land parcels
5 Isolation of alternative uses for identified land parcels
6 Selection of preferred uses for parcels
7 Identification of procedures to assure that uses are limited to the selected alternatives
8 Implementation of controls to assure public compliance with mandated procedures

Table 8-5 suggests potential involvement patterns at each general phase of planning activity. The chart is by no means a definitive treatment of planning phases and participation, but simply attempts to estimate the degree and depth of potentially desirable and appropriate public involvement. It suggests, for example, that the greatest degree of personal involvement is required of individuals who are involved in all phases. This usually arises from formal appointment to commissions or election to public office.

However, the relatively low level of involvement suggested in participation level 2 may have a highly significant beneficial effect, while a high level of personal involvement (levels 4 through 8) may not. That is, the collective impact of individual participation through influential organizations could be much higher than initiatives by active individuals or small groups. Likewise, an increased level of awareness and understanding created through mass media presentations may have a highly significant impact on public support (or lack thereof) for planning. This is only to say that each of the "levels" of participation noted in Table 8-5 are potentially important.

The totals at the bottom of the chart suggest the greatest depth of public involvement may be in selection of goals, policies, and preferred uses

Table 8-5 Phases of Planning and Public Participation Levels*

Participation level	Planning phases								Degree public is involved
	1 Goals	2 Policy	3 Data	4 Suitabilities and limits	5 Alternatives	6 Preferred use	7 Procedures	8 Implementation	
1. Media exposure	X	X			X			X	4
2. Organizational involvement	X	X			X			X	4
3. Response to surveys	XX	XX	X		XX	XX		XX	11
4. Volunteer input	XX	XX		X	XX	XX		XX	11
5. Public hearing input	XX	XX		X	XX	XX	X	XX	12
6. Committee or commission appointment	XX	XX	XX	XX	XX	XX	XX	XX	16
7. Seeking elected office	XX	XX	X	XX	XX	XX	X	XX	14
8. Serving in public office	XX	XX	XX	XX	XX	XX	XX	XX	16
Depth of public involvement	14	14	6	8	14	12	6	14	

*An × in the matrix expresses in elementary form the likelihood of a given level of public participation in a particular planning phase. ×× denotes both participation and a formal input to the planning phase. The total of ×'s on the lower margins suggest the degree and depth of participation and input.

and in the implementation process, while the least public involvement is likely to be in the most technical tasks of data collection, determination of suitabilities and limits, and delineation of procedures for implementation. One implication that can be drawn from the chart is the variety of participation possibilities beyond the traditional "public hearing" process. Public hearings may be valuable for formally seeking and recording the input, both critical and supportive, from special interest groups or actively interested individuals. But hearings are by no means the only useful means to engage public attention to planning issues or decisions.

The allocation of participation levels in Table 8-5 is merely illustrative and may not accurately describe or prescribe participation within any jurisdiction. However, the chart can serve a useful analytical function if applied to a planning program. It can be used to estimate or describe the existing situation, suggest alternative, potentially desirable levels, or as an educational device to help planners, public officials, and citizen groups decide how they might develop a more adequate public participation scheme.

If an effective planning process is to be implemented, more vigorous, systematic, and persistent educational processes may be required. This suggests the deliberate introduction of an additional participation level in Table 8-5 to supplement participation levels 1 and 2: educational programs that go beyond mass media and organizational presentations, to include formal classes, workshops, and other organized attempts to generate more widespread public interest, preparation, and willingness to make a larger input to planning through participation levels 4 through 8.

If the various forms of potential public involvement in each phase of the planning process are to be realized, deliberate efforts seem in order to support such involvement. Recent federal and state planning and environmental legislation have provided funding to support participation, which suggests increasing recognition of the value of public input.

Planning professionals can help provide access to information relevant to public decisions, while assisting the formation and education of citizen planning groups. The current complexity of planning organization requires a more professional and systematic effort to involve citizens if realism and legitimacy are to be incorporated into the implementation of effective planning process.

Chapter IX

The Organization and Operation of Rural Planning Programs in the State of Washington

with
James C. Barron and C. Dirck Ditwiler

States vary widely in the degree of formalized planning for rural regions, but if programs exist they tend to be generally similar in organization and operation. Several states have highly developed legislation which guides planning and provides substantial state-level support, while other states have virtually no formalized rural planning programs. The state of Washington is at some point between the extremes and illustrates the organization and procedures for rural planning in reasonably typical fashion.[1]

Washington has operated under planning enabling legislation since

---

[1] Much of this material is adapted from William R. Lassey. *The organization of planning programs in Washington*. Pullman: Washington State University, Cooperative Extension Service, College of Agriculture, June 1975 (Extension Monograph 3982).

1935 but does not require statewide uniformity or provide significant state funding support (as of 1976). Planning programs exist in each of the 39 counties—although wide variation exists between counties in comprehensiveness of activity.

County commissioners have ultimate responsibility for planning programs and planning decisions outside incorporated cities or towns (excluding state or federally controlled land). They actually wield more executive and legislative power than any other elected decision maker in most rural regions of the United States (see Figure 9-1). The commissioners appoint a planning commission which serves in an advisory capacity to the county on planning-related issues. County commissioners have the further option of forming a planning department, directly employing a planning director and delegating responsibility to the director; or the commissioners can delegate employment of a planning director and supervision of planning programs to a planning commission. If the commissioners form a planning department, it functions as a part of county government similar to other county departments; the planning commission is then advisory directly to the department and only indirectly to the county commissioners. In the latter circumstance, the authority of the planning commission is more directly influential, although its duties remain essentially the same.[2]

A county or city may join with one or more other counties, cities, towns, school districts, port districts, and other private and public units or jurisdictions to form a regional planning commission or council. Regional planning commissions are empowered to undertake a planning program comparable to a single county, except that enactment of official implementation controls is reserved to the individual participating jurisdictions. Initiation of a regional planning program, definition of boundaries, selection of boundaries, selection of officers, and securing or allocating costs of operation are reserved to the governing bodies of the participating organizations. That is, the regional planning commission or council has no power of its own, except as specifically allocated to it by agreement among members of the commission, and implementation can be undertaken only through its members.

A planning director and staff are usually employed by the county commissioners or planning commission to undertake studies and administer controls and regulations. Whenever a planning agency is organized, and a zoning ordinance is enacted for any part of the jurisdiction, a board of adjustment must also be created, or a professional zoning adjuster may be appointed. Members of the board of adjustment or the zoning adjuster are appointed by the county commissioners. Principal responsibilities of the

---

[2] These organizational alternatives are prescribed in the "Planning Enabling Act," Revised Codes of Washington, Chapter 36.70, as amended through 1972.

Figure 9-1   Role of the county commissioner. County Commissioner Bill Mahan, Kitsap County, Washington. County commissioners are the most influential elected decision makers in most rural regions of the United States. They are responsible for the planning function in county government and usually hold both executive and legislative power; they must develop policies and enforce regulations, particularly in states which do not have strong planning or land-use legislation mandating rural planning activity. Local government remains heavily responsible for any efforts to effectively plan for rural regions, despite strong state and federal initiatives in many other public decision arenas. (*Photo by W. R. Lassey.*)

board of adjustment or zoning adjuster are to receive requests for changes or variances in zoning ordinances, to conduct hearings to secure evidence related to the changes, and to make recommendations to the county commissioners on zoning changes.

County health and engineering departments usually have direct ties with planning departments. In most instances, permits and approvals are required from the health department for any proposed sewer or water system, while engineering departments have similar responsibilities for roads and other physical construction. Several rural counties have joint planning and engineering departments or other organizational mixtures which combine planning functions with other county responsibilities. This occurs largely in low-population rural counties in which funds are not perceived as adequate to support staff with sole responsibility for planning.

Informal Planning Linkages[3]

Informal relationships usually exist between planning departments and a variety of local, regional, state, or federal units, such as:

County assessor
County auditor
County parks and recreation department
City councils
School districts
Port districts
Public utility districts
County public works departments (usually comparable to engineering departments in smaller counties)
Irrigation districts
Library districts
Fire districts
Local community colleges or other colleges
Boards of realtors
Sportsmans' associations
State Department of Natural Resources
State Office of Community Development
State Department of Ecology
The Cooperative Extension Service, Washington State University
Indian tribes
The Soil Conservation Service, U.S. Department of Agriculture
Forest Service, U.S. Department of Agriculture
Corps of Engineers, U.S. Department of Defense
Farmers Home Administration, U.S. Department of Agriculture
U.S. Department of Housing and Urban Development
U.S. Environmental Protection Agency
Federal Aeronautics Administration
Cooperative area manpower programs

[3] A survey of county and regional planning departments was undertaken in 1973 and 1974 and provides some insight into the styles of planning currently used, while providing indicators of success or failure associated with alternative approaches. The primary objective was to obtain a description of planning processes and techniques in the state to show both similarities and differences among planning departments. A second objective was to provide a basis for further investigation on critical issues.

Data were collected by a combination of personal interviews and mail questionnaires. A total of 35 planning departments provided responses; 22 by personal interview and 13 by mail. In most respects the questions asked by both methods were identical. However, the personal interview obtained greater detail on some topics. In each case the planning director was interviewed if he or she were available; otherwise the senior staff person responded.

This list is not intended to be comprehensive but indicates the great variety of organizations which may relate to local planning.

Regional Planning

Regional planning programs are usually organized primarily to *coordinate* and *interrelate* planning activities of counties (or within a single county), towns, cities, and special districts (such as ports), or other units within the jurisdictional area. In those "regions" which encompass only one county, there is wide variation in the degree to which "county" and "regional" planning are distinguished. In several counties, "regional" is essentially equivalent to "county" with respect to activities of the planning staff; that is, the regional planning department serves town and rural areas in the entire county and is the only planning unit in the county. However, in other instances, regional planning departments function entirely as coordinating units and undertake no specific planning activity; in these instances the regional planner attempts to link together the various jurisdictional units in the county region so as to increase the completeness and comprehensiveness of planning efforts.

Planning commissions or councils are the responsible decision-making units for regional planning departments and include elected local officials, appointed officials, and citizens as representatives from the legal jurisdictions which choose to join the regional program. Although county commissioners are represented on the council and may have significant influence on decisions, they have no more official authority than representatives of other jurisdictions in the region. However, in many counties the regional planning commission receives its primary support from the county; the county commissioners therefore exercise considerable control through budget allocations. The degree of county commissioners' influence depends heavily on the number and size of other jurisdictions in the county; if there are one or more large cities, urban officials may exercise influence equal to or greater than county officials.

A governor's proclamation divided the state into 13 planning "regions" of two or more counties. However, this scheme was not readily accepted by most counties, in part because of what seemed to be an arbitrary base for combining groups of counties. Those regional groupings which did emerge were not always in conformity with the boundaries recommended in the original designation. The state has now essentially abandoned the multi-county grouping concept and accepts the county or city as the basic units for most substate planning purposes.

However, multipurpose regional planning units were operational in 1976. Many other multicounty activities are organized for specific programming functions, such as law and justice planning and comprehensive health planning. The largest of the multipurpose groupings are the Puget Sound

Governmental Conference and the Columbia Regional Association of Governments. Both of these units encompass a major metropolitan area (Seattle-Tacoma and Portland-Vancouver) and attempt to provide planning coordination across a variety of jurisdictional boundaries. Both units are attempting to design and establish standard policies for growth and development, environmental protection, and a variety of other measures to encourage a higher quality physical, biological, social, and economic system.

The other multicounty regions are more modest in scope of activities, but each is attempting to provide a coordinated regional perspective for planning and governmental services. The Benton-Franklin Governmental Conference (surrounding the tri-cities of Pasco, Kennewick, and Richland) is attempting to design an innovative and integrated structure for an area that has unique and difficult problems because of the close proximity of three growing cities surrounded by an intensive agricultural area and a major atomic energy production and research facility.

The Cowlitz-Wahkiakum Regional Planning Conference is located near the mouth of the Columbia River and contains a rapidly urbanizing complex (Kelso and Longview), as well as substantial areas that are undeveloped. The region is the focus for a new experimental program called "Washington Partnership" which attempts to develop local and state collaboration in physical and human resource planning, through special funding and technical assistance from state and federal sources.

The Olympic Regional Planning Council is responsible for a region surrounding Olympic National Park, bordered by Puget Sound and Pacific Ocean coastline—characteristics which have encouraged rapid growth of recreation, tourist, and retirement facilities and communities. The council attempts to provide a regional focus for planning of land use and development.

The Grand Coulee Conference of Governments was organized because of a common concern about development associated with Coulee Dam and reservoir. Its activities have been limited to joint consultation among governments on issues associated with that concern, and little other formal planning activity has resulted.

Organization of Planning Departments

The organizational structure of departments varies widely. In rural counties employing only a single staff person, the planning functions are largely limited to fulfilling legislated requirements, such as shoreline management plans, solid waste disposal plans, and supervision of any zoning ordinances that might have been adopted.

In the larger departments, there are usually at least three major subdivisions: (1) long-range, advance, or comprehensive planning; (2) current planning; and (3) administration of existing plans, ordinances, and regulations.

Other subdivisions noted in one or more departments include:

1 Shoreline planning (largely related to the Shorelines Management Act)

2 Special studies (such as water quality management plans, water and sewer plans, solid waste management plans)

3 Environmental planning (which may include shorelines and river basin planning, as well as other special plans relating to environment)

4 Small communities (to develop comprehensive or special-purpose plans for smaller towns in the county)

5 Environmental impact statements (in certain counties, the planning departments have been designated to prepare all environmental impact statements required of local government under state and federal environmental policy acts)

6 Research (undertakes the studies required for all planning functions)

7 Community development (essentially comparable to physical planning related to expansion of urbanization, such as new subdivisions, new sewer and water extensions, etc.)

8 A-95 review (in larger counties and multicounty regions, the planning department is often designated as the unit for reviewing all proposals for new federally funded programs or special grants; this activity is intended to increase the likelihood of coordination between programs and avoidance of overlapping or conflicting proposals)

9 Community or human services (attempts to coordinate all social programs in the region)

This list of possible subdivisions is not exhaustive, but represents most organizational subunits now in operation.

Human Services Planning

No provision is made in the Planning Enabling Act for the inclusion of "social" or "human resource" planning functions; however, these functions have increasingly become a part of both county and regional planning programs by direction of local elected officials, and usually with state or federal funding support.

A human services division is usually formed with responsibility for one or more of the following functions:

1 Comprehensive health planning
2 Law and justice planning
3 Manpower development
4 Housing
5 Alcoholism
6 Mental health
7 Drug abuse

   8 Child development
   9 Economic opportunity for low-income residents
  10 Mental retardation
  11 Recreation
  12 Older citizens

Several counties and/or regions are attempting to develop a more systematized method of planning and coordination for human services development, as well as physical and economic development. Human resource planners are increasingly becoming legitimate members of the planning staff.

Other counties and regions have experimented with direct coordination of physical and human resource planning functions within a single office or department. Elected local government officials generally recognize the proliferation of programs within their jurisdictions and indicate a preference for avoiding overlap, while improving the general quality of available services. However, no uniform organizational scheme has emerged by which this can be accomplished.

Usual Planning Elements

Each planning agency operating under the Planning Enabling Act is expected to prepare a "comprehensive" plan for the "orderly physical development" of the county or region. Such a plan is to include:

   1 A land-use element designating the proposed location and uses of land for agriculture, housing, commerce, industry, recreation, education, public buildings, and other public and private uses
   2 A circulation element indicating the location, routes, and extensiveness of major transportation facilities, utility lines, major transportation terminal units, and other means for transporting goods or people
   3 A conservation element for the development and utilization of natural resources
   4 A recreation element indicating the location and extent of all public sites for current or future leisure activity
   5 A transit element, as a special phase of transportation, indicating present and potential public and private means of passenger service
   6 A public services and facilities element
   7 A public buildings element
   8 A housing element
   9 A renewal and/or redevelopment element for elimination of blighted areas
  10 A financing element indicating the means for providing funds to undertake capital improvements

Table 9-1 Distribution of Planning Staff Time among Functions—35 Departments

| Function | Time distribution of planning staff | | | | Mean % |
| | 0–10% | 11–30% | 31–50% | Over 50% | |
	Number of departments				
Long-range planning	12	13	7	3	24.4
Short-range planning	10	19	5	1	19.5
Administer ordinances, etc.	10	9	15	1	27.2
Respond to officials and citizens	18	16	1	0	13.1

Allocation of Time[4]

Planners often assert that long-range planning does not receive adequate attention due to more immediate demands on their time. Table 9-1 illustrates the distribution of planning staff time among four functions: long-range planning, short-range planning, administering ordinances and regulations, and responding to local officials and citizens.

There is clearly a wide variation among planning departments. The mean proportion of time spent by all departments on long-range issues was 24.4 percent, but this is not a very useful statistic given the variation. The average allocation of time to short-range planning is somewhat smaller, but again with wide disparity among departments.

Administration of ordinances, regulations, and related activity takes the most time. In some instances the planning staff is not responsible for administration and enforcement, while other counties' or regions' regulation functions have not yet evolved. The mean is 27.7 percent, but if those nine departments which reported no staff time are omitted, the mean proportion for administration and enforcement increases to 37.2 percent. Responding to local government official and citizen requests requires less time than any of the other three major functions.

The data shown above are for allocation of time by the entire planning staff; Table 9-2 shows a more detailed breakdown of activities for the person (usually the director) responding to the survey.

Goal setting or clarification of planning objectives would seem to be an important role for the directors or senior staff. On the average, however,

---

[4] Much of this section is adapted from James C. Barron, William R. Lassey, & C. Dirck Ditwiler. *A search for new approaches to planning in Washington.* Circular #595, Agricultural Research Center, Pullman: Washington State University, 1976.

Table 9-2   Distribution of Planning Directors' Time among Specific Activities*

| | Time distribution of planning director | | | | |
| | 0–10% | 11–30% | 31–50% | Over 50% | Mean % |
Activity	Number of departments				
Goal setting, clarification	19	2	1	0	5.0
Research, information, analysis	6	14	1	1	11.9
Educational or citizen participation	16	5	1	0	6.4
Project plans—sewers, transport, etc.	20	2	0	0	3.1
Advising local officials	17	4	1	0	7.0
Evaluate plots or subdivisions	14	8	0	0	5.4
Enforcement of zoning, etc.	18	3	1	0	5.1
Evaluate variance requests	21	1	0	0	1.7

*Personal interview data only, 22 respondents.

only 5 percent of their time is so allocated.[5] The major use of time appeared to be in the collection, analysis, and preparation of information. Education or citizen involvement in planning absorbed 6.4 percent, on the average. Advising local government officials is an important function for many planning directors; nearly one-half reported 10 percent or more of time allocation here.[6]

Immediate demands and crisis situations had the major impact on how staff time was allocated: "brushfire" situations of various kinds, mandated programs from the state (i.e., shoreline management and water quality programs), and responding to pressures as they arise.[7] Several directors emphasized citizen involvement as a major future requirement in allocation of staff time.

Planning directors indicate that long-range planning, goal setting, education, and citizen participation are receiving less attention than they may deserve. If planning is to be effective in assisting decision makers to positively influence the future course of events, there must be time for reflec-

[5] It should be noted that planners were asked to volunteer how their time was allocated. They may have had varying definitions of what constitutes "goal" or "policy" setting. To the extent this was true, the data could be somewhat misleading.

[6] Some rural counties have only a part-time planner who functions principally as an executive assistant to the county commissioners even though his or her title may be "planning director."

[7] A more detailed analysis of the effects of mandated programs is provided later in this chapter.

tion, analysis of decision alternatives, and involvement of appropriate people and interest groups. Figure 9-2 illustrates the consequences of such a deliberate approach in one community, which changed from a state of decline to a prosperous and unique attraction for both local people and visitors.

Implementation of Plans

Zoning is the predominant technique for putting a physical plan into practice; its widespread use often leads members of the public to think it is equivalent to "planning." A variety of other tools are available to planners, however, and in recent years vigorous efforts have been devoted to the search for new alternatives. Dissatisfaction with the limitations of zoning has been primarily responsible for this effort.[8]

Planners were asked to list the methods used to implement plans within their jurisdictions. There was no restriction on how many methods could be listed. Table 9-3 compiles all the responses in five general categories; the number in each cell indicates how many times that general approach was listed and in which order of priority (first, second, third, or lower).

Regulations and ordinances include zoning, subdivision controls, building permits, health regulations, and other miscellaneous rules. This was clearly the preferred method of implementation. It was listed as first choice by 16 departments and as second choice 11 times. (Note that these numbers sum to more than the number of respondents. For example, five responses were combined under "regulations.")

Environmental controls were nearly always in a lower level of priority. The Shoreline Management Act was listed eight times in this category.

---

[8] One of the most noted critiques of zoning is Richard F. Babcock. *The zoning game—municipal practices and policies.* Madison: University of Wisconsin Press, 1966.

Table 9-3   Present Methods of Implementing Plans*

Method of implementation	First choice	Second choice	Third and lower choices	Total among all choices
	Number of departments			
Regulations, ordinances	16	11	6	33
Environmental controls and policies	0	3	16	19
Special assessments and performance standards	1	1	5	7
Public facilities and capital improvements	0	1	4	5
Public review	1	1	8	10

*Personal interview data only, 22 respondents.

Figure 9-2 Revitalizing rural towns. Rural towns with leadership adequate to the task can often create a common Main Street theme which transforms them into a unique place and an attractive destination for tourism. Winthrop, Washington, was able to change its image from a declining rural service center to a featured historical Western town, while also improving service to permanent residents. (*Photos by W. R. Lassey.*)

Special assessments and performance standards are relatively new methods compared to zoning but were cited seven times. The judicious placement and timing of capital improvements and public facilities can also be used to implement plans. The public provision of sewers, water supply, transportation services, or other utilities heavily influences land use, but was noted only five times. The final category, public review, can lead to voluntary implementation through improved public understanding, acceptance of plans, and voluntary compliance.

The data demonstrate a variety of implementing tools in use, but the major emphasis at present is clearly on regulations and ordinances. Newer approaches and innovative techniques are beginning to appear but do not yet replace direct regulations.

Present performance is not necessarily the preferred or desired means of plan implementation. Table 9-4 summarizes the methods *proposed* to make plan implementation more successful. Planners would like to see greater flexibility and innovation: changes and increased flexibility in zoning included impact zoning, density zoning, and conditional use permits; general governmental flexibility and cooperation included suggestions for intergovernmental cooperation among counties, between counties and cities, and through regional organizations; greater flexibility in property taxation was emphasized. There is considerable sentiment for stronger regulations as a means to better implementation.

Improved staff capability is considered critical to effective implementation. Improved professional competence is needed, but, more importantly, adequate staff resources are needed to provide the information and analytical base for decisions. Greater public involvement is considered to have major potential for achieving improved plan implementation.

These data clearly indicate that planners in Washington are interested in exploring new and improved methods for planning, particularly departures from regulatory planning in the direction of entrepreneurial or systems planning.

A cautionary note is in order with respect to the data in Table 9-4. Planners are not suggesting that regulatory measures be entirely abandoned in favor of more innovative approaches. Regulations and ordinances would probably still remain the first preference but should be supplemented by other methods.

Success or Failure of Planning

Earlier chapters of this book assert that planning must assist decision making. Since public decisions are rarely made with unanimous agreement, there is always a subjective element involved in weighing success or failure.

Table 9-4   Proposed Methods of Implementing Plans*

Method of implementation	First choice	Second choice	Third and lower choices	Total of all choices
	Number of departments			
More or stronger regulations	4	5	5	14
Planning flexibility and new approaches	10	5	7	22
General governmental flexibility and inter-governmental cooperation	0	1	6	7
Improved data base and staff capability	2	2	5	9
Greater public involvement	3	2	4	9

*Personal interview data only, 22 respondents.

Table 9-5   Major Reasons for Success of Planning Efforts*

Reason	First choice	Second choice	Third and fourth choices	Total of all choices
	Number of departments			
Cooperation of local officials	10	1	0	11
Citizen awareness and support	5	5	1	11
Quality of planning staff	3	3	3	9
Application of regulations or guidelines	0	4	4	8
Interagency cooperation	0	1	3	4

*Personal interview data only, 22 respondents.

Planners are certainly not a disinterested group when it comes to evaluating the relevance of planning to governmental decisions; nor are they likely to be very objective. Nevertheless, the very nature of their work compels other officials to think seriously about the results of their efforts.

Table 9-5 illustrates major bases for success. Cooperation of local officials, citizen awareness, and public support were clearly considered most important. Local officials cooperate in several ways; they provide resources, give verbal support (or criticism) to the planning department, and accept ultimate responsibility for planning decisions. Citizen awareness and support is almost certain to be closely related to support from local officials. If a large segment of the public is informed and supportive, it follows that they will have some influence on elected officials.

The quality of the planning staff is an important factor in successful planning. "Quality" requires professional training, continued professional growth, and adequate technical supporting resources. A staff of several people with sufficient training would be more likely to provide consistent and reasonable application of regulations than a one- or two-person staff which is overburdened by details.

Many public agencies at local, regional, and state levels can contribute to planning programs. If they work well together in sharing and analyzing information, it would seem logical to expect improved total results.

Lack of success (see Table 9-6) is principally a consequence of disinterested citizens or public officials. Lack of coordination among units and levels of government as well as poor interagency collaboration were recognized as important deterrents to planning. Conflicting expectations between state and local government could introduce additional negative factors, as could inappropriate political influence and inadequate staff.

It should be emphasized that the issues reported here are entirely from

Table 9-6 Major Reasons for Lack of Success of Planning Efforts*

Reason	First choice	Second choice	Third choice	Total of all choices
	Number of departments			
Lack of citizen interest or support	10	3	0	13
Lack of support from local officials	5	2	1	8
Lack of coordination or interagency cooperation	1	4	2	7
Political influence	2	2	0	4
Planning staff inadequacies	1	1	1	3

*Personal interview data, 22 respondents.

the perspective of planners. A different set of priorities might emerge from a survey of public officials or citizens.

EFFECTS OF NEW PLANNING-RELATED LEGISLATION[9]

The state of Washington recently assumed the initiative in resource use and environmental quality. Two state planning laws mandate local government participation and thus have broad implications for local development processes: the Shorelines Management Act of 1971 (SLMA) and the State Environmental Policy Act of 1971 (SEPA).

The very nature of these acts makes it clear that they are intended to influence, in a direct way, the development and use of the natural resource base in local areas. The need for direct state influence on decisions affecting environmental quality can be rationalized on several fronts. For example, in many local areas there is:

1 A general resistance to centralized (albeit local) planning—stemming from a long history of laissez-faire growth
2 Inadequate planning resources to effectively incorporate resource management and environmental quality dimensions into local development plans
3 Meager experience in using statuatory powers to control growth, coupled with the absence of local processes to identify objectives toward

---

[9] Much of this section is adapted from C. Dirck Ditwiler, William R. Lassey, & James C. Barron. *The impact of mandated legislation on local planning activity in the state of Washington.* Circular #596, Agricultural Research Center, Pullman: Washington State University, 1976.

which statutory powers may be applied (this is especially true for rural areas which are often endowed with a relatively unspoiled natural resource base)

4   A lack of incentive to explicitly take into account the adverse environmental impacts that a local decision may create for neighboring communities

The objectives of the SLMA and the SEPA, though not unanimously endorsed, have received widespread support. The legislation seeks to achieve the objectives by use of a mixture of prescriptions and incentives directed at local entities, rather than by assigning responsibility only at the state level. The strategy is presumably designed to maximize local community freedom within the strictures set forth in the legislation. However, local freedom is not achieved without cost: this approach places more direct burden and responsibility on local planning entities and influences the very nature of local planning structures and processes. It is obvious that some of the impacts on local planning entities are intended; prescriptions and incentives are designed to elicit certain activities considered as necessary conditions to achievement of the desired results.

Impact on Resources

Although the SLMA and the SEPA mandate a broad range of activities for local planning entities, they fail to offer more than modest technical and financial assistance. For example, although the SLMA declares that it establishes a cooperative program between state and local governments, the local government bears the major long-range brunt of technical and financial responsibility.

If required planning activity is accompanied by an adequate budget, the mandated activity need not involve a reshuffling of local priorities since the local entity can accomplish the job by acquiring new staff or hiring outside consultants. However, if funds are not adequate to cover all costs, or if the required activity serves to impact adversely on ongoing programs, then local priorities will be modified by the mandate.

Collaboration in Local Planning

Increased collaboration among public agencies is one of the principles that legislation attempts to incorporate into local planning processes. Collaboration among local, state, and federal agencies is considered desirable since it is usually assumed that efficiency and effectiveness will be enhanced. Needless competition and inefficient use of services are avoided (see Figure 9-3) when public agencies work together.

The inclination to collaborate arises from specific legislative or agency directives, or indirectly from basic data/expertise requirements which are not available in any one agency. Specific directives tend to result in the establishment of formal although perhaps tenuous relationships. The call

Figure 9-3 Public agencies and collaboration. Rural areas have benefited substantially from services provided through the Cooperative Extension Service and other public agencies which either manage public lands or deliberately attempt to initiate planning and development activities. Unfortunately there is often a severe lack of information sharing and collaboration among such units, which can lead to competition or inefficient use of already limited services. Joint planning and collaborative programming might provide better service at lower cost. (*Photos by W. R. Lassey.*)

for collaboration creates both (1) a need to develop interorganizational linkages and (2) pressures and strains on these linkages. The latter occurs in part because many efforts are "one of a kind" and therefore no opportunity occurs to develop habit patterns. Local planning departments in Washington relate to a wide variety of local, regional, state, or federal units. Nearly 20 such collaborating units have been identified (Ditwiler et al., 1976).

Local planning departments often seek to establish and/or utilize formalized vertical or horizontal collaboration. Thus, a county may have a need to develop linkages with state or federal entities on the one hand, or cities and towns on the other. Horizontal linkages occur when counties cooperate with one another or with incorporated towns, as demonstrated in regional planning units. While county or regional planning departments have developed effective linkages to other organizations, many planning units feel largely frustrated with attempts at collaboration.

The absence of general collaboration continues to exist in spite of the fact that many pressing problems for both city and county emerge from impacts generated by development in urban or town fringe areas. Many planning departments recognize this problem and are trying to improve the small city-town-county planning relationship.

It is apparent that effective collaboration does not happen by virtue of legislative or administrative mandate. The prospects for effective collaboration are not particularly bright when visible costs in terms of limited time and heavy work pressures are coupled with tenuous and often largely intangible benefits of collaboration. In spite of widespread support for the desirability of collaboration, mandated requirements may not produce success in the absence of an explicit and well-defined collaborative process. Further, once achieved, effective collaboration often generates secondary requirements such as centralized units to collect, process, and disseminate data and prevent activity overlap. Meeting these requirements would place additional stress on a meager planning budget.

THE LEGAL AND ORGANIZATIONAL BASIS FOR RURAL PLANNING[10]

There are four primary legal bases for rural planning in Washington. The first of these arises from the state constitution, which provides that "any county, city, town or township may make and enforce within its limits all such local police, sanitary, and other regulations as are not in conflict with other laws" (Article IX, section II of the State Constitution).

The legal statutes include three legislative acts, all of which enable, but do not require, local jurisdictions to undertake planning. The first of these was enacted in 1935, as noted earlier, and was entitled the "Planning Commission Act" (Revised Codes of Washington, Chapter 35.63). It was the basic act providing a clear opportunity for counties, cities, and towns to plan.

The "Optional Municipal Code" (Revised Codes of Washington, 35A) provides for a broader range of powers than the first act, but only for cities and towns. In particular it allows the legislative body of a city or town to create a planning agency as part of local government, which must develop a comprehensive plan with several required elements.

The "Planning Enabling Act" (Revised Codes of Washington, 36.70) applies to counties and is considerably more specific than the earlier acts. Its provisions are described in greater detail at the beginning of this chapter.

Although these are the principal enactments under which planning is presently (1976) guided in Washington, a variety of other laws rather directly affects the process and the results, but they will not be detailed here. An extensive discussion of these provisions is available in the document cited in the previous footnote and is available from the State Office of Community Development.

State Organizations Associated with Rural Planning

The State Planning and Community Affairs agency was created in 1967 (Revised Codes of Washington, 43.63A.010) to assist local planning and development. An executive reorganization in 1973 created a merger between this legislatively mandated agency and other agencies to form the State Office of Community Development, which now has principal responsibility for supporting and encouraging rural (as well as urban) planning. It is housed with the governor's office and attempts to coordinate local planning at the state level while providing a conduit to local jurisdictions for federal programs and funding of wide variety.

The State Department of Ecology and the State Department of Natu-

---

[10] Much of the material for this discussion is drawn from a report prepared by Haworth and Anderson, Inc. *Land use planning in the state of Washington: The role of local government.* Olympia: Washington State Office of Community Development, July 1976.

ral Resources also have a highly significant influence on rural planning because of their legislated responsibility for state land-use programs and management of state land. For example, the State Environmental Policy Act and the Shorelines Management Act, both discussed earlier, are administered by the Department of Ecology. The Department of Social and Health Services also has substantial influence because of its mandated responsibility for maintenance of public health, including protection of water supplies and waste management. Several other agencies could readily be noted and described, but these will serve to illustrate the variety of state influences on and responsibilities for rural planning.

THE FUTURE OF RURAL PLANNING IN WASHINGTON

Although a variety of legal bases exists, and several state agencies have important responsibilities related to planning in general, and rural planning in particular, no mechanism currently exists to assure reasonable coordination between the legislative enactments or the agencies designated to undertake various dimensions of planning activity. At the local jurisdictional level this has led to confusion and conflict of time and priorities, as noted earlier in this chapter. Local jurisdictions responsible for rural planning usually lack the resources to manage the integration of programs and agency activities as well as they would prefer. Many local officials observe that increased responsibility imposed by legal mandate and the pressures of increased rural population require strengthening of local government capacity to plan for and manage the rural sociophysical environment. The legal tools and state or federal agency competency appear to exist, but the local levels of government lack the tools to adequately use the resources available to them.

Chapter X

The Netherlands and the United Kingdom: Rural Planning in Practice

Among industrialized democracies, the Netherlands and the United Kingdom probably have the most advanced systems for rural planning. This chapter describes the general outline of planning systems in both countries and draws comparisons with the methods and processes discussed in earlier chapters.

THE NETHERLANDS

The Dutch have been highly energetic in implementing rural planning. The Netherlands is the most densely populated country in the world (990 persons per square mile) and has historically felt intense pressures to use land and space to full advantage, while instituting advanced planning and technology to satisfy the needs of an increasing population. The Dutch exhibit an impressive tradition of inventiveness, creativity, and pragmatism in rural planning, which contributes directly to one of the highest levels of productivity and conservation among the nations of the world.

National planning and development policies are heavily concerned with the character of individual and community life. This concern is manifested in a highly visible and impressive effort to preserve the opportunity for individual choice of living environments, access to comfortable housing, ease of movement to work and recreation, healthfulness, and beauty of the natural environment, while maintaining individuality (Strong, 1971, p. 208).[1]

The Netherlands has a three-level system of government—national, provincial, and municipal—which corresponds roughly to federal, state, and county levels in the United States; however, the Dutch municipality encompasses not only urbanized areas but the surrounding rural countryside as well, without the distinction between town or city and county governments that exists in most of the United States. The municipality is a much more autonomous and powerful government than the United States county. There is a long tradition of municipal dominance over planning and development decisions, except for certain activities—such as water management—which are recognized as requiring provincial or national responsibility.

The tax structure is of particular significance in Dutch governmental organization for planning. Most taxes are collected at the national level and then distributed to municipalities and provinces on a formula basis. Roughly 90 percent of all municipal revenues are distributed through the national government. This allocation is based in part on development plans prepared by municipalities.

The weakest level of government has traditionally been the province, although this is now in the process of change as the need for regional planning and management becomes more evident and as the national government has tried to deal directly with some 935 municipalities. Eleven provinces are more manageable units for many purposes (Strong, 1971, p. 236).

Planning Organization and Process

The first major legislative act establishing municipal planning procedures occurred in 1901; the other major enactments expanded planning requirements in 1950 and 1962. The first legislation was concerned primarily with provisions for housing and community services, while the later enactments extended planning to physical, economic, and social issues among rural territories and populations. At the national and provincial levels a diverse group of agencies participates in a council for physical planning, which consists of cabinet ministers for housing, transportation, water, agriculture,

---

[1] This section is based on the author's investigations while serving as a visiting scholar in the Netherlands during 1972 and also draws from Anne Strong's excellent summary *Planned urban environments: Sweden, Finland, Israel, the Netherlands, France.* Baltimore: Johns Hopkins Press, 1971.

fisheries, economics, cultural affairs, recreation, social work, finance, domestic affairs, and defense.

At the operational level the principal responsibilities rest with the ministries themselves, while the council for physical planning serves a coordinating and review function along with the council of state. These councils provide a democratic structure for decision making which reflects a strongly held national value—that the government's role in planning is to lead and advise, but not to force. There appears to be a general acceptance of the need for planning at all levels; the need for both direct and indirect expenditures and incentives to assure that the plans are realized is widely recognized. Direct state controls on private development are viewed with extreme distaste, but are accepted in certain instances when national interest is clearly at stake.

Once the national council for physical planning reaches a decision, requests are issued to provinces and municipalities for implementation of the policies, which in fact have the force of law even though they are stated as "requests." If a municipality or province is directed to act as a consequence of national policy, it can request the national government to reimburse it for any costs involved, over and above those required for municipal planning purposes. Although provinces and municipalities are required to implement national policies resulting from planning decisions, the administration of planning at province and municipality levels remains autonomous; there is no direct chain of command originating at the national level.

The provinces have responsibility for regional planning, involving subunits of provinces and usually including several municipalities. Both national and regional plans are essentially advisory, with final decisions resting at provincial and municipal levels. Specific provisions are made in the legislation for the involvement and review of regional and national plans by municipalities and private citizens. Objections and criticisms must be considered and formal responses by the planning authorities are required—although the degree of modification in plans is not necessarily related to the intensity of objections. In other words, the involvement and review process does not have the force of negative "votes" which might constitute some kind of majority disapproval of the plan; government officials and planning agencies retain substantial authority over the final direction which plan implementation should take.

Municipalities have final responsibility for implementation within their jurisdiction, through a nonbinding master plan and a more detailed mandatory development plan. The development plan covers all undeveloped areas, rural territory, and any urban areas considered for redevelopment and alteration. Building or construction permits are not granted unless a proposed development is in accordance with the mandatory development plan; strict enforcement is very much the rule. The development plan covers land use, water use, future road locations, sites for future public facilities, and other types of proposed development. Type of use, boundaries for each use, density of housing, building types, and other details must be included.

As in national and regional plans, specific provision is made for complaints and objections, which must be reviewed and considered by planning authorities before the final plan is implemented. Once enacted, the development plans allow for expropriation if an owner refuses to develop in accordance with the plan. Compensation is paid when land is expropriated, and recompense also may be claimed if the plan unreasonably restricts owners in the use of their land (such as a requirement that land be left in its existing or natural state). The amount of compensation allowed is the fair market value at the time of expropriation plus any losses incurred as a direct result of expropriation. The national legislation specifically regulates compensation for damages resulting from planning decisions. All landowners can apply for compensation whenever they believe that they have suffered unreasonable and uncompensated losses on the value of their property. The municipal council hears and approves or rejects the application— which may be appealed to the national level if the landowner is not satisfied with the municipal decision.

The clear demarcation between town or city and farm is one of the most noticeable effects of the strict and complete adherence to established planning guidelines. There is essentially no strip development along roads or highways, and housing is confined to designated areas, as is commercial and industrial activity. There is little evidence of derelict or unused land, and the countryside retains a neat and cared-for appearance, as do housing and other structures. Greenbelts (rural areas) have been maintained between major cities.

There is little evidence of social suffering in the form of poverty or human neglect. For example, aged persons invariably receive pensions and are provided adequate housing, which if not luxurious, is certainly substantial and capable of meeting more than minimum needs.

Rural Planning and Redevelopment

A major redevelopment program for rural regions of the Netherlands is currently under way. A long-term program of land consolidation will make holdings more efficient and improve the organization and design of agricultural areas. Many farms throughout the country are considered too small for current production methods; it was estimated when the redevelopment program was initiated that 65 percent of the land should be reparceled. Roughly 50 percent is either already redeveloped or is in process. The development effort focuses partially on water management, provision of land for future urban development, new or improved roads, and conversion of poor agricultural land to recreation or nature areas.

A full-scale effort to redevelop a rural region is preceded by a detailed planning process, involving careful studies of the existing physical, biological, economic, social, historical, and cultural situation; maps are drawn of all existing structures, including villages, farm buildings, roads, canals, and other private and public facilities. Particular attention is given to the land-use patterns, emphasizing existing and potential efficiency of use. The studies include most of those factors noted in Chapter III, Figure 3-1, and Tables 3-1 through 3-14. However, the major emphasis is on the food and fiber production system, with less attention to recreational, forestland, and other resource or production systems (Bijkerk, 1968).

Once these studies are complete, interrelationships among the study results are examined and projections made about the likely and desirable future status of the area for agricultural production and other uses. The heavy emphasis at this stage is on definition of an efficient and productive farm unit. Designs for more efficient farm units are developed and compared to the existing land-use patterns. A painstaking process is then initiated to redesign existing farm units: expanding size, projecting needed new or reconstructed buildings, indicating needed canals and roads, and suggesting changes in landscape design (i.e., planting trees, realigning fences, etc.).

When these preliminary projections and alternative designs are completed, reports are prepared for public scrutiny. Farmers and other citizens have an opportunity to review the alternatives and make suggestions. Rural redevelopment plans must be approved by affirmative vote of 50 percent of the farmers and landowners affected. Once the landowners have voted to participate in the redevelopment scheme, they no longer have the right to withdraw if they do not like the final plan for redevelopment as it emerges. The final decisions on the shape of the plan rest with technical experts and public officials.

Since the major goal of the redevelopment scheme is to increase the size and efficiency of farm units, while improving the general physical design of the rural region, population shifts are required. This means that farmers and other residents must make a choice about remaining on the land unit, with expanded responsibilities, or shifting to other occupations. They may move elsewhere to farm—to new land developed from drainage of sea water in the polders, for example (if they qualify)—or they may retire and receive a pension in addition to compensation for their farm. In any case, major disruptions occur in social organization and social structure. It is not usually possible to satisfy all participants, *if* redevelopment is to produce the intended improvement in agricultural production capability, as well as increased average incomes and more adequate social services. Major conflicts often occur, but these are resolved finally when individuals must choose to remain in the area or leave, or when arguments are sufficiently convincing that the responsible political and governmental officials make changes in the plans which satisfy some of the protesters.

However, the Dutch population—and their representatives—are generally convinced that rural development of major scope is essential to the future of agricultural and rural regions; the determination to carry on with the change process, despite the disruption of cherished social and cultural patterns, is firm and persistent. Because Dutch society is generally homogeneous in basic values, national origin, and other characteristics, the drastic changes are incorporated in a relatively short period, and general satisfaction with the new system seems to emerge.

When the final plan is adopted, a systematic and long-term process of physical and landscape reconstruction begins. Most of the land is kept in production during this period—either by the farmers who have been operating the land or by hired government workers if the land has been purchased for reallocation; once the realignments are made, the individual who will farm the land participates in the initiation of the new farm organization, with the help of technical experts employed by the Rural Redevelopment Authority and agricultural extension agents responsible for the rural area. During the transition period, much of the land is managed directly by the Rural Redevelopment Authority.

Changes in economic and social services to the area are generally the responsibility of cooperating government agencies, usually the ministries responsible for such services in other parts of the country. Much of the responsibility rests with the local municipalities which have had responsibility for political administration of the region. In some instances municipal boundaries are expanded or realigned to improve local government administrative efficiency under the new land-use system, although such changes are the exception rather than the rule.

Government research institutes have undertaken continuing studies of the redevelopment areas in an effort to determine the effectiveness of the changes. These studies suggest a tendency of redevelopment programs to be somewhat conservative. There is strong evidence that the new farms very quickly appear too small for advanced technology and the income expectations of farmers; the farms should have been made even larger and economic organization more drastically altered. Consequently, the more recent redevelopment efforts are greatly increasing the size of units and are introducing more drastic changes.

However, the studies generally conclude the redevelopment effort has been highly successful in improving the productivity and efficiency in agriculture, while producing a landscape with more potential for recreation and other public benefits (Bijkerk, personal communication, 1972).

Regional Rural Planning in the Polders

The construction and development of the polders (land claimed from the sea) is an impressive example of regional rural planning. Originally, the purpose for draining of new land was to increase agricultural production,

Figure 10-1   Rural landscape in the Netherlands. The Dutch have undertaken one of the most massive rural planning and development projects in history, in the process of developing agricultural and urban land from the sea to form the polders. The towns and farms have been planned in intricate detail, with a distinct separation of town and countryside, to produce a pleasing, productive, and utilitarian landscape, while providing for the social, political, economic, and other structures required for a functional rural society. However, as the photographs indicate, the landscape appears highly standardized and orderly, in contrast to the more naturally picturesque countryside in the United Kingdom. (*Photos by W. R. Lassey.*)

but more recently the purpose has broadened to include provision for urbanization, recreation development, and deliberate efforts to create green
space which contributes to maintenance of ecological cycles. The landscape
which evolves appears orderly and well-managed (see Figure 10-1). Relatively new and advanced concepts of town and countryside planning have
been used to create rural service centers and regional cities, in which com-
pactness of population settlement is achieved while allowing for park and
recreation areas as well. When compared to the unplanned urban sprawl so
evident in many parts of the United States (and many European cities), the

neatness and attractiveness of the new towns is most impressive. However, they also appear highly standardized, largely because diversity arising from creative individual initiative is not generally evident.

A major "innovation" for a democratic society is public ownership of most land and buildings in the entire polder area. The farmland and town structures are leased on a long-term basis to users, who pay a fixed rental fee to the government for the privilege of use. This enables the government to maintain control over land use and land management; either apartments, houses, and business establishments in the towns are constructed by the government and leased, or the land is leased on a long-term basis for the private construction of business structures or dwellings. A consequence of this policy is the strict separation of rural and town areas by function; industry is localized, as are various types of housing and recreation. No encroachments of urbanization are allowed on land reserved for agriculture. Farmers are carefully selected to generally assure success of farming enterprises; likewise, business executives wanting to settle in the polder towns are screened to assure the potential success of their enterprise. Very little is left to chance in the polders, which places a heavy responsibility on the authorities who must make the critical planning decisions.

The Dutch System and Planning Models
The Dutch approach to rural planning conforms rather closely to the methods outlined in earlier chapters. Over the past half-century a series of highly professional government research institutes and university research centers has evolved; these institutions tend to be problem-oriented and directly associated with planning processes. Each of the institutions is largely financed by the national government and draws heavily on highly trained professional staff for the preparation and implementation of plans. There is a "macrosystem" of planning linkages that functions very much like the design illustrated in Chapter I.

Most of the elements described in Tables 3-1 through 3-14 are operational. However, Dutch planning and governmental process has been dominated by the engineering, physical, and biological science professions, often without effective inputs from other fields—particularly the social sciences. Only in recent years has serious consideration been given to the issues illuminated by social and cultural knowledge.

Much of the formal planning activity for small municipalities is undertaken by consultants. There are several large and experienced firms in the country, which serve as part of a team for achieving specific planning objectives. University faculty are often employed by these firms on a part-time basis. However, as in the United States, consultants do not always provide the continuity and buildup of basic planning knowledge and experience that is crucial to effective long-range planning. Larger municipalities have therefore employed full-time planning staff, while smaller governmental units retain consultants on a continuing basis. The national and provincial governments employ professional planners, who help assure the needed continuity.

Possibly the major drawback in Dutch planning (as elsewhere) is the difficulty of integrating and interrelating the various fields of relevant knowledge. The highly specialized nature of individual disciplines and sub-disciplinary understanding often leads to suspicion and disrespect because individual professionals do not appreciate the potential contributions from other fields (Constandse, 1973; Bijkerk, 1972).

A second major difficulty arises from the autonomy of municipalities and the consequent hesitation to approach planning on a regional basis. A large number of regional plans have been produced, but there remains a lack of sufficient incentive—in the form of required action, compensation of affected municipalities and individuals, and tax distribution policies—to encourage a regional approach to management of those areas of national significance which overlap provincial and municipal boundaries.

Possibly among the most important inadequacies of Dutch planning is citizen input to planning policy, particularly in rural and remote areas. Although specific provision is made for individual criticism and objection to plans, there is the very strong feeling among citizens that the authorities are in control, and objections will simply be "absorbed" without any substantial changes; consequently, there is a hesitancy and some feeling of helplessness about offering statements critical of either the formal plan or the processes used to implement the planning controls.

The very complexity of the planning processes and control mechanisms makes it largely impossible for most citizens to understand what is transpiring until it affects them directly, which is often too late to effectively object. Nevertheless, for those individuals who are sufficiently persistent, the planning laws require that public authorities pay attention to the objections of individuals or groups—and modify plans or compensate affected individuals if the objections are justified. The appeal process can extend to the national levels, for review by the ministries and the Council for Physical Planning—which can overrule local authorities if it is clear that injustice has been done. But such a process is immensely time-consuming and expensive, which means that such appeals are only rarely undertaken (Strong, 1971, p. 252).

This last inadequacy may arise in part because the Dutch implementation process rests heavily on "information-education" and "force-coercion" change strategies (see Table 8-3), rather than a more active-learning and public-involving approach. Social action has not been incorporated into the Dutch planning process in a manner that facilitates and emphasizes citizen involvement in the preparation and implementation of plans. Participation of individuals is left largely to citizen initiative, with little tendency for active seeking of public involvement or input.

Finally, the organization of planning in the Netherlands is not systematized sufficiently at the municipal and provincial levels to assure comprehensiveness and integration of physical, economic, social, and ecological planning. Yet the total consequence of actions by specific government ministries at the national level, based on segmented plans and legislatively mandated programs, has produced a society and environment which exemplifies more advancement in providing for human and ecological needs than most other countries. The "system" seems to be working despite the inadequacies noted here; modifications are constantly in process to correct what seems to be weak in the planning system, partially because the research institutions provide a continuing supply of evaluative data.

THE UNITED KINGDOM

While the Netherlands has been notably successful in implementing systematic physical planning, the United Kingdom has demonstrated a more cohesive effort to wed physical, economic, and social planning—and has recently begun to place increased emphasis on involvement of broad segments of the public in consideration of rural planning and environment. The British put an extraordinarily high value on individual freedom of choice—and manifest this in the planning process by encouraging and facilitating widespread debate in the mass media, public meetings, and political decision processes.

The United Kingdom is in the process (beginning in 1973) of implementing a widespread reorganization of local government, which attempts to improve representation and which incorporates the planning process as a central function and tool of each government level. The central decision authority rests at national or county levels (a county in the United Kingdom corresponds roughly to the state in the United States but has more direct authority and responsibility than either the state or the county). Within the county there are district councils and parish councils at more local levels, but these units have only review powers with respect to planning and have little authority. The main authority rests with the county, based on legislative direction from Parliament.

Planning Organization and Process

The responsibility to prepare and implement local plans was given to county authorities by the Town and Country Planning Act of 1947. Further consolidation and elaboration of local planning authority and responsibility is contained in planning acts of similar title passed in 1962, 1968, and 1972. Increased requirements for public participation in all dimensions of planning process were a major feature of the 1968 act. The picturesque countryside of the United Kingdom (Figure 10-2) reflects the care and attention that planning processes are attempting to preserve.

As in the Netherlands the planning responsibility of county authorities encompasses rural and urban areas, although larger urban areas have a separate authority and responsibility. The legislated planning requirements are essentially identical for both rural and urban areas. The plan must consist of two parts: a *structure plan* is comparable to a master or comprehensive plan in the United States; it sets out general proposals for development and other use of land within the jurisdiction, with particular emphasis on improvement of the physical environment and management of traffic. Social and economic planning are directly tied to physical planning within the county government structure but are separately staffed.

Local *development plans* fill in the details of the structure plan. These more specific plans delineate the kinds of development or restriction of development that will occur and indicate where activity should be allowed or restricted. Considerable flexibility is allowed at the local level to determine how the structure plan for the county is to be implemented. The process requires continuing opportunity for public input—which must be formally considered and acknowledged by local authorities. It is quite possible for public input to take detailed form, so that plans formulated by local authorities can be substantially altered before final adoption.

All structure plans must be approved by the national Minister for the Environment (formerly the Minister of Housing and Local Government), while local plans must be approved by the elected county officials. However, citizens can appeal decisions of the local officials directly to the minister if there is evidence that decisions are not in full accord with legislative requirements or that unfairness is involved in administering planning controls. A major difference between British and American or Dutch planning legislation has been the British emphasis on making elected local officials fully responsible for physical, social, economic, educational, welfare, and other components of planning. The planning function is an inherent and continuing responsibility of elected government officials, although the specific and detailed preparation and administration of plans are undertaken by professional planning officers. Planning issues and decisions are incorporated more directly into the political process than is the case in most constituencies in the United States.

Enforcement procedures are equally as strict as those in the Netherlands. Planning permission is required for essentially any alteration of the physical environment: alteration of buildings, new construction for industry or housing, removal of trees, and virtually all other kinds of physical change. If planning permission is not obtained, local authorities have the power to require restoration to the original situation insofar as that is possible. If a breach has occurred, the local planning authority serves an en-

Figure 10-2 Preservation of rural countryside in the United Kingdom. The countryside in the United Kingdom mixes the rolling, tree-decorated hills and fields with the incursions of new towns and orderly advancing urbanization. There is evidence of careful planning for preservation of the historically beautiful landscape and for the new housing and urban settings required for population distribution outside the major cities. (*Photos by W. R. Lassey.*)

forcement notice, which may be appealed to the Minister of the Environment if it is considered unjust or inapplicable. The enforcement of restoration cannot occur until the Minister has ruled on the appeal, thus largely protecting the right of property owners from arbitrary administration of planning controls at the local level.

Local authorities have the legal power to acquire land on a compulsory basis if needed to implement local development plans, with compensation provided at current market value. This provision is intended to alleviate speculation and escalation of land values arising from planning decisions. Development rights have essentially been placed in public hands, so that ownership does not imply a freedom to develop land at will; that right is reserved for public decision.

The Countryside Act of 1968 makes special provision for greater public access to rural areas by giving authority to the national Countryside Commission for the designation of "areas of outstanding natural beauty." Specific provision is made for compensation of landowners under the act, not only for losses suffered when land is designated for preservation but also for establishment of country parks, picnic areas, campsites, and a variety of other uses. Specific provisions are made for preserving trees and maintaining footpaths or horse trails. The act is intended to give the public greater access to the countryside, while assuring landowners compensation for services provided.

A Case in Point: Mapledurham Estate

Landowners are finding the rural planning requirements to be both exasperating and helpful, depending on the nature and location of the rural land.[2] Mapledurham Village is a historic and well-preserved headquarters for Mapledurham Estate, which encompasses roughly 4,000 acres along the Thames River in Oxfordshire County. The Estate is located at the border of Reading and is part of a designated area of outstanding natural beauty. Since Reading is roughly 45 miles from the center of London on a main-line commuter railway, the villages and environs around Reading are an attractive residential location for individuals working in London or nearby urban centers. Mapledurham Estate is thus faced with pressures from urban-based individuals seeking a rural retreat, while planning officials are determined to enhance and preserve one of the more magnificent rural environments in the area.

The Estate is divided into seven farms, with highly diversified production—including two dairying operations, beef cattle production, and several kinds of field crops. Extensive timber acreage is regularly harvested for

---

[2] The author had occasion to observe the consequences of planning controls while living in Mapledurham Village near Reading, Berkshire, during the early part of 1973.

commercial sale. Hunting rights are sold to a group of Londoners, and a gamekeeper is employed to supervise game and hunters. Fishing rights along the Thames River are likewise sold for a fee to a fishing club. The Estate owners established a "country park" along the river for weekend use, for which they charge a user fee. Mapledurham House—the Estate headquarters and a magnificent Elizabethan mansion built in the late sixteenth century—is open for visitors on weekends for a fee. The village itself is extraordinarily picturesque, with a narrow, winding main street at the end of a dead end and very narrow one-lane road. Footpaths and bridlepaths cross the Estate at several points, and public access via these thoroughfares is required by law.

The Estate is a private enterprise but has received considerable public funding support in return for providing public access to the premises. The owners of the Estate received a grant from the government for restoration of the mansion and for establishment of the country park. They also received compensation for preserving trees, which might have been cut for commercial timber. Hundreds of hikers, auto tourists, and horseback riders use the Estate for recreation, but maintenance of paths, roads, and other facilities (other than the main entry road) are the responsibility of the Estate. There is constant demand to rent housing units available on the Estate—all of which are well over 100 years old—and there is persistent interest (among entrepreneurs and real estate developers) in subdividing parts of the Estate for housing development.

However, planning controls strictly forbid construction of any new housing on the Estate or in the Village itself—even by the few individuals who are already residents and landowners. Construction of farm buildings is restricted by provisions that require conformity to building codes, height limitations, and architectural style. Maintenance or reconstruction of existing buildings is allowed, but with strict limitations on major change. Any physical changes on the landscape require planning permission, unless they are directly a part of the farming operation and do not in any way interfere with the natural beauty of the area. Planning permission requirements for new farm buildings or other changes is a long and often frustrating process for the Estate administrators, who have difficulty appreciating the right of public authorities to regulate their activities so closely. However, the right of public decision over land use is clearly established, and owners have no choice but to conform.

A major point of controversy between the Estate managers and local planning authorities is the issue of modern farm management requirements. If the managers are to keep the agricultural and recreation operations efficient and viable, in a period of rapidly changing farm technology and public recreational interests, they must constantly adapt and upgrade their procedures and equipment to produce products and maintain the character of the landscape. Meanwhile, planning officials are usually little versed in agriculture or farm-based recreation and have little understanding or appreciation of management needs; they tend to be much more concerned about preserving the landscape and restricting development than with maintaining or increasing the viability of a commercial enterprise. The Estate managers are therefore engaged in a constant dialogue with planning officials, to secure permission for changes which they consider necessary (and educating the planners to farm management needs in the process), while the planners try to explain the rationale behind the restrictive ordinances and planning decisions.

The Estate owners feel strongly that the planners are not prepared to deal with rural agricultural and recreational planning issues and need a much more complete education about the character and requirements of rural development. On the other hand, the managers are often perceived by the planners as affluent country gentlemen and ladies who want to make unnecessary profit from "public" trust land while failing to understand the requirements of planning legislation. Although there is something of a standoff between planners and the land managers, the level of understanding and mutual appreciation seems to be gradually improving.

The Estate is part of a "structure" plan for the County, which designates it as an area of outstanding natural beauty; this designation is not a controversial issue. Rather the very local and day-to-day development planning activity generates the major controversy. The larger goals of planning are clear, but substantial disagreement exists about the values on which local objectives should be based, and debate is constantly reported in the public media about how objectives are to be implemented on any specific parcel of land—such as Mapledurham Estate. There are some rather fundamental differences (between urban citizens and their rural counterparts) about the priorities for land use; urbanites (planners or citizens) tend to think in terms of developing rural areas for the enjoyment of visitors, while rural landowners or residents tend to be much more dependent on the land—and therefore want to preserve or develop the land for productive or residential purposes.

Although Mapledurham is not "typical" of rural areas in the United Kingdom in every sense, it illustrates the difficulty of designing and implementing rural planning in a social and physical environment where the values of a variety of interested members of the rural and urban public converge. Although a great deal of time is consumed in the resolution of differences, the Estate has maintained (at least until 1974) a modestly profitable operation from the mixing of agriculture and recreation, while preserving and enhancing an exceedingly delightful rural environment.

Professionalization of Planning

The variety and detail of decisions required under the Town and Country Planning Acts and the Countryside Act require a highly professional planning staff in each county, usually consisting of a variety of disciplines with special training in planning process and method. Two universities provide specific training in countryside planning, and several others offer urban and regional planning degrees at the graduate level. The county planning staff usually includes a strong contingent of lawyers responsible for interpretation and implementation of the planning provisions. The county planning director is responsible to the executive, legislative, and judicial units for planning decisions; however, local government relies heavily on professional staff for the great majority of interpretations and decisions.

The highly developed nature of local government planning, particularly for rural areas, has led one authority to conclude that the United Kingdom has the most effective system of comprehensive land-use planning of any democratic nation (Wibberly, 1973). The reorganization of local government instituted in 1973 should improve the status of planning effectiveness to an even greater degree.

Generally speaking, the British planning system closely approaches the planning models and systems introduced in earlier chapters. However, these systems have been implemented only hesitantly in the remoter rural areas of the United Kingdom. In those locations close to major urban centers, such as Mapledurham Estate, planning systems are highly developed; but in the less populated areas of Scotland, Wales, and England, there is a tendency to allow population decline and haphazard development to occur, much as it does in many parts of the United States. Nevertheless, the mechanisms are there, and the creation of an institutional structure to implement the established policies in remoter areas is legally and politically possible if sufficient pressure is exerted on public authorities (Green, 1971; Ashton & Long, 1972).

Public Participation in Planning

As noted earlier, the British are making a concerted effort to increase public involvement in planning process and planning decisions. The participation scheme outlined in Table 8-5 is comparable to the formal process proposed by the so-called Skeffington Report (Committee on Public Participation in Planning, 1972).

Participation is defined by the writers of the report as "the act of sharing in the formulation of policies and proposals. . . . Participation involves doing as well as talking and there will be full participation only where the public are able to take an active part throughout the plan making process" (p. 1). However, the point is further made that "the completion of plans—the setting into statutory form of proposals and decisions—is a task demanding the highest standards of professional skill and must be undertaken by the professional staff of the local planning authority" (p. 1). In other words, strong emphasis is placed on both the lay role and the professional role in planning, as well as on the responsibility of locally elected authorities to assure that both roles are supported. The recent emphasis is on greater opportunities for discussion of important planned changes while they are still at the formative stage and can be influenced by the people whose lives they will affect.

The public media in the United Kingdom have taken this new emphasis quite seriously and have generally chosen to give heavy emphasis and coverage to planning process and critical decisions. Public officials are constantly questioned by newspaper, radio, and television reporters about their stand on planning issues and are called upon to explain their votes or decisions. The concern with rural planning issues receives heavy emphasis, particularly in the print media.

The Skeffington Report recommends the appointment of "community development officers" who would work with planners, local officials, and citizens to implement public participation—particularly among those groups and individuals who are least likely to initiate participation. The community development role corresponds to "directed change" or "education" roles, noted in Figure 1-2. It is apparent to members of the committee who prepared the Skeffington Report that special effort by trained professionals is needed if disadvantaged members of the population are to be heard and have an input in planning. The report further notes that participation requires special communication techniques that are much more personal and specific than mass communication.

SOME COMPARISONS

Although the Dutch take biological factors into account in the planning process, the British are much more openly conscious of ecosystem considerations and are clearly attempting to institute advanced methods of environmental analysis, although with varying degrees of success in rural territories (Green, 1971; Weller, 1967; Wibberly, 1973). The British are not as prepared to accept the uniformity and order that is characteristic of Dutch countryside and social order; this is apparently the basis for a very strong effort to preserve areas of outstanding natural beauty (including structures) which further enhance the historic attractiveness of the countryside.

Both the Netherlands and the United Kingdom have well-developed professional skills related to planning, although social-behavioral professionals are less involved than might be desirable. British sociologists are heavily oriented to historical-social theory, particularly as it relates to urban society; there is a severe scarcity of either sociologists or psychologists with rural concerns. Hence, the schools which purport to educate land-use and social planners tend to lack scientifically based behavioral science content and ignore much of the potentially relevant social theory, particularly as it applies to the implementation of comprehensive rural planning.

As a consequence, the completeness of rural planning systems throughout the United Kingdom is mixed indeed—with wide variation between counties and within counties. The contrast with the Netherlands in this respect is striking. The Dutch landscape tends to be much neater but also more uniform, and the application of existing rural land-use and social planning rules is more uniformly imposed. This may arise in part from the more authoritarian tradition in the Netherlands and in part from cultural-geographical-historical factors which distinguish the two countries. But the contrast may also arise from differences in the implementation strategies and action processes. The British education system and general historical process have placed strong emphasis on individual freedom of growth and choice, at least for those individuals who demonstrate high intellect and who achieve the upper streams in educational process. A pronounced spirit of independence and individuality, particularly within the privileged stratum of society, is evident in the continuing debate through the public media. One consequence is a high level of conflict between farmers or land owners and the professional planners (as noted for Mapledurham), with resolution of issues requiring a long process of negotiation.

The Dutch have involved behavioral scientists to a greater degree than the British and seem to have achieved somewhat greater success at implementation of planning on a countrywide basis. British social geographers have in many instances assumed the role of behavioral scientist in the absence of sociologists or other behavioral disciplines and have usefully applied social research methods in planning efforts.

If rural planning in the United States is to benefit from the experience of these two countries, it may help to understand the models used and how they seem to have functioned in achieving the established goals. The references noted in this chapter contain considerable detail on the legal and operational aspects of rural and regional planning in the two countries and provide a rather complete description of the issues and problems encountered.

Chapter XI

Problems of Rural Regional Planning Illustrated: Major Recreation Development

Increased leisure time and the demand for rural recreation opportunities is one of the major issues with which rural and regional planning must deal. Major new recreation developments are initiated regularly throughout the United States, but particularly (in recent years) within the sparsely inhabited valleys of the mountain West. One such development has been documented in detail, beginning with a baseline study prior to initiation, followed by careful monitoring and measurement of impact during planning, construction, and early operation.[1] The following discussion of impacts generated by the new recreation development provides a useful opportunity to illustrate the concepts developed in earlier chapters, although no formal plan has been implemented for the study region.[2]

[1] Documentation and analysis were undertaken by Montana State University, under a project entitled "Impacts of Large Recreational Developments Upon Semi-Primitive Environments," funded by the National Science Foundation. The research was initiated in 1970 and extended through 1976, under NSF Grants GI-38, GI-29908X, and GI-29908X1. The author served as one of the principal investigators in the early stages of the study.

[2] *The Gallatin Canyon Planning Study* was prepared by the Murray-McCormick Environmental Group, Sacramento, Calif., in 1972 but has not been implemented.

The development, "Big Sky of Montana," is financed by several large corporations, principally the Chrysler Realty Company.[3] Chet Huntley, the late prominent newscaster for the National Broadcasting Company, was responsible for initiating the project and served initially as chairman of the board of directors.[4] The site is located in the West Fork area of the Gallatin Canyon, roughly 45 miles south of Bozeman, Montana, and 45 miles north of Yellowstone National Park. It is adjacent to the Spanish Peaks Wilderness area, and is otherwise largely surrounded by land under United States Forest Service or Burlington Northern Railroad control (roughly 85 percent of all the land in the region under study is controlled by these two units, usually in the alternate-section checkerboard pattern established when land was allocated to railroads in the last century). Big Sky of Montana initially purchased ranches containing 8,720 acres, and acquired an additional 1,985 acres (total: 10,705) as a result of land exchanges between the United States Forest Service and Burlington Northern (although the exchange was protested by private groups and was under litigation for several years).

The project is a four-season multipurpose development, including winter sports of several kinds, golfing, horseback riding, tennis, fishing, backpacking, and numerous other activities which can readily be undertaken in the area. Condominiums are available as well as lots for construction of individual houses. A summer village surrounding the golf course caters to purchasers of property as well as tourists and local residents. A winter village roughly 6 miles away at the foot of the ski facilities serves winter visitors and property owners, but is also available for summer use. Initial projections anticipated sale of 1,600 residential lots and 1,600 condominium units. The area was designed to accommodate 10,000 residents and visitors at any one time. This clearly represents a substantial "new town" development in a relatively isolated area, and will in all likelihood become the service and trade center for the resident population of the surrounding region, as well as for visitors and owners within the Big Sky development. The initial investment at Big Sky had surpassed $60 million by the end of 1975, and total investment will eventually include many more millions of dollars.

Lots of ¼ to 5 acres were initially offered for sale at $6,000 to $25,000 each. Condominium units sold from $29,000 upward, with the greater proportion priced at more than $42,000. The first single-family homes to be completed were valued at an average of roughly $65,000. All homes and

---

[3] Also, the Burlington Northern Railroad, Continental Oil Company, Montana Power Company, Northwest Orient Airlines, General Electric Pension Fund, Meridian Investing and Development Corporation, and Chet Huntley.
[4] Until his death in 1974.

condominiums must be attached to the central water and sewage systems, and restrictive covenants are in effect for all buildings. Seventy percent of all land in the development is to remain in its natural state.

The area is made particularly attractive by the presence of spectacular Lone Mountain—an impressive peak of 11,000 feet, on the slopes of which ski lifts are located. High mountains and peaks are visible in every direction from the valley in which the development is centered. Proximity to Yellowstone National Park, the Spanish Peaks Wilderness area, and a national forest make Big Sky an excellent location from which to explore large areas of magnificent and uninhabited (by resident human populations) territory. The region has been noted for outstanding fishing, hunting, camping, backcountry horseback riding or backpacking, and other activities oriented toward enjoyment of relatively unspoiled nature. A much more detailed description of the development is contained in reports from the Big Sky of Montana Corporation and progress reports of the Gallatin Canyon Study.[5]

General Description of the Region

The Gallatin Canyon area encompasses roughly 950 square miles. Its natural beauty is nationally and internationally famous (Figure 11-1). The upper part includes a corner of Yellowstone National Park, from which the West Gallatin River originates, flowing roughly 60 miles through the canyon before entering the Gallatin Valley, The region is enclosed on each side by mountain peaks, except for several stream drainages and smaller valleys. The canyon floor and the valleys contain all of the privately owned property in the region (other than Burlington Northern land), much of which is devoted to guest and livestock ranches—the predominant commercial and recreation activities in the region until the advent of Big Sky. Summer homes and permanent residences occupy other private property.

Bozeman is the largest city (1970 population, 18,670) within close driving distance of the Canyon and serves as a commercial and tourist center, as well as county seat for Gallatin County. It is the home of Montana State University (roughly 8,500 students and 600 faculty), is situated on a north-south and east-west crossroads for rail, air, and motor traffic, serves as an entry point for Yellowstone Park visitors, and is located 16 miles from Bridger Bowl, one of the most popular ski areas in Montana.

West Yellowstone is located at the upper end of the Canyon and has a fluctuating seasonal population, ranging from roughly 750 people in winter to 10,000 in the peak summer season. It is the most direct access point from

---

[5] Big Sky has published numerous brochures and other accounts of intended development. The most complete statements of progress and results of initial research studies are contained in several volumes published by the Institute for Applied Research, Montana State University, Bozeman, Mont. The May 1973 issue of *Planning*, a monthly journal of the American Society of Planning Officials, contains a description and commentary on the development, pp. 16–22.

the west and north to Yellowstone Park via U.S. Highway 191, which connects northeast Idaho with southwest Montana; an airport operates in summer, served by two commercial airlines (Western and Frontier).

Ennis is the county seat of Madison County in which more than half of the Big Sky development is located (including the winter village and ski facilities). However, Ennis is not now accessible (1976) to the area by a direct road connection (construction of such a road is one of the key planning issues under discussion).

Rural Planning Issues and the Gallatin Canyon Region

The region is confronted with several of the issues discussed in Chapter II, particularly (1) urbanization of land and people, (2) inadequacies of local government, (3) shortage of rural services, (4) despoliation of natural resources, (5) increases in leisure and recreation activity, (6) inadequate transportation systems, (7) functional specialization of towns, (8) legislative and legal inadequacies, (9) shortage of financing for rural planning, and (10) inadequate education for planning.

The potentially damaging human impacts on the region are a direct consequence of the interest exhibited by urban residents in acquisition or use of land for satisfaction of leisure, recreational, or investment interests. Much of the private property in the Canyon is owned by individuals from urban locations; a high proportion of the visitors to the area come from urban areas; and new developments are catering primarily to urban (and affluent) populations from larger cities throughout the United States. The area is viewed in some respects as an extension of "urban space" and as an outlet for enjoyment of the aesthetically and ecologically pristine rural environment, while also providing the satisfaction of high technology, physical comfort, cultural variety, and other "urban" conveniences.

The inadequacies of local government are illustrated by the unwillingness of county officials to assume leadership in provision of government services and failure of either state or local governments to initiate planning controls. Much of this hesitancy to act arises from inadequate legal or legislative provisions by state government. In this instance, the county commissioners from two counties are the only legally responsible "bodies" for governance of the region. Yet, traditionally, commissioners take action only through specific instruction from legislative acts; in this instance, there is no existing legal statute requiring county government initiative. Several attempts have been made to organize citizens of the area to seek additional government services and to institute planning regulations. Some of these efforts were modestly successful: solid waste disposal was provided for part of the area; fire protection services were instituted; a planning study was completed; and various ad hoc groups were formed to protect wildlife or to undertake other specific activities.

(a)

(b)

Figure 11-1 Recreation development. The Gallatin Canyon is one of the most magnificent natural areas in the United States; the highway corridor is the only evidence of human impact in those parts which are within the national forests. The new recreation-based town is introducing structures and people in large numbers, but generally with careful attention to establishing a blend with the natural landscape and with a strong commitment to maintenance of large areas of open space. However, any planning is undertaken by private recreation developers, since no regional or county plan is current-

(c)

(d)

ly operational. (*a*) Condominiums in Meadow Village, Big Sky. (*b*) Big Sky sewage lagoons showing aeration bubbles. (*c*) Skiing at Big Sky. (*d*) The highway corridor, Gallatin Canyon. (*Photos from David G. Stuart et al., Impacts of Large Recreational Developments upon Semi-Primitive Environments: The Gallatin Canyon Case Study, Institute for Applied Research, Montana State University, Bozeman, Mont., 1974, pp. 85 and 128. Reprinted by permission.*)

Economically productive natural resources are in relatively short supply. Timber harvesting has removed much of the most valuable lumber, occasionally leaving the landscape scarred and aesthetically displeasing. Because the Spanish Peaks area is in wilderness status, no natural resource extraction of any kind is presently allowed. Commercial minerals have not been mined in the region, and little evidence exists that immediately available or economically productive quantities can be exploited. Wildlife resources are abundant in most parts of the area. However, commercial development of the West Fork or surrounding areas will displace some of the grazing and trail areas for elk and other wild game (Picton, 1972).[6]

Increase in demand for leisure and recreation space is probably the central impact on the region. The great bulk of new activity is recreation or leisure related. Commercial recreation and related development will make the area much more visible and accessible; it is therefore quite likely that individuals seeking a pristine but comfortable rural environment will visit the region in expanding numbers and for increasing time periods. It is in many respects an ideal setting for families with extended vacation time or for retired people who will want to enjoy the amenities of an outdoor life in beautiful natural surroundings. Since most of the facilities are open to any member of the public with ability to pay, it is difficult to predict accurately the total number of individuals who might eventually direct their leisure and recreation time to this region. Use of the area will undoubtedly multiply as a consequence of the Big Sky complex, and any overflow will cause an increasing impact on the surrounding environment and commercial facilities.

No air or rail transportation systems regularly serve the immediate area, although such services are available at both major towns in the region (Bozeman and West Yellowstone). Commercial truck and bus traffic use the existing highway extensively. However, the highway has apparently not been overburdened by traffic in either summer or winter.

The "new town" in process of creation will specialize in four-season recreation. Manufacturing or other nonrecreation-related commercial activity will be severely limited (but under present circumstances could develop on surrounding private land). The permanent population will also be limited on property controlled by Big Sky, but will likely increase on surrounding private land.

Inadequacies of legislative and legal provisions for controlling development have been paramount issues since the announcement of the Big Sky

---

[6] All references to the authors in the following pages are based on work undertaken as part of the National Science Foundation–sponsored research project, usually from Jezeski, James J. (Ed.). "Impacts of Large Recreation Developments Upon Semiprimitive Environments." Progress report, Vol. II, Disciplinary Appendix. Bozeman, Mont.: Montana State University, Center for Interdisciplinary Studies, 1973.

development. Action with respect to some of these inadequacies has been undertaken in the interim, such as change in the liquor laws to facilitate large commercial recreation developments. New legislation encourages initiation of planning by counties, while existing legislation requires formal sanction by existing landowners before planning controls can be instituted, regardless of the degree of despoliation or destruction of environmental amenities. Environmental impact statements are required for public developments of large magnitude, but the only laws which directly limit small developments are related to health requirements and water or air pollution (except on federally controlled National Forest areas or on Big Sky property where restrictive covenants apply).

One of the obvious obstacles to effective planning for the area is the limited funding available to local or state government for planning purposes. Gallatin County has appropriated only a very modest planning budget, and the state has not seen fit to supply adequate funds at either the state or local level. The federal government, through the U.S. Department of Housing and Urban Development, has been responsible for the bulk of the financial incentives to encourage planning. As a consequence, the local planning department staff has little time or resources to initiate long-range regional planning activity. The region in question is served by a small staff responsible primarily for the area immediately surrounding and including the city of Bozeman; marginal attention is given to countywide or regional planning.

Funds for the Canyon planning study were supplied in part by the Big Sky Corporation as a contribution, and in part by the state department of planning and economic development from federal and state sources. There was essentially no local contribution, except in time and energy of an advisory group of citizens and officials. The planning study team was severely underbudgeted and had to rely heavily on data supplied from Montana State University research; had it not been for the availability of the research data, it is highly questionable whether the planning report could have been completed in any reasonably comprehensive manner.

Finally, appreciation of the potential usefulness of careful planning by citizens and local officials is clearly problematical. Evidence from surveys would suggest that the level of understanding about components and requirements for effective planning is minimal (Williams, 1972). Many local citizens have either a very limited conception of the potential role of planning in achieving an improved level of environmental and human welfare, or they equate planning with totalitarian and undemocratic values—which obviously makes them quite antagonistic to the very concept of planning. This latter attitude was exemplified in a series of articles in the local weekly paper during 1971 and 1972 (*Gallatin County Tribune*, 1971–72). Planning is considered by many rural residents as a clear infringement on individual rights; those who might be concerned about destruction of parts of the natural ecological system are willing to risk damage in the interest of protecting their own freedom to develop property as they wish. Personal freedom is essentially equated with property rights.

THE ELEMENTS OF RURAL AND REGIONAL PLANNING

The Gallatin Canyon Study sought baseline information for each of the elements which might be affected by the entry of a major development (discussed in Chapter III and summarized in Tables 3-1 to 3-14). A discussion of these elements as they apply to the Gallatin Canyon region, and a brief description of the available data, will help to illustrate the relevance of each category.

Physical Factors

The Gallatin Canyon and surrounding region have a variety of unique physical characteristics which predetermine in some respects the impact of human activity. The composition of rock and soil on the slopes in some locations imposes a potential hazard of earth movement in as much as 15 to 20 percent of the region. Roughly an equal proportion of the area is subject to slump or rockslides. Several faults are evident, one of which led to a 1959 earthquake causing severe shocks in the entire region; the most serious result was the displacement of roughly 37 million cubic yards of broken rock from a half-mile of mountainside in the nearby Madison River Canyon and a severe shifting and displacement of nearby Hebgen Lake. The existence of faults implies that the area has been, and may continue to be, subject to periodic earthquakes, necessitating construction which will withstand substantial shock from earth movement (Montagne, 1972).

Thirteen active and fifteen inactive landslides are mapped in one area (the Porcupine Creek drainage); the investigators recommended that all construction should clearly be avoided on active landslide areas and should be undertaken only with extreme caution and special provisions on inactive landslides which could be reactivated by perturbation resulting from human activity or earthquakes. Ice was discovered within the entire length of a rock glacier on Lone Mountain, scheduled to be the site of a triple chair lift for a ski facility. It was therefore necessary to move the lift location to an older and inactive part of the rock glacier, providing much greater stability and safety (Montagne, 1972). Snow avalanche dangers were noted on Lone Mountain, for which provisions must be made during the ski season: snow surveys and reduction of danger by explosives or use of artillery to displace potential avalanches prior to entry of skiers.

Much of the flat land surface of the valleys in the region consists of porous rock which often provides a good building base but also allows for very rapid percolation of water and sewage—thus endangering the purity of underground and surface waters if care is not taken in the location and construction of sewage disposal systems.

The geologic surface features are clearly an important component of the aesthetic attraction of the region and affect location of residential and tourist structures. This point begins to illustrate the interrelationship between geologic studies and other data—in this instance the sociology of recreation and the economics of site selection; that is, the geological structure directly affects costs of construction and the kind of population likely to engage in recreation activities.

The area contains a fossil forest which begins in Yellowstone National Park and consists of hundreds of petrified trees from 27 successive buried forests; potentially outstanding scientific and recreational value is evident. It is this kind of information which geologists can supply only through detailed and extensive study, but which is clearly crucial to adequate planning for future use of the area. Much more could be described about the bedrock and surficial geology of the area; however, the discussion to this point should sufficiently illustrate the fundamental relevance and applicability of such information in planning for this type of rural region.

Soils of the Gallatin Canyon area were rated for a wide variety of potential uses: suitability for drainage of septic tank filter fields, building foundations, construction of campgrounds or roads, and other uses directly related to projected or probable development. Ratings are based on criteria arising from guidelines used by the U.S. Soil Conservation Service, the National Cooperative Soil Survey, the U.S. Forest Service, and the Montana Department of Health and Environmental Protection: surface texture, slope, flood hazard, depth to bedrock, permeability, stoniness, drainage, available water-holding capacity, salinity or alkalinity, rockiness, course fragments, depth to water table, hydraulic conductivity, percolation rate, organic matter, frost heave potential, and moisture consistency, as well as other factors (Olson, Leeson & Nielson, 1973). Some 117,500 acres of soils were rated by these criteria, in cooperation with the U.S. Forest Service and the U.S. Soil Conservation Service.

Limiting soil properties and hazards were investigated and keyed to a map of general soil interpretations for selected uses (Olson, Leeson, & Nielson, 1973). The limitations existing in selected parts of the region include: flooding or ponding hazard, seasonally high ground water, excessive slope, thin surface layer of topsoil, slow permeability, rapid permeability, groundwater contamination hazard, erosion hazard, unfavorable organic matter content, susceptibility to frost heave, high shrink or swell, unfavorable clay content, piping hazard, shallow depth to sand or gravel, existence of gravel, cobble and stone, slippery or sticky when wet, shallow depth to bedrock, low bearing strength, salinity, sandy texture, tree downfall, or unfavorable compaction characteristics. Soil limitations would obviously apply only to selected kinds of human activity. Classifications of limitations were therefore made for 10 kinds of potential uses and keyed to the soil map:

1 Foundations for low buildings
2 Septic tank filter fields
3 Road and parking locations
4 Lawns and landscaping
5 Camping areas
6 Picnic areas
7 Playgrounds
8 Trails and paths
9 Sanitary landfills
10 Pond sites

Resource overlay maps, slides of soils, landscapes and land uses, and other interpretations of soil and land relevant to rural planning were prepared.

Water supply is a central consideration in the region under study, because of its purity, abundance, recreational uses, and the need to supply adequate quantities of quality water to local downstream users. The stream flow from the West Fork area and other forks of the West Gallatin River has been measured regularly since 1970, largely by the installation of partial flumes or gauging stations. The intent is to measure any changes in level of stream flow over time which might be attributable to development activities or geological changes (Williams & Hanson, 1973).

Ground-water measurements are being taken in several wells in the West Fork region. Precipitation and snow measurements were instituted for determination of water content and contribution to total precipitation.

Water law and water quality are closely related to usability of existing supplies and are also under analysis. However, these are legislative and legal issues (in the case of water law) and biological issues (in the instance of water quality) and are discussed later (Bowman, 1974).

Air quality was initially determined to be extremely high in the study area. Measurements determined air temperature, humidity, wind speeds, composition (including particulate matter or pollution), and several measures of interaction among soil, water, and air. Maximum and minimum temperature probabilities were calculated for the West Fork area, on a daily basis; such data can assist in the prediction of human comfort levels for potential outdoor activity at any given period of the year. Honeysuckle plants were used to determine the budding, blooming, and withering times, as an aid in determining likely seasonal plant life and kinds of plant life which will flourish within temperature and humidity limitations. Measurements of day and night temperature ranges and air velocities helped to determine the likelihood of inversions and air pollution. The lower portion of the Big Sky development could develop inversion and pollution problems if control of emissions is not exerted (Caprio, Ottenbrett, Bordeau, & Lancaster, 1973).

Because of the unique landforms in the region, the climate is not necessarily typical of similar elevations at the same latitude elsewhere in the world. Bioclimatic measurements of air temperature, humidity, speed, and composition, along with precipitation measurements, are therefore important in planning for development, if human activity potential is to be reasonably predictable.

Biological Factors: Vegetation

The natural botanical characteristics of land and water in the region are a direct derivative of the physical features. Plant growth on land and in water heavily influences the species and characteristics of animal life. Much of the uniqueness of the region rests on the attractiveness of combined physical, botanical, and zoological features.

Although the study examines a number of plant life characteristics as they relate to potential future development, no attempt was made to document and map the complete vegetative attributes (except for the immediate West Fork area). This may be one of the more significant gaps in the study from a planning standpoint, since it will be difficult to measure change over time in plant ecology (although many of these characteristics are already well known without additional detailed study).

Specific attention was directed to measurement of vegetative baselines in campgrounds and on (or near) trails, including potential impact of air quality on vegetation and animal life. A campground study determined the relationship between foot or vehicle traffic and vegetative cover, by measurement of bulk density of soil in developed and underdeveloped (projected) camping areas. Bulk density was determined to be related to soil infiltration rate and plant species complexity in campgrounds. The data are incomplete for indexing the utility of plant association in evaluating suitability for intensive outdoor recreation activity, but further work should indicate whether this is possible and useful (Hehn, 1973).

The study of vegetation near mountain forest and meadow trails indicates that many plants characteristic of the forest floor tend to disappear at the edge of the trails, depending in part on the intensity of trail use, but decrease or disappearance of plant types is limited to 1 to 2 meters from the edge of the trail. Other plants (such as mosses) appear to be quite tolerant for trail use. Some new plants appear at trail edges which are not common on the forest floor, but tend not to increase for more than 1 or 2 meters into the forest. The study isolates which types of plants appear to be most and least tolerant to trampling, whether on the edges of trails or in other areas where trampling levels are high (Weaver & Dale, 1973). Studies of air quality impact on plant life have demonstrated useful methods for measuring air pollution—through quantification of air ion levels as direct correlates of air quality (Sharp, 1972).

Animal Life

The Gallatin elk herd has created considerable controversy because it is one of the most impressive collections of wildlife in the Rocky Mountain area; both hunters and wildlife preservationists have a high interest in maintaining the herd. Intrusions of human activity have a decided impact on location, size, and movement of the elk herd because elk do not cohabitate with humans and need large grazing areas if their numbers are not to decline. Populations of mountain goats, bighorn sheep, mule deer, black bear, and moose exist in the West Gallatin area; however, research has been limited primarily to elk and mountain sheep (Picton, 1974).

Fourteen aerial big game distribution surveys were conducted in 1971 and 1972 to locate various species and their habitats. Ground surveys were conducted in 67 sections of land (one section equals 640 acres). The surveys indicated that some type of big game existed in nearly all parts of the 150-section study area, with elk and mule deer by far the most extensive, although sizable populations of bighorn sheep were noted; one of the largest populations of such animals in North America resides in the Spanish Peaks area, numbering possibly 200 animals.

Pressure on these herds will clearly occur, as a consequence of winter range disturbance, displacement of elk by recreation developments and other construction, logging, and intrusions by one kind of game on the range of other species. Logging alone could reduce the use of such areas by 50 to 60 percent, and initial disturbance of summer elk range is estimated to be as high as 42 percent of all available range in the study area. Habitat fragmentation and other impacts resulting from human activity affect the elk in far greater proportion than the actual territory disturbed.

In addition to hunting, wildlife has obvious value for aesthetic purposes. Studies of travel in the area indicate at least 36 percent of all Sunday afternoon traffic stops to observe wildlife. Direct economic benefits from hunting and wildlife viewing were estimated to exceed $450,000 during fall and winter 1971 to 1972. Indirect social-aesthetic benefits were obviously substantial as well. Wildlife have a strong influence on the biological balance of the area and serve as a major visually satisfying outlet for a high proportion of residents and visitors.

Aquatic Life

Fish probably have greater economic and recreational value than other wildlife for both resident and nonresident populations. A 2-year survey was made on two sections of the Gallatin River used for fishing, to determine fishing pressure and estimate the economic value of fish on somewhat the same basis as wildlife. These estimates resulted in calculations of more than 300 annual days of fishing per mile of stream during 1971 and 1972 (Graham, 1973).

One important indicator of water quality and fish population is the condition and extent of aquatic invertebrates—tiny animals which inhabit water. The biota occurring in water are extremely sensitive to physical and chemical changes in water composition caused by human or animal activity. Measurements were taken on a monthly basis at 11 stations on the West Fork and West Gallatin over an 18-month period, followed by a year of sampling at 3-month intervals. This enabled the investigators to establish baselines from which changes over time can be measured (Roemhild, 1973).

The results indicate that essentially no significant increase in pollution occurred through the end of 1971. These measurements were highly sensitive to the changes in the stream resulting from construction activities in 1972, but no persistent pollution had been added by the end of 1972, although the composition of insect populations had altered in certain locations. Except where stream beds had been realigned in one location, the fish habitat and food supply had not changed significantly.

Microbiological and chemical analyses of water were undertaken at 27 surface locations and 38 ground-water sampling sites above and below the developable areas. Collections were made twice per week initially, once a week during the first summer, twice per month for later summer periods, and once per month in winter. Bacterial counts of coliform and fecal streptococcus were made from each sample, as measures of potential sewage pollution. Physical measures of temperature, conductivity, and turbidity were taken; and chemical measures were made of alkalinity, hardness, and a series of other chemical content factors (Stuart et al., 1974).

The bacteriological quality of the West Fork was considered very high, comparable to requirements for closed municipal watersheds. Physical and chemical characteristics were also indicative of very high quality for both surface and ground water. Measurements over time indicated that early entry of development activity actually improved the water quality, because it resulted in a decrease in livestock and wildlife populations, which had made a higher contribution to fecal content than did the human population. After 2½ years of study it was concluded that ranching, construction, and weather had more to do with water quality than the entry of humans—as of the end of 1973. However, it is predictable that without careful protective measures, higher populations in later years of the development could have a detrimental effect on water quality.

Overall it is quite clear that biological measurements can be sensitive indicators of the impact of human activity. There is a powerful interaction between human intervention and the behavior of plants and animals, in terms of biological reaction to human behavior and with respect to human reactions to biological change. Presumably if both kinds of behavior are clearly understood, as well as the interaction effects, control might be exerted to assure some optimum balance between human activity and biological consequences.

The Cultural-Historical Record

Archaeological evidence suggests that people have inhabited the Gallatin Canyon area at least intermittently for the last 10,000 years. Permanent settlement probably did not occur until relatively recent times, largely because of harsh winter seasons. Penetration by whites began after the Lewis and Clark Expedition of 1804–1806, primarily by trappers at first, followed by gold seekers in the 1870s, and when Yellowstone Park was created in 1872. During the decades of the 1880s and 1890s lumbering, ranching, and mining were pursued in the Canyon by a few pioneering individuals. Neither lumbering nor mining reached significant proportions until later in the twentieth century, but several livestock and dude ranches were the major economic enterprise in the Canyon until very recent years (Malone, 1973).

Possibly the most significant feature of Gallatin Canyon culture and history is the failure of area residents to form any permanent type of formalized local community or government. The area has persistently contained a population of individualists with little ongoing inclination to collaborate. Visitors from outside have maintained a powerful interest in the magnificence and pristineness of the Canyon area. The federal and state governments have exercised continuous influence on biological and physical development (or nondevelopment) because most of the land is under control of the U.S. Forest Service; the wildlife and water have been largely controlled by the State Department of Fish and Game. As noted above, the only other major outside landholder has been the Burlington Northern (formerly Northern Pacific) Railroad which controls roughly 20,000 acres in checkerboard mix with Forest Service land.

The first road through the Canyon was completed in 1911 and was preceded in 1909 by a railway to Gallatin Gateway near the mouth of the Canyon. These two transportation linkages were expected to vastly increase the use and development of the area, which they did to a limited degree (but probably not to the extent that promoters had foreseen). Bus tours through the Canyon to Yellowstone National Park began in 1926, and the road was improved and entirely paved by 1930. This opened the way for tourism to begin in earnest—the only economic activity to reach major proportions in the Canyon, although it was able to support a relatively small population—primarily in the midsummer months.

The area attracted increasing numbers of individuals who were interested in enjoying its serenity, pristineness, wild game, and rural atmosphere.

Summer homes began to outnumber permanent residences in the 1950s, and temporary visitors (to dude ranches, campgrounds, and picnic areas) far outnumbered local property owners. Attempts to build a dam across the river at the West Fork or near the Canyon mouth failed, as did oil exploration efforts in the late 1940s. Lumbering was the only major enterprise which met with considerable success, apart from dude ranching.

Several citizen associations were formed in the 1950s and 1960s but usually with limited goals and short-term participation. None developed into a "representative" organization allowing the property owners to unify; the inclination to remain individualists, or even isolationists, prevailed for a high proportion of the permanent residents. Only the Gallatin Canyon Women's Club and the local school board have met continuously through the years, probably because their activities have persistently avoided controversy. All other organizational efforts have seemed to polarize residents into enough subgroups so that no clear majority of opinion on any issue has been attained; hence, organizational efforts seem invariably to have ended in stalemate or simmered in disagreement and considerable intergroup hostility.

The most recent events to regenerate organizational effort and controversy have been (1) the land exchanges between the Burlington Northern Railroad and the U.S. Forest Service—through which both parties were attempting to overcome the management difficulties of the checkerboard ownership pattern—and (2) the entry of major commercial recreation and land development (Big Sky of Montana). These two issues caught the full thrust of current debate over economic development versus environmental preservation, and also generated statewide and national attention. "Outsiders" selected the Gallatin Canyon as a kind of battleground in which to test the strength of the environmental movement in opposing the potential negative impacts of economic exploitation (Malone, 1973).

Social-Psychological Issues

An interview survey of property owners was undertaken during the summer of 1970 as a part of a study of social factors. Influential leaders from outside the Canyon were also interviewed. Of the 331 property owners and residents identified, 282 (85 percent) completed the questionnaires. Roughly 18 percent were full-time residents, 70 percent were summer- or part-timers, and 12 percent were nonresident property owners. The survey sought information on a wide variety of issues, attitudes of property owners toward these issues, characteristics of respondents (educational levels, ages, etc.), and behavior with respect to events and activities in the Canyon (Lassey & Williams, 1971).

Later surveys examined special groups, such as hunters, fishermen, campers, snowmobilers, and sightseers. In each case the purpose was to determine characteristics of visitors, how they were using the Canyon, their attitudes toward the area, and economic impact of their activity.

Surveys were supplemented by several other methodological devices to obtain a clear picture of social events, organization, and behavior: (1) observation of significant organizational meetings and activities, (2) collection of newspaper and magazine articles describing events and activities, (3) regular contact with nonlocal agencies, organizations, and groups having a clear impact on Canyon events, and (4) continuous informal interviews with key influentials within and outside of the Canyon.

The announcement that the Big Sky of Montana Development was to be located on the West Fork occurred in February of 1970 and was public knowledge at the time of the initial survey of property owners. However, no development had yet taken place, and little detail about the proposed project was available. At this stage the great majority of the property holders (70 percent) expected the Big Sky Development to respect the environment and take measures to avoid despoilation. However, there was considerable concern (54 percent) that the peripheral developments could do serious damage to the attractiveness of the area. Most property owners (76 percent) at this point were in favor of some kind of zoning regulations to control commercial and residential development; however, the proportion of those supporting such action was much lower among permanent residents.

Efforts to institute planning procedures were deliberately disrupted, however, by individuals who held values highly antagonistic to any kind of public control over use of private property. As noted above, a Bozeman weekly newspaper, which served as the principal local news media for the Canyon area, carried a continuing series of editorials and articles highly critical of any efforts to plan and zone—based on ideological viewpoints supporting individualism and inappropriateness of government "interference" with private property rights.

Although this antiplanning ideology clearly did not influence all of the property owners, it was promoted vigorously and gained sympathy from enough permanent residents to undercut organization of a land-use planning district. When a later attempt was made to initiate countywide planning, the antiplanning group caused its defeat by petition. However, neighboring Madison County, in which part of the development is located, initiated county planning efforts.

There was considerable confusion and misunderstanding among property owners about the meaning of "planning" and "zoning." The terms were often equated; or planning was considered only as a mechanism for preparing to zone. Little positive potential was recognized for dealing with opportunities or problems through planning, apart from land-use control. There was little recognition of planning as a practical process for protecting property and environmental values, or as an even broader mechanism to assist with a design for social, economic, and other services.

A descriptive characterization of attitudinal and behavioral population characteristics revealed four general types, on a continuum ranging from "preservationist" to "developmentalist." A computerized analytical device was used for establishing response patterns from questions answered by property owners (Williams & Gilchrist, 1973). The four general types included (1) preservers, (2) protectors, (3) promoters, and (4) developers.

"Preservers" tended to oppose the Big Sky Development, because they thought it would adversely affect the natural environment; they had little confidence in promises by the developers to focus on environmental preservation; they felt development would detract from their personal enjoyment of the area. Roughly 27 percent of the population were preservation-oriented. "Protectors" represented 13 percent of the population and had many characteristics in common with preservers; but they had greater confidence in the integrity of the developers and were very much in favor of planning controls to assure that all users of the region be required to meet environmental protection standards. "Promoters" were the dominant category (45 percent) and were highly favorable to Big Sky. They did not believe the development would have negative effects; on the contrary, they were confident it would considerably enhance the desirability and attractiveness of the area. They rather uniformly supported the need for planning and land-use controls. "Developers" had some characteristics in common with promoters, but were opposed to land-use planning, and viewed the entry of the Big Sky Development as an opportunity to reap profitable commercial advantages through land-development activities. They represented 14 percent of the property owners.

The four-part continuum was based on analysis of all individuals holding property in the Canyon; analyses limited to permanent residents reveal quite a different picture, with a much lower proportion in the "promoter" group and a higher proportion in the "developer" and "protector" categories (much greater detail on the educational, income, occupational, and other characteristics of the types is available in study reports by Williams and others, 1973 through 1975).

Similar characterizations were made of the temporary visitors to the Canyon, including hunters, fishermen, campers, snowmobilers, and sightseers. Major events and activities involving these and other groups were documented in detail, as indicators of the existing and potential behavior of individuals and organizations as the development proceeds.

This information is quite clearly useful in understanding the planning orientation of the population. In this instance the record is clear; regardless of how important it might seem to exercise controls to protect the ecological system and the long-term value of the area for residential, recreational, or other uses, the existing population has not been able to reach agreement on how this should occur—apart from controls on public land (which require environmental impact statements) and health standards.

The Political-Legal-Governmental Framework

"Political" and "legal" factors might better be treated as separate sets of issues for many purposes, but in the planning arena they must be closely tied. The legal provisions for planning invariably arise from political process, and the failure of political process is a primary cause of inadequacy of legal tools for planning. Elected officials have historically lived outside the Canyon and have shown little initiative in exercising their limited powers to affect Canyon territory or population.

National and state governments have tended to intrude in the area without taking the values and preferences of residents or landowners into account. Hence, the Canyon has been heavily affected by outside political or administrative decisions, but largely by imposition.

As noted earlier, Montana legal statutes do allow for the formation of either countywide planning or more limited rural planning districts. In both instances the legislation is permissive—that is, planning can only be initiated with the approval of local officials and qualified voters in the county or district. There is no legal means to organize or impose planning control by local or higher levels of government without the consent of residents. This means that without effective and progressive government, and a citizen population favorable to the concept of planning as a device for positive action in meeting environmental and human goals, there is no possibility of formalized planning implementation.

The two recent efforts to organize, first through the Gallatin Canyon Property Owners Association in 1970 (which was abortive because of intense internal conflict) and later through the Gallatin Canyon Association, have failed to achieve effective action—although efforts to develop other local services were moderately successful. Neither of the recent organizations had legal standing nor significant political influence, except as a legitimizing organization for the Gallatin Canyon Planning Study [which has yet (1976) to be seriously considered for implementation, although it was approved in principle by the Association].

Big Sky of Montana Corporation instituted a number of planned community services, such as fire protection, sewage disposal, a water system, and other amenities. These services were sponsored entirely at the initiative of corporation officials—although the development plan includes the intent to transfer control over these activities to the residents of the Big Sky property. Some of the services, such as fire fighting, are also available to other residents of the Canyon (who have collaborated to form a volunteer fire department).

The ineffectiveness of political, governmental, and statutory means to initiate effective preparation for the future of the Gallatin Canyon has been a major frustration of the Big Sky Corporation, concerned citizens, and officials at all levels. Some of the "outsider" groups with an interest in environmental preservation have used the courts to delay potentially damaging activities in the Canyon such as (1) the land exchanges between the U.S. Forest Service and Burlington Northern and (2) construction of a highway through the West Fork area to the Big Sky winter village. The recent requirement of environmental impact statements for all development projects on public lands or projects initiated by public agencies has provided a legal entry for protesters. The requirement has forced public and private agencies to be much more explicit about their projected impact on the environment.

One of the major long-term legal questions is related to water rights. A study was undertaken of the existing claims to water in the Canyon, as a means of determining how much of the total supply might already be appropriated and how much total water might be available for recreation and other uses. Information about appropriated surface water was incomplete, but there appears to be no evidence of overappropriation of water; sufficient volume exists for additional developments (Bowman, 1974).

The Economic Base

The principal purpose of the economic studies was to establish some means of estimating the consequences of development and to interrelate the economic impact with other variables. The economic issues can be summarized more explicitly by listing the measurements undertaken:

1 Flows of income generated by Big Sky
2 Increased employment
3 Induced business activity (apart from Big Sky, but created at least in part by it)
4 Changes in land ownership, land use, land development, and land prices
5 Public costs and income generated (expenditures versus taxes)
6 New capital investments
7 Investments made for environmental protection
8 Potential alternative use of resources

These specific measures are to be used for development of a predictive method or model to estimate the generalizability of this example for other major recreation developments (Thompson & Hash, 1973).

The key elements in measuring impact were (1) increased population, both temporary and permanent, (2) increased economic activity in terms of individual and business incomes, and (3) changes in land and other natural resource uses generated by economic activity. The first element was measured principally by establishing a population baseline for permanent residents, temporary residents, and traveling visitors—the latter of which is by far the most complex and significant in a study of recreation impact. It involved measurements of traffic volume, length and nature of visitor activity, and expenditures for each kind of activity (lodging, food, equipment, etc.).

To measure changes in economic activity it was necessary to extend the study well beyond the Canyon, to include particularly Bozeman and Gallatin County, although the investigators were well aware that the impact would extend into the state and national economy as well (however, measurements outside the local region were beyond the study capabilities). The baseline measures included surveys of business activity and volume, collection of data on indicators such as telephone hookups, bank debits and deposits, vehicle registration and assessments, and total employment change; these activities were then monitored over time.

To measure changes in land use, data were collected on land transfers beginning in 1965, prices involved in transfers, tax assessments on land, and changing property tax volume in the two counties most directly affected by the Big Sky development. Land-use changes were recorded, as were the changes in land character as a result of use.

Early results clearly indicate substantial increases in population, business activity, land exchanges, and land values as the Big Sky investment occurred. But the analysis has not proceeded sufficiently to estimate the detailed impact on the immediate and larger region. Isolating the specific impact is difficult because population influx and a land exchange "boom" were already under way before the announcement of the Big Sky development, and similar land-use alterations were occurring in other locations comparable to Montana (Thompson & Hash, 1973).

Design and Construction

Because the Gallatin Canyon contained relatively few alterations of human design prior to 1972, baselines were established as a means of noting structural and landscape changes and to isolate how the new designs affect visual character of the landscape.

A complete photographic and descriptive record was completed for all structures in the Canyon. Colored photographs were made of the physical and biological terrain throughout the area. The structural inventory included all buildings, outbuildings, and bridges. The buildings were classified as to type of use, ownership, construction characteristics, age, and geographical location. Maps were drawn to illustrate the data by location (McKroskey, 1970).

The "seasonal" residences (62 percent of all structures) were by far the most numerous; 9 percent were permanent residences, and 17 percent were dude-ranch cabins. Seasonal employee residences accounted for 5 percent and motel units 3 percent. Commercial structures of various kinds represented the remainder. Log construction accounted for 58 percent of the structures, and wood frame with wood siding another 33 percent; 2 percent were mobile homes, and 1 percent stone or concrete block; the remaining 5 percent were of mixed materials. In addition to these characteristics the record included size of buildings, foundation type, basement and floor construction, roofing material, garages or carports, fireplaces, heating systems, existence of electricity, kind of heating fuel, bedrooms, bathrooms, plumbing, extent of occupancy, water supply, sewage disposal system, garbage disposal, communication (telephone, radio, etc.), and date of construction. Characteristics of site improvements or landscaping and general condition of structures and sites were rated.

The bulk of the buildings were located in largely "unimproved" wilderness locations at some distance from other structures, with only a narrow gravel trail entering the sites. Except for a small proportion of residential land close to the highway, the buildings were not readily visible nor aesthetically offensive to the critical observer.

The main highway through the Canyon generally followed the natural contour, but required displacement of the river or mountainsides in numerous locations where inadequate construction space was available. Regrowth of plants had obscured the bulk of visual blemish (at the time of the baseline study). However, the new road entering the West Fork required much more obvious displacement of both river and soil. The highway design required relocation of the West Fork for a short distance, construction of a new flow channel, and construction of a concrete bridge.

New designs of structures and entry of mobile homes in large numbers were highly visible intrusions as the Big Sky Development proceeded. Within the Big Sky complex careful attention was given to maintenance of a rustic design that blended with the sagebrush, pine trees, and grass which were the predominant vegetation. Landscape design of golf courses, ski runs, and residential yards were similarly controlled so as to blend with the existing landscape. However, the final effect of the effort to "design and construct with the environment" remains to be evaluated. Initial observation suggests that the Big Sky Development is generally maintaining a much more pleasing visual atmosphere than some of the new structures on its periphery.

Interrelating the Basic Data
The process of interrelating information from the variety of subcategories described above is an extraordinarily complex task, and not readily resolved, regardless of the importance of considering "all factors" relevant to

a planning or study region. The original intent of the Gallatin Canyon project was to achieve an "interdisciplinary" approach and to build a system of interrelationships and mutual understanding among investigators. Each part of this intent proved to be a substantial challenge which was not entirely surmounted after 3 years of project activity.

Major emphasis was given to the potential use of the data: (1) for specific planning in the project area, (2) for transfer potential of the concepts, results, and implications to other locations facing similar impacts, (3) for private decisions on recreation development, and (4) for public policy or legal tools needed to guide and regulate major recreation development. For each of these potential uses of data an attempt was made to identify (1) the full range of primary activities related to the development, (2) the key decision-making issues involved in these activities, and (3) the most significant variables or baseline factors which should affect planning activities and decisions.

Illustrative Interrelationships

It would require a major volume to examine all of the potential interrelationships among the factors or elements studied; this section is therefore limited to a description of the interaction among a selected set of variables, to illustrate the relevance of each basic knowledge category to the Gallatin Canyon in particular and rural or regional planning in general. The illustrations are based on specific recreation activities which form part of the Big Sky Development, but which are also potential activities in a wide variety of other rural regions.

The mass of available data, and the wide variation in level of measurement (i.e., from *numbers* of aquatic invertebrates in water, to *attitudes* of fishermen toward the number of fish available for catching) makes quantitative interaction analysis difficult and sometimes of uncertain reliability. The variables are therefore interrelated primarily at conceptual and relational levels. That is, relationships between variables (number of fishermen related to physical accessibility of the fishing stream) are diagrammed and described; and the direction of relationships is tested (i.e., numbers of people fishing will increase where streams are accessible and when catches are consistently successful). When the levels of measurement were clear and could be specified, statistical relationships were computed, sometimes involving data from two or more disciplinary bases.

Consequently the ability to predict relationships into the future is limited to general conclusions that appeared evident on the basis of descriptive data rather than readily quantifiable relationships. For example, because of climatic conditions (air inversion layers) in the West Fork area, it is readily possible to predict (at a *high* confidence level) that as motor traffic and heating of homes or condominiums increases, the degree of air pollution will rise. However, the exact mathematical relationship between number of automobiles or fireplaces and increased air pollution is not clearly established. Measurement methods for locating visual air inversion levels, and health-damaging air pollutants, were improved as part of the research. Increased predictability of climatic conditions and more advanced measurement methods will be directly helpful in planning to optimize air quality in the Gallatin area (as well as other locations).

The conceptual and relational chart in Table 11-1 illustrates important interactions and provides an initial basis for planning and development guidelines used by the Big Sky Corporation and the consultant planners.

THE PUBLIC PLANNING PROCESS

The consultants responsible for the Gallatin Canyon Planning Study were strongly oriented to an ecologically based approach to analysis. They undertook several major stages of activity: (1) goal selection, (2) environmental resource inventory, (3) sensitivities analysis, (4) delineation of alternative land-use concepts, (5) comprehensive plan and guidelines, and (6) environmental impact summary.

Planning Goals

The Planning Study Committee (selected in part by the Gallatin Canyon Association but officially appointed by the state governor) was appointed to assist in the formulation of general goals and specific planning objectives. A series of meetings between consultants and the committee resulted in several general goals (Murray-McCormick Environmental Group, 1972):

    1 Prepare suitable land use alternatives for the environmental enhancement of the entire region to be strengthened by recommended guidelines that provide control of the physical environment.

    2 Develop and maintain cooperation and coordination of government agencies—local, state and federal—responsible for the creation and preservation of the present quality of life in the Gallatin Canyon area.

    3 Coordinate planning efforts including goals, plans and programs of local, state and federal agencies relating to open space, recreation facilities and scenic preservation for residents and tourists that visit the Canyon area annually.

    4 Enhance the social, cultural, and recreational activities in the Canyon while preserving the ecological and environmental values of the region.

    5 Protect and preserve the existing ecosystem from unnecessary alteration and disturbance.

In addition to these general goals a series of much more specific objectives were recorded, as guidelines for the consulting firm, as the basis for preparation of a formal plan, and as long-range intentions for the preserva-

Table 11-1   Illustrative Interrelationships

Element	Physical	Biological	Cultural-historical	Social-psychological	
Skiing-related	Potential avalanche	↔ Destruction of trees; destruction of small animals	↔ Past avalanche destruction	↔ Skier fear of dangerous slopes; skier avoidance of dangerous ski areas	←
Summer home or condominium construction	Soil instability on slopes	↔ Restriction on vegetative types; plant destruction by erosion; stream turbidity and decline of aquatic invertebrates	↔ History of soil loss and erosion	↔ Limitations on hiking; limitations on freedom to build	←
Fishing	Turbidity of streams	↔ Decrease in aquatic invertebrates; decrease in fish	↔ History of "blue ribbon" trout streams in the area	↔ Discomfort of fishermen with stream; decrease in social activity of fishing; decline of aesthetic value	←
General recreation development	Inability to control physical stability of geological and soil features; probable deterioration of physical systems	↔ Inability to control biological (or ecological) balance of nature; probable deterioration of natural systems	↔ Historical and cultural basis for individual rights in use of land and property; value system emphasizing individuality as opposed to social control	↔ No control over individual or social behavior related to land use or social service; individual and group freedom to use property as they wish	←

Political-legal		Economic		Design		Construction
→ Requirement to remove avalanche precipices; legal statutes to protect citizens from avalanche danger	←→	Increased cost of skiing required by avalanche control; destruction costs of avalanches	←→	Lift and structure design to withstand avalanches; design of ski runs to avoid avalanche areas	←→	Construction of lifts and structures to withstand avalanches
→ Regulations to avoid construction on unstable slopes and soils	←→	Increased construction cost; increase of erosion abatement costs	←→	Landscape design to stabilize soils; building design to account for soil instability	←→	Construction of roads, lifts, landscape, structures to avoid instability consequences
→ Potential imposition of statutes to limit turbidity; imposition of legal regulations on stream use and input of pollutants	←→	Decreased financial benefits from fishermen expenditures; decrease in tax revenue; increase in costs of administering regulation	←→	Improved design to avoid influx of turbidity to streams; improved landscape design to withhold turbid elements	←→	Improvement of construction procedures to prevent turbidity
→ Failure to form a legally constituted planning and zoning district	←→	Freedom to initiate individually selected enterprises; freedom of land speculation and rising land prices	←→	Individual freedom to design or fail to design structures and location of structures; no control over landscape design	←→	Freedom of individuals to construct whatever they choose wherever they choose

tion and development of the region. The objectives touch a wide range of issues and contain values and ideals with which few citizens or officials could publicly disagree; however, many landowners found fault in their potential constraining effects on private property development.

Environmental Resource and Sensitivities Analysis
The bulk of the "environmental resource" information used to develop alternatives was derived from original research undertaken by the consultants as part of the Montana State University Gallatin Canyon Study, or from earlier studies. Geological, climatic, hydrological, vegetative, soil, fish and wildlife, settlement, circulation, land ownership, development, and growth patterns were described and analyzed for "sensitivity" to development. The basic premise was that each place in the landscape has an "intrinsic suitability" for certain human uses or activities (McHarg, 1969). A land sensitivities map was constructed to depict the natural and cultural constraints to various types of development, with emphasis on recreation potential.

Land-Use Alternatives
On the basis of these analyses, three alternative land-use approaches were outlined to demonstrate the development possibilities for the Canyon:

1 Full development while respecting the natural constraints
2 Curtailment of present trends with no further developments, and assuming that the land exchanges between the U.S. Forest Service and the Burlington Northern Railroad would not occur
3 A composite of the first two, emphasizing clustered development consistent with the identified natural and cultural sensitivities

After reviewing these alternatives with the local planning study committee a "synthesis" alternative was developed, incorporating some features of each of the original possibilities. The synthesis called for preservation of the Canyon as a uniquely natural scenic area. It proposed controlled development; that is, utilization of the area should be governed by regulations which preserve the natural scenic environment through coordinated public and private land management. Development activities would be clustered in those areas along U.S. Highway 191 most suitable for construction while minimizing visual intrusion on the landscape and limiting interference with natural ecosystems.

Improvements on U.S. Highway 191 might be required to accommodate better traffic movement, but should be limited to addition of stopping points and rest areas for truck and recreation vehicle traffic; no widening beyond two lanes would be allowed.

However, the consultant planners projected feasible alternatives only in terms of "physical" possibilities for implementation; social, economic and political feasibility were not examined in detail. The data available from the Gallatin Canyon Research Study on the social-psychological and political character of the local population and larger surrounding region were not considered in the planning report.

The Comprehensive Plan

The comprehensive plan sets forth policies which could guide the physical growth of the Canyon, including distribution of population, the intensity of building and commercial development, the transportation system, and other land uses.

The land-use element was divided into five major sections:

1   Natural areas, including riparian or water-related locations, primitive or wilderness areas, and high elevations or mountain peaks
2   General forest areas
3   Residential areas
4   Commercial areas
5   Recreational areas, including dispersed activity, commercial recreation, and trails

The transportation element was concerned with:

1   Redesign and development of U.S. 191
2   Access roads from the main route
3   Trail systems for off-road vehicles, horse travel, and hiking

A public facilities and services element outlined recommendations for:

1   Water supply
2   Sanitary waste disposal
3   Solid waste disposal
4   Fire protection
5   Schools

IMPLEMENTATION GUIDELINES: CRITIQUE AND DISCUSSION

Each major element of the comprehensive plan outlines policies which could serve to fulfill the major goals outlined earlier. It is deliberately general, rather than attempting to specify in detail how each policy should be implemented for all locations in the Canyon.

The general guidelines are not operationalized by precise implementation procedures; the individual property owners in the Canyon remain free to interpret and subscribe to the plan as they wish, with no responsibility to make decisions on the basis of the policies outlined. This makes it possible and probable that the plan will remain largely an artifact of Canyon history, unless the legal muscle is provided through organized enforcement. Since it is oriented entirely to "physical" issues, with no design or detailed proposals for social, political, or economic development of the region, the crucial organizational support fabric which will ultimately be responsible for guiding development is left to a highly uncertain fate.

The "action-planning" concept, as outlined in an earlier chapter, is clearly not operational (as of mid-1976). Although some components of such an approach were incorporated (citizen involvement in goal setting and discussion of the draft plan), the most crucial attributes of organization, legal mandate, and staffing for the "action" component are missing; without incorporation of these features, planning in the Canyon may be a rather empty exercise serving more to frustrate than to facilitate effective and planned development. The quality of life and environmental goals are likely to be less than optimally attained.

Although the State Division of Planning and Economic Development successfully fulfilled some of the governmental guidance functions (monitoring and facilitating, particularly), under present Montana statutes they were not legally able to assume what were essentially local government functions. Management, feedback, and evaluation by state or local agencies were at best intermittent and minimal.

Quality of Life and Environment

The principal goals of planning activity in the Gallatin Canyon focused on achievement of quality individual and community life, and a quality physical, biological, and economic environment. The meaning of "quality" is the subject of vigorous debate among residents of the region and visitors from outside. However, this "uncertainty" is not unique to southwestern Montana. There are few explicit guidelines to indicate how much deterioration of the existing ecosystem can occur without serious negative influence on environmental quality, and there is widespread disagreement over how much development can take place without overpopulating rural regions or despoiling environmental and social amenities associated with high-quality environment.

Standards of environmental "quality" were established partially on the basis of measurable deterioration using methods described in the Montana State University research. These measurement methods provide a basis for legal statutes defining the specific standards required, and the minimal quality levels to be allowed.

Strategies of Change and Organization

The formal efforts at instituting planning in the Gallatin Canyon have so far been frustrated in part by at least three major factors: (1) a value bias against public control of land-use decisions affecting privately held land, (2) inadequate understanding of regional planning as a problem-solving and goal-achieving approach, and (3) inadequate organization for effective design and management of the planning and action process.

Value bias is extremely difficult to surmount. The "planning process and participation model," as outlined in Chapter VIII, was partially followed during the efforts to prepare an acceptable regional plan. There was a continuing opportunity for participation of local citizens and interested outsiders; however, the manner and timing through which this "opportunity" was provided proved less than satisfactory to many leaders and citizens. The State Division of Planning and Economic Development was largely responsible for the process, with the assistance of the consulting firm; both were criticized strongly for failing to sufficiently involve and inform the local people. However, the state agency assumed the leadership role only because local leadership and local government were apparently not able or willing to organize and manage formal planning. The state agency staff and the consultants were both largely unfamiliar with the social and political character of the area—even though both state and private planning professionals were technically competent.

In retrospect it seems quite clear that a much more carefully designed social-change strategy would have helped. The strategy used was essentially based on the "information-education" model (see Table 8-3) involving public meetings, mass media presentations, speeches, and publication of numerous written and visually explanatory documents; most local people were able to identify the planning effort as an ongoing process, and their knowledge of planning procedures was probably increased considerably. A few individuals may have undergone attitudinal, ideological, and behavior change through involvement with the process. However, misunderstanding prevailed, and only a relatively small proportion of the total population was heavily involved. Because the legal requirements did not exist to institute planning by "force," this strategy was not seriously attempted, although many individuals interpreted the actions of the state planning department as an effort to coerce local citizens and local government. The "active-learning" change strategy might have been more successful but would have required substantially more effort.

It seems likely that a planning procedure with credibility and continuity will require a permanent, professional, and sophisticated organizational base—possibly somewhat like the model illustrated in Chapter XIII. The "temporary systems" components of the model were fulfilled by the university and consultant studies—although this has so far included only "basic" and "applied" research, with no substantial effort to fulfill "change agent" or "educational" roles. The NSF-financed research has generated a large data pool and has undertaken analysis and projections, which would be available to a permanent planning team.

The major gap is clearly the "implementation" and "change agent" activities—obviously crucial steps if the planning effort is eventually to serve a useful purpose. This is not to say that the local planners are at fault; rather, it means that local government has not recognized, nor had the legal mandate to incorporate, planning as an instrument to improve local government effectiveness in planned development.

Chapter XII

Education of Planners
and Public Education for Planning

Roughly 5,000 students were enrolled in planning schools in 1973: 1,000 in bachelor degree programs, 3,500 in master's degree programs, and about 300 were pursuing Ph.D.s. This contrasts with a total enrollment of only 1,000 in 1963. Growth of the field as a profession has clearly been extraordinary, as further indicated by a near-doubling of the number of schools offering planning degrees during the same period (from 28 to 54) (Perloff, 1974, p. 168).

However, only a small number of schools have emphasized environmental and natural resource considerations, and as of 1976, very few programs emphasized rural regional planning. The major planning schools have given primary emphasis to three core areas: (1) planning theory, (2) planning methods, and (3) interaction or interrelationships between social, economic, political, and spatial elements of *urban* systems. Planning theory and planning methods are still largely derived from other disciplines; only recently have professionally trained planners begun to make major original contributions to knowledge about the field (Perloff, 1974, pp. 170–171).

Perloff suggests a number of dilemmas which presently confront planning education (Perloff, 1974, p. 173):

> **1** The conflict between educating for generalist skills as opposed to specialist skills.
> **2** Training for high level technical skills versus preparation for humanistic understanding as a basis for planning.
> **3** Focusing on current problem solving as opposed to a more abstract concern with future goals and opportunities.
> **4** Emphasis on scholarly research as compared to professional practice.
> **5** Stressing substantive content and products in planning as opposed to planning as a public involvement process.
> **6** Focusing education on carefully selected full-time students as compared to stressing preparation of a variety of students, including extension programs for up-dating professionals and educating citizens about planning.

Although these dilemmas as outlined by Perloff would seem to imply a choice among one or the other of two extremes, that need not be the requirement. Given adequate understanding of educational needs it should be possible to provide for both ends of the continuum by maintaining a balance between the extremes—while strengthening the total educational experience for full-time students, practicing professionals, and citizen planners. However, basic institutional changes may be necessary to meet the particular needs for continuing education and public education in planning.

Planning curriculum content focuses heavily on urban problems and urban regions, with little special attention to the uniqueness of rural communities or environmental systems with low population density. University departments of planning tend to be located in design or fine arts divisions, often with a strong dependence on architecture or engineering as the major supporting disciplines (Hartman, 1970, p. 218). A study of the county and regional planning departments in the state of Washington illuminates this issue rather forcefully; most professional planners are trained in urban planning or related fields such as geography, or have no professional preparation in planning. A high proportion of planning staff members admit inadequate preparation for work with rural or small town residents (Lassey, Barron, & Ditwiler, 1974).

Support for increased and coordinated efforts toward improved planning curricula focusing on rural regions comes from a variety of sources. Professional associations such as the American Society of Planning Officials have given encouragement to the initiation of such programs to meet the recognized need for greater emphasis on rural planning during the next decade. Local and state rural development committees (consisting of representatives from state and federal agencies with rural concerns) have placed major emphasis on rural planning and have articulated the need for improved academic preparation and in-service education of planners, public officials, and citizens.

Local, state, and federal agencies regularly employ individuals to fill planning-related positions who do not have appropriate preparation. Agency heads indicate there is both a need for new professionals with specific training in planning for rural regions *and* opportunities for graduate-level in-service training (Hobson & Lassey, 1974).

New land-use planning legislation has been passed in several states. The statutes already passed or bills under consideration each call for considerable expansion in the number of positions for professional planners at local and state levels (Council of State Governments, 1975). Federal land-use planning legislation has failed by only a few votes in recent sessions of the United States Congress and may eventually succeed. Existing environmental legislation has heavily impacted planning activity in most states. Should federal land-use legislation be enacted it may further increase the demand for professional planners at national, state, and local levels, particularly for nonurban areas. The proposed legislation calls for expanded requirements and increased funding for state and local jurisdictions (*National Land-Use Policy Legislation*, 1973).

Federal departments, such as Agriculture, Interior, Housing and Urban Development, and Commerce, have each placed increased emphasis on state, regional, and local planning assistance and are employing planners specifically for work in rural regions. This is particularly notable in the U.S. Forest Service, Soil Conservation Service, Bureau of Land Management, Economic Development Administration, and Farmers Home Administration. The Rural Development Act of 1972 places increased emphasis on planning in rural areas; guidelines prepared for implementation of the act give specific responsibility to federal and state agencies for increased emphasis on local, regional, and state planning (Rural Development Act, 1972). New federal programs in water-quality maintenance, coastal zone management, and air pollution abatement each call for comprehensive planning.

Private planning firms and corporations are seeking professionals trained in rural-oriented planning, as a means of strengthening their service potential or to more effectively manage privately held corporate lands.[1] Many rural jurisdictions cannot fund a planning department and must depend on private consulting firms for a variety of planning services. The record of consultant effectiveness in rural areas is regularly questioned by local officials and citizens, largely because the consultant planners have little appreciation for uniqueness associated with rural jurisdictions.

---

[1] William R. Lassey: Personal interviews with local officials, representatives of private consulting firms, and corporation officials (Boise-Cascade, Weyerhaeuser, Burlington-Northern), 1972–74.

Possibly the greatest shortcoming of many professional planners who attempt to work in rural areas is their inability to understand and empathize with value systems of rural residents and the character of social, political, and economic organization.

Revised Curriculum Content

A new or revised approach to education of rural planners is therefore called for. The curriculum and educational process discussed below would overlap considerably with the existing content of urban or regional planning education in many colleges and universities; it simply replaces the focus on urban design and urban structure with greater attention to the content and process which fits the requirements of a rural environment and population.

Table 12-1 outlines the major knowledge and skill areas needing emphasis. This is not to imply that every planner working in rural regions should become fully acquainted with each of the content areas noted; rather, the curriculum would require integrating seminars or courses, gaming-simulation, internships, and research, which introduce students to the full range of variables and which provide an opportunity to interrelate content.

Rural planners will usually need a thorough understanding of the physical and biological foundations of the natural and created systems on which life depends. A reasonably complete understanding of the economic and social factors which impinge on or characterize rural areas, as compared to urban regions, is essential. Understanding of cultural and historical uniqueness of rural communities, and political and governmental systems, is equally crucial. Preparation in design of adapted biological and physical systems for rural areas is important as a basis for proposals and specific plans for transportation, public utility, landscape, and other rural community requirements.

In addition to basic knowledge and skills, a planner must be able to interrelate a multiplicity of factors which impinge on decisions about the future and must be prepared to anticipate probable future events. Skill in developing feasible goals and objectives would be improved by increased understanding of the opportunities and constraints imposed by rural socio-economic-environmental systems.

Understanding of educational and communication processes is important if planners are to facilitate citizen involvement in policymaking, planning, and implementing processes. Planners must understand the mechanisms and processes for assuring that plans are implemented, monitored, and evaluated within the prescribed policies.

Any single planner would be frustrated in an attempt to become expert in each of these areas; but enough understanding must exist so that a planner can function as part of a planning team with full cognizance of the relevance of each component of rural planning organization and activity.

Table 12-1   Curriculum Topics for Rural Planning Professionals

Physical:
  Geology
  Physical geography
  Soil structure
  Hydrology
  Meteorology and climatology
  Energy resources

Economic:
  Rural land economics
  Rural public finance
  Rural development economics
  Rural transportation economics
  Rural demography

Cultural-historical:
  Rural cultural history
  History of planning in rural areas

Design:
  Rural landscape design
  Town layout and design
  Rural utility system design
  Rural transportation system design
  Cartography for planning
  Rural recreation system design

Interrelationships:
  Systems theory
  Ecological systems
  Statistics
  Computer systems

Planning theory and process:
  Planning organization
  Elements of planning
  Regional planning process
  Land-use planning in rural areas
  Human resource planning
  Planning regulation and enforce-
  ment
  Evaluation of planning programs

Biological:
  Botany
  Zoology
  Microbiology
  Limnology
  Ecology

Social and psychological:
  Human ecology
  Rural social organization
  Sociology of rural community
  Rural social institutions
  Planned social change
  Complex organizations
  Social research for planners
  Social planning methods

Politics, government, and law
  State and local government
  Planning law
  Public administration

Education and communication:
  Design of educational process
  Audiovisual presentation
  Mass communication
  Interpersonal communication
  Public involvement process

Projections:
  Demography
  Feasibility analysis methods
  Physical-biological resource con-
  straints

Integrating experiences:
  Simulation of rural community sys-
  tems
  Simulation of planning decision
  process
  Rural planning internship

Experience-based education for students and practicing planners will usual-ly constitute an important supplement to classroom instruction in helping to integrate the subject matter categories noted in Table 12-1.

The Design of Experience-based Education for Planning Professionals

If education for potential planners is to be sufficiently practical and immediately relevant to the solving of rural problems and realization of development opportunities, the learning process must be heavily devoted to experiencing and dealing with real issues. There is a variety of means to achieve this, many of which have been successfully tested. Three learning devices seem worthy of special note:

1   Gaming-simulation, in which participants are engaged in structured exercises with realistic opportunities to consider issues about which decisions must be made; participants are required to involve themselves in "simulated" issue resolution.
2   Direct participation in ongoing planning processes, through temporary internships with local or state units, private firms, or federal agencies engaged in rural planning.
3   Research on rural planning problems, in which participants would systematically seek firsthand information about planning issues, reactions of participants, and planning process.

Although each of these learning devices is listed as a separate possibility, they may often be appropriately overlapped. Each method will provide a somewhat different kind of experience, from which substantial learning and skill could be derived under adequately organized conditions. The important point is that students will be much better prepared to apply the knowledge gained from lectures, books, films, and other kinds of exposure to theory and practice, if they can engage directly in the activities about which they are attempting to learn.

Gaming-simulation has been widely used in military training, business, education, more recently in urban planning education, and in a variety of other circumstances (Taylor, 1971). The approach has been sufficiently tested to make its use worthwhile as an initial instructional device for helping budding planners understand the factors and the roles that form the basis for planning constraints and possibilities.

Although the value of gaming-simulation seems evident, the cost in time, space, and equipment relative to other educational methods may at first seem formidable. Very few simulation games relevant to rural or regional planning are available in a form which can be adequately operated in the conventional lecture or studio period. Most games have operated in specially designed circumstances, evening sessions, weekends, or special workshops. The Community Land-Use Game (CLUG) was developed at a cost of roughly $73,000 (through a Ford Foundation grant) and retails for $125 as a package. It requires a minimum of four hours of steady playing time and is much more useful if extended to several days. [A variety of other game-simulations is discussed in detail by Taylor (1971) in a very useful analysis of instructional planning systems.]

The experience of those who have helped to develop game-simulations or who have adapted them for class use suggest several attributes of potential value:[2]

1 The preparation for and management of a game-simulation is a useful learning experience for an instructor. Serious thought must be given to teaching objectives and the concepts to be communicated, and the instructor must also realistically consider the kinds of roles, issues, constraints, and problems of planning.

2 Games appear to help the student take a more sophisticated and comprehensive view of planning situations. They help participants to distinguish between significant issues and trivial events or concerns. Attempting to play various roles within the planning framework helps the student to understand and appreciate the characteristics and inclinations of persons who function in those roles on a permanent basis.

3 Gaming-simulation appears generally to be highly interesting and motivating to participants if it is well designed and managed. It provides an opportunity for participants to judge their own progress, knowledge, and skill, as part of the feedback from other players and from the results which occur as a consequence of participant decisions. Instructor evaluation is therefore largely unnecessary in the game situation. Student self-teaching is facilitated.

Gaming-simulation can be considered one approach among several which involve participants directly in learning through experience—by creating a synthetic environment which illustrates the conditions, activities, and behavior within a real environment. The participants are placed in a decision-making context over an extended period of time, but within a relatively controlled and risk-free environment. Some of the related techniques are listed in Table 12-2.

One of the most useful attributes of the approach is the opportunity it provides for participants to organize facts and insights, while emphasizing the interconnectedness and interrelationships among fields of knowledge; it is by nature "interdisciplinary," and (assuming skillful management of the process) can overcome some of the barriers between academic fields associated with planning. This is its principal recommendation as a learning context for ecologically based rural planning.

Gaming-simulation and the related approaches briefly described in Ta-

---

[2] Adapted from John L. Taylor. *Instructional planning systems: A gaming simulation approach to urban problems.* Cambridge University Press, 1971. Adapted by permission of Cambridge University Press.

Table 12-2 Experience-based Learning Approaches

	Usual nomenclature	Approximate definition
Reality	Internship	Participating in actual work situations with defined learning objectives
	Case study	Descriptions of actual situations similar to the learning objective
	Problem solving	Written solutions to sequence of problems drawn from actual situations
	Incident process	Reactions to contrived incidents which represent decision situations
	Role playing	Formal opportunities to simulate roles of individuals involved in decision making or problem solving
	Gaming-simulation	Structured group process simulating a real situation, in which a sequence of decisions and results occur over time and are related to simplified problem situations
Abstraction	Machine or computer simulation	All data inputs and decisions arise from mathematical representations of reality

Source: Adapted from Taylor, 1971, p. 11.

ble 12-2 can help fill the gap between the generalized textbook-lecture learning model and practical experience required for effective work in planning offices. But more than that, cognizance is taken of several alternative educational methods which arise from knowledge about human learning:

1 The importance of active and intensive involvement of the learner in self-discovery
2 Introduction of decision-making experience in realistic settings, with rapid and regular feedback indicating the consequences of decisions and adequacy of performance
3 Creation of environmental conditions conducive to self-pacing, self-monitoring, and openness to learning from errors
4 Potential for diversity of stimulation through combinations of educational media, ranging through auditory, manipulative, verbal, and visual experiences

Finally, gaming-simulation at its fullest potential involves the participant in a "systems" approach to learning from experience involving models of reality with clear and direct similarity to the circumstances of the community, region, or other planning environment. When combined or integrated with conventional teaching experiences, as well as direct participation in ongoing planning programs and research on planning problems, gaming-simulation can provide the process by which potential participants in planning can learn to operationalize and use the appropriate concepts in advance of involvement in positions of responsibility.

Internships or Direct Experience

An internship is intended to provide some type of supervised preprofessional work experience. This would ideally involve exposure to the combination of research and fieldwork that make up a high proportion of activities undertaken by the practicing planner in a public agency or private firm. A good internship should:

1 Expose the student to political process as it relates to planning
2 Introduce the student to a wide range of projects and activities in a planning office
3 Provide the intern with responsibility for a complete project, including conceptualization of a major problem to be resolved, data collection, analysis, recommendations, and a final written and visual product
4 Include a major opportunity for the student to apply theory and prior study to practical professional work

Internships may involve compiling current and previously published information, or the collection of original data, which will be of direct benefit to public agency officials and private citizens in management or development decisions. Such activity will usually increase library search skills, mathematical or statistical ability, writing competence, and the student's specialized vocabulary.

Fieldwork experience will require the student to participate in the development and/or implementation of plans or programs for a public agency or private firm. This should involve the identification of policy alternatives and the impact of potential policies on decisions by public officials. Experience in administration and management should also be provided, particularly program organization and implementation, evaluation of policy and program results, budgetary processes, allocation of personnel and material resources, and establishing and maintaining work priorities.

A well-designed internship can help the student develop professional attitudes, technical skills, and self-confidence through exposure to practicing planners in work situations; the experience should increase sophistication in effects of planning process on individuals and communities.[3]

---

[3] For further discussion of internships see the manual *Student internships*, published by the Planning Advisory Service, American Society of Planning Officials, Report #246, May 1969, and later supplements.

Research or Thesis Preparation

Original research can be among the most illuminating and informing means of learning, particularly if related to the direct experience as described above and if the research contributes to the solution of important problems. Student involvement in an ongoing research program may often be more valuable than a student-originated project, depending in part on the prior experience and preparation of the student. However, research experience is likely to be most valuable if the student is involved in conceptualization of the problem to be studied, design of the methods of data collection and analysis, conduct of the investigation, analysis of the data, and preparation of written and visual parts of the report. Competence in rigorous research is among the most critical skills required of planners and can best be learned through direct involvement; requiring a high-quality thesis may be the most effective means to test student ability to undertake and report on research.

The research process can achieve many of the same learning opportunities noted above for gaming-simulation but also provides the context for some of the direct experience (or observation of direct experience) provided by internships. Since gaming-simulation, internships, and research each provide somewhat different learning experiences, beyond the conventional classroom situation, a combination and integration of each learning method would presumably provide the most complete preprofessional preparation. A student who participates in each kind of learning opportunity should be in good position to enter professional work with immediate effectiveness.

The future of the planning field will depend heavily on the quality and timeliness of research by graduate students and their professors. Planning research can be an important tool in preparing students for specialized activities in which specific courses are not available. A strong research program is clearly basic to a sound educational effort (Perloff, 1974, p. 172).

Special Training Requirements for Action Planning

Planners who are to be involved directly in initiating programs may need basic understanding about social action. They must understand themselves well enough to know how they affect other people. They must understand the various action roles, as well as technical functions, they will have to perform. Their effectiveness will depend heavily on an ability to learn from experience while relating their new knowledge to the understanding they already possess. They must be able to translate the technical skills acquired through formal education to the realities of practical situations; this is essential if they are to effectively communicate with rural individuals who have acquired most of their knowledge from experience rather than through formal learning.

There is often a vast gulf between rural or small town leaders, government officials, and the "professional" planners who presumably come to help them. Because of an inability to "empathize" or understand situations from the point of view of these local leaders, professionals are often perceived as useless in helping achieve the goals defined at the local level. Planners must be effective in reducing the distance between their point of view and the local point of view; this requires keen observation and a high degree of sensibility to the personalities and preferences of rural citizens.

However, regardless of the planners' skills at the interpersonal level, rural planning and action is bound to be charged with emotion, disagreement, and conflict; the long-term interests of many influential individuals will be challenged by the changes required. Planners must learn to accept a certain degree of conflict and understand how to work with conflicting points of view. Land-use or human service plans will often have a profound effect on the balance of local power; if they are to be effective, rural planners must have a well-developed understanding of political process and persuasive skill to moderate resistance from individuals or groups who would subvert the larger interests of society to protect their own often selfish interests.

Involvement in decision and action processes will quickly destroy the effectiveness of planners unless they are perceived as highly responsible and legitimate persons. They must subscribe to and function according to a professional ethic which is based in honesty and commitment to public rather than private or personal interests and goals. The ends pursued must justify the means of pursuit (Friedman, 1969).

There is obviously much more that could be said about the design and content of a curriculum for rural planners. However, the preceding discussion suggests the general substantive content and educational process appropriate to rural planning education.

Public Education for Planning

A carefully designed education-communication strategy is essential if local officials and citizens are to understand and actively participate in rural planning efforts. The issues raised in Chapter II, and the problems noted above which require special education for planners, suggest the importance of helping citizens to understand the public issues and processes associated with future societal and environmental enhancement. Further, a better understanding of the role of planning, in policy development and local government effectiveness, is crucial if informed decisions are to be made about future use of natural resources, design and development of rural communities, and preservation of the physical, biological, and social support systems.

There is obviously a wide variety of subject matter which public education for planning might include; Table 12-1 might be used as a source of content possibilities for public as well as professional education, and the methods suggested for professional training might be adapted in part for public education. However, a much more limited and basic approach seems appropriate for rural citizens who have had very little exposure or experience with planning concepts.

The most relevant potential content areas can be briefly summarized:

1 The policy alternatives for minimizing negative human impact on the environment in the locale where participants live

2 The fundamentals of ecology, with particular emphasis on the cycles required for maintenance of life-support systems

3 The relationship between basic scientific knowledge and the factors or elements of knowledge required for informed planning

4 The rationale for planning: a means of preparing for the future with forethought, rather than arbitrary control over individual freedom

5 The basic phases of planning process

6 The existing legislation and organization for planning

7 The requirements or methods for implementing the results of planning

The responsibility for public education about planning has heretofore been widely diffused and insufficiently systematic. It may be crucial for federal, state, and local governments to designate specific responsibility for design and conduct of educational efforts. State land-grant university extension services have a long-standing role and reputation in education efforts to improve rural communities. Extension offices are located in nearly every county throughout the United States and have access to local communities and local leaders. Extension faculty generally have contact with local government officials and could collaborate with them in the design and development of local educational programs, with assistance from university specialists in planning, other planning professionals, and educational design specialists.

Community colleges and local school systems might also play a useful role, by offering basic courses on planning topics, for interested citizens, members of planning commissions, and local officials. The public media have been used extensively to present planning-related content in some communities but usually cannot deal with the topics in great detail. However, much more sensitive use of the media for public planning education would clearly seem desirable.

A variety of additional possibilities for public education exists as part of citizen participation in planning efforts; involvement may be the single best means of public education, since it can often be substantially more effective than formalized learning situations in altering attitudes and behavior.

Chapter XIII

Adapting Rural Planning and Development Organization and Process

Research and experience have multiplied what we know about rural people and their environment. An abundance of institutions and agencies have been created to supply information and programs for rural regions. This has led to a proliferation of professional competencies in specialized agencies and organizations but has not usually produced an adequate formal mechanism for interrelating and integrating programs or services at the local level. An improved rural planning and development program design and process is needed which can systematically merge the interests and programs of public agencies with the interests and priorities of local officials and citizens.

An Organizational Model for Planning in Rural Regions

The adapted institutional design in local jurisdictions should provide for greater involvement of the public and must incorporate a wider array of agencies and organizations. The specific organizational structure will vary according to local preferences or requirements but should contain several major elements:[1]

1 *A planning management unit which relates directly to executive, legislative, and judicial decision processes of local government and which has direct ties to external or higher level government planning and development agencies.* This unit should have overall responsibility for planning within the local jurisdiction and would become the central source of consultation and information on key planning issues (see Chapter II) for jurisdictional decision makers.

2 *A subunit (or staff competence) which has responsibility for generating and creating access to basic information required for the planning function.* The subunit should be capable of securing access to applied and developmental research results which provide the physical, biological, social, economic, political, and other knowledge on which planning should be based (see Chapters III, V, and VI).

3 *A subunit for analyzing, interpreting, and projecting information as a basis for both short-range decisions and long-range goal formation.* Such a subunit might rely heavily on external assistance from centers or resource people with competence in applied research, modeling, projection, and processes for reducing data to comprehensible forms. The subunit would be responsible for developing data in maps and other visual and verbal forms that are useful to citizens and decision makers (see Chapter VII).

4 *A subunit with competence in public involvement and implementation of planning decisions.* Such a subunit would deliberately design, organize, and support public input and public involvement in the ongoing planning process, and would be responsible for helping citizens understand the consequences of decisions—such as regulations, ordinances, limitations on property rights, and social programs. The subunit might rely heavily on educational organizations, such as community colleges, cooperative extension staff, and private organizations with educational interests (see Chapter VIII).

A generalized diagram of a local planning unit is outlined in Figure 13-1. The lower section is labeled "temporary systems" since much of the work involved could be the responsibility of existing organizations or individuals to which a permanent local planning unit would have access.

Installation of an effective unit would necessarily require a broadly trained planning administrator who has a high level of management skill and a clear understanding of and appreciation for the political-governmen-

---

[1] The proposed organizational design is outlined in greater detail in William R. Lassey. Changing conceptions of rights to the use of land: social and organizational implications. In James C. Barron (Ed.). *Land use policy.* Pullman: Washington State University, 1974, pp. 46–61 (Cooperative Extension Service Bulletin).

tal process. Specialized staff would be required who could fulfill the other roles called for.

Table 13-1 sketches out a planning process and participation scheme, suggesting the major interaction points between planning officials and the citizen public (Committee on Public Participation in Planning, 1972). The scheme proposes a continuing dialogue among elected and appointed officials, lay leaders, and citizens. Interaction will presumably take place in a variety of settings, including public meetings when formal debates are in order. The professional staff will usually prepare exhibits, such as maps, models, and written explanations, which can be displayed in public locations and at meetings or in the media. Audiovisual media would help clarify and explain the intent and implications of proposals and alternative possibilities. If the public is to be meaningfully involved, it will be particularly

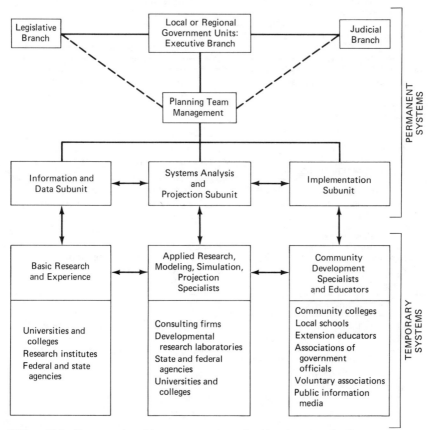

Figure 13-1 Permanent and temporary systems for planning organization.

Table 13-1   A Planning and Public Participation Process

Planning authorities		The public		
Elected repre- sentatives in local government	Appointed or elected planning boards or councils	Organized groups	Mass media (TV, press, etc.)	Inactive but affected citizens
Planning professionals ◄———►		**Articulate spokesmen for the public**		
1. Announcement of intent to plan ◄———		►Awareness of problems or opportuni- ties needing attention; formal meetings		
2. Isolation of issues needing at- tention through planning ◄		►Discussion and debate about plan- ning-related issues		
Review and response ◄				
3. Collection of data relating to the relevant issues, through ex- isting reports, surveys, census findings, research, etc. ◄		►Provision of information on plan- ning issues, response to surveys; rec- ommendations		
4. Analysis of data and information◄———		► Discussion, comment, interpreta- tions, involvement in data analysis		
5. Publication of study reports, with planning objectives ———		►Review, discussion, comment, criti- cism; media reports and interpreta- tions; formal meetings		
Review and response ◄				
6. Prepare alternative proposals for realization of planning goals ———		►Review, discussion, comment, criti- cism; statements of preferences; formal meetings		
Review and response ◄				
7. Prepare and publish proposals, ——— containing priorities, rationale, procedures for implementation		►Formal review and debate; submis- sion of criticisms and recommended alterations; formal meetings		
Review and response ◄				
8. Review and publish a formal set ——— of plans		►Filing of formal objections for re- view by higher level authorities; formal meetings		
Review and response ◄				
9. Implementation of acceptable ——— plans		► Continuing discussion, debate, pro- posals for change		
10. Review, revision, and continuous ◄ updating of plans and implemen- tation procedures				

important to explain the use of, or failure to use, proposals, criticisms, and recommendations offered by individuals or groups of citizens.

Systematized public participation requires a commitment to assist citizens in learning how to express themselves, while increasing their basic understanding of the issues and priorities to be considered. A constant and continuing educational process, involving interaction between citizens, policymakers, administrators, planners, and other "experts" is similarly implied, although this will probably involve only the most interested and articulate of citizens in the more public forums. Television, the print media, and radio can serve to indirectly involve a much wider group. A continuing investigative and educational process, to illuminate the most effective means for this continuing dialogue, would seem essential if it is not to become sterile and eventually stultifying.

Educational institutions must become more involved with local, state, and federal governments in developing improved processes for application of knowledge and building collaborative and integrated working relationships.

Education and Linkage Building

Professionals from agencies and organizations in rural regions need more advanced knowledge about:

1 The basic requirements for effective rural planning and development

2 Needed contributions from the wide array of organizations and agencies serving rural regions

3 Specific needs, problems, and opportunities for improvement of rural regions and communities

4 Collaboration and problem-solving skills

Citizen leaders require a similar educational and involvement experience which would enable them to:

1 Understand more clearly how local problems and opportunities are related to the larger forces at work in society

2 Learn in greater detail about the nature and resources of agencies and organizations available to assist with rural development

3 Increase their confidence and skill in providing more effective and informed local leadership

4 Increase their skill in working collaboratively with agency and organizational professionals in resolving problems and realizing opportunities

Neither organizational professionals nor community representatives have been accustomed to approaching rural planning and development from a holistic and integrated vantage point. Old habits, attitudes, and working methods will not be easily adapted to the new requirements. A continuing educational process must therefore become an institutionalized and integral part of a long-term rural planning and development strategy (see Chapter XII). This is not to imply that planning is devoid of continuing education (see Figure 13-2); rather, an opportunity exists for more systematic and long-term efforts specifically focused on *rural* planning issues.

Educational and collaborative efforts probably will not occur without thorough preparation and continuing organizational and logistical support from rural planning and development professionals who have a grasp of required actions and considerable skill in working with organizations and communities. New or redefined roles are called for which provide continuing support for collaborative efforts. New administrative and support roles must also evolve; it cannot be presumed that we already know precisely what kind of professional support will be required as the planning and development process unfolds.

Figure 13-2 In-service and continuing education for planning. In-service education for professional planners or other participants in the planning process is increasing. Professional planning organizations, public agencies, and colleges and universities are collaborating in a variety of such efforts. However, very little systematic effort has been undertaken to define the range of knowledge and skill required as a basis for devising a definitive continuing education program. (*Photo by W. R. Lassey.*)

Interrelationships among Local Jurisdictions and Public Institutions

The development potential of a region is delimited by available internal and external resources. Appropriate development is dependent upon the ability of local governmental jurisdictions to draw upon both internal and external resources. Rural jurisdictions do not generally have sufficient internal resources to unilaterally plan and develop on the basis of existing goals, plans, or potential alternatives; they are therefore dependent upon external resources (often urban-based) channeled through educational institutions, public agencies, and other organizations (public or private) from outside the jurisdiction or the region. The institutions, agencies, and organizations control professional and/or financial resources intended for application to the development problems of rural regions, but these external resource units are dependent upon informed decisions by representatives of local jurisdictions for the appropriate allocation of resources.

Research and Evaluation

Continuous learning from structured data collection, monitoring of experience, and application of relevant knowledge is essential if continuous adaptation of rural planning and development organization and process is to occur. Participants in the process must acquire the capability to examine their procedures with sufficient rigor that a firm connection can be made between behavior of individuals, organizations or local jurisdictions (communities), and development results.

More specifically, research and evaluation can help assure:

1 Clarification of which elements ought to be included in the planning and development process

2 Tracing and monitoring phases of intervention and field activities, to assure understanding of technical requirements of the process

3 Design and development of measurement instruments to assure reliable and valid data documenting significant events

4 Measurement of economic, social, and governmental changes in the region, such as: (*a*) changes in capital investment flow from outside the region; (*b*) changes in local investment activity; (*c*) changed employment patterns; (*d*) migration and demographic changes; (*e*) land-use changes

5 Assessment of effectiveness for educational or training events

6 Printed and audiovisual reporting and dissemination of new knowledge arising from the experience

The "Temporary System" of Consultants

Within the United States and in most other countries, a high proportion of formal planning and development programs is undertaken by consultants. A consultant is usually defined as a professional person or firm who is engaged temporarily to complete a task or series of tasks and who is then released without obligation by either employer or consultant. This enables a public or private organization to acquire needed skills and/or knowledge as needed. The use of consultants in the fields of engineering, law, architecture, economics, and a variety of other disciplines has a long and honored tradition.

Because physical and social planning is a relatively new enterprise, when compared to other professional fields, the quality of consultants and rules for consulting are not yet well developed; hence, the adequacy and completeness of "community" and "regional" plans prepared by consultants are often subjected to severe criticism by public officials and citizens. However, plans prepared with informed consultant assistance could be highly useful in those jurisdictions which cannot afford to support a planning staff with the important competencies.

Part of the difficulty in adequately using consultants arises from lack of public knowledge about what ought to compose "planning." Furthermore, much of the planning consultation has so far been undertaken by architect-planners and engineers; in these instances the focus has generally been limited to preparation for the "physical" needs of communities, i.e., transportation, waste disposal, buildings, parks, shopping areas, and related structural components of towns and cities. Although most plans contain sections on social and economic issues, these have tended to be least developed and elementary when compared to physical plans. Human services planning is often limited to facility location and structures for welfare, health, aging, and other social services.

To be most useful, consultants must increase their understanding about unique features of rural regions and populations, while responsible public officials must learn to evaluate ecologically and socially sound planning. Consultants may function more usefully if they develop a long-term association with the jurisdictions which they serve—so as to acquire more profound understanding of the total local milieu and to assure cognizance of implementation issues and requirements. If this were the case, the probability of greater quality, completeness, and acceptability of consultant-assisted planning would undoubtedly increase.

Although academic faculty have responsibility for teaching students the knowledge and skills required for planning, few professors have had sufficient practical experience—through consulting, professional practice, or research—to achieve a broad and holistic conception of the field. Greater involvement of teachers and researchers with operational programs seems essential; this could increase comprehension of the issues, while providing a pool of available professional skills. There are numerous examples of experimentation with this role among academic faculty, but the process has not been sufficiently institutionalized to make it fully legitimate with higher education administrators, public officials, citizens, or professional planners.

Students who seek planning competence are likely to be more satisfied and better prepared if they can work with faculty who have firsthand and continuing contact with the subject matter of their specialization. A part-time consultant role for faculty may contribute substantially to the further professionalization and adequacy of full-time consulting. More realistic standards and guidelines for high-quality work could thus be transmitted to students and, through professional communication channels, to those already at work in the field.

THE FUTURE OF RURAL PLANNING[2]

In the struggle for consensus on new policies and new approaches to planning, what are the implications of the changes proposed in these pages? What will be the effect on local government? What kinds of skills are required? Who should be involved? What kind of institutions will emerge?

Some local government units have already made significant progress toward adapting their structure and processes to accommodate new approaches to planning. Shifting away from a regulatory approach may be the most difficult adjustment to make. Government agencies have usually focused on enforcing "bureaucratic" rules to keep their staff members on an even course. Once the rules are established, there "appears" to be little need for creativity, innovation, or probing for new methods. Agency staff often assume their job is largely a matter of administering programs or regulations. This simplified view of local government responsibility is clearly obsolete, but it continues to prevail in many jurisdictions.

If local governments are unable to provide the resources for effective planning, fail to open up planning and decision-making processes to public scrutiny, and fail to work closely with citizens, it is entirely possible that planning responsibility will continue to shift away from local government to the state or federal decision level. Much of the present controversy over land-use planning is focused on the issue of local versus state versus federal authority. Effective planning will require that local government provide a climate encouraging flexibility and innovation, while working with regional, state, and federal governmental units.

Citizen awareness and support are a major basis for success of planning efforts. Local government officials (including planners) and citizens each have important responsibilities if the process is to be improved. There must be a flow of communications between citizens and government and an openness to respond positively to information and alternative choices. Public involvement is implicit in the new approaches to planning; the planning function of government cannot be left to the technicians (Friedmann, 1973).

[2] These concluding comments benefit from the insights and recommendations of my colleague, Dr. James C. Barron, Agricultural Economist, Washington State University.

The skills required to undertake adequately conceived future planning are likely to be very different than the skills involved in more conventional problem solving or crisis intervention. Extension of present trends is used widely in regulatory planning. However, trend forecasting does not predict the turning points or fundamental shifts which alter the direction of the future. More attention to potential major shifts in resource allocation and social organization is essential if major errors in planning are to be avoided.

An accurate assessment of public values and priorities is needed. A number of states are undertaking such studies; a case in point is the "Alternatives for Washington" program, which involved large numbers of citizens and leaders in designing desirable futures for their state. Efforts to obtain this information require substantial resources, highly sophisticated research, and advanced public involvement methods.

Improvements in rural institutional performance will be highly important in successfully shifting to new and more functional approaches to planning. Two kinds of changes in institutional performance are essential: (1) improvement of institutional *efficiency*, i.e., streamlining or adapting existing institutions so they work more effectively in providing leadership for changing conditions; and (2) institutional *innovation*, or the development of new institutional forms with responsibility for resolving issues that cannot presently be effectively treated. As the emphasis shifts from planning in reaction to the past toward planning that shapes the future, it is likely that both institutional efficiency and innovation will be critical.

References

Ashton, J., & Long, W. H. (Eds.). *The remoter rural areas of Britain.* Edinburgh: Oliver & Boyd, 1972.

Babcock, R. F. *The zoning game—Municipal practices and policies.* Madison: University of Wisconsin Press, 1966.

Barkley, P. W., & Seckler, D. W. *Economic growth and environmental decay: The solution becomes the problem.* New York: Harcourt Brace Jovanovich, Inc., 1972.

Barron, J. C., Lassey, W. R., & Ditwiler, C. D. *A search for new approaches to planning in Washington.* Pullman: Washington State University, 1976 (Agricultural Research Center Circular #595).

Beal, C. Rural development: Population and settlement prospects. *Journal of Soil and Water Conservation,* 1974.

———. Rural population growth more than a 'transient fad.' *Western Wire,* Vol. *1*(2). Corvallis, Ore.: Western Rural Development Center, December 1975.

Becker, H. S. Personal change in adult life. In W. G. Bennis, K. D. Benne, & R. Chin (Eds.), *Planning of change* (2nd ed.). New York: Holt, 1969, pp. 255–268.

Bennis, W. G. Post-bureaucratic leadership. *Trans-action,* July–August 1969.

———, Benne, K. D., & Chin, R. *Planning of change* (2nd ed.). New York: Holt, 1969.

Berry, Brian J. L. The question of policy alternatives. In C. Lowell Harriss (Ed.), *The good earth of America*. New York: Columbia University, The American Assembly, 1974, pp. 158–60.

Bijkerk, C. Rural reconstruction and development. In *A decade of research in land and water management, 1957–67*. Wageningen, The Netherlands: Institute for Land and Water Management, 1968 (Technical Bulletin #6).

———. Personal conversation, Wageningen, The Netherlands, 1972.

———, Linthorst, Th. J., & Van Wijk, C. *A method of a machine processed survey of the division of rural areas, as practiced in the Netherlands*. Wageningen, The Netherlands: Institute for Land and Water Management, 1970 (Miscellaneous Reprint #102).

Blann, J. Personal communication, Aspen Ski Corporation, October 1975.

Block, W. J. *Rural zoning: People, property and public policy*. Bozeman, Mont.: Cooperative Extension Service, April 1968 (Bulletin #331).

Bolan, R. S. Community decision behavior: The culture of planning. *Journal of the American Institute of Planners*, September 1969, *35*, 301–10.

Bosselman, F., & Callies, D. *The quiet revolution in land use control*. Washington, D. C.: Council on Environmental Quality, 1971.

———, ———, & Banta, J. *The taking issue*. Washington, D.C.: Council on Environmental Policy, U.S. Government Printing Office, 1973.

Boulding, K. E. Reflections on planning: The value of uncertainty, *Technology Review*, October–November 1974, p. 8.

Bowman, C. C. *Water right laws as they affect land acquisition and construction*. Bozeman: Montana State University, 1974 (Research Monograph No. 6).

Branch, M. C. *Planning: Aspects and applications*. New York: Wiley, 1966.

Caprio, J. M., Ottenbreit, S., Bourdeau, D., & Lancaster, L. *Climate of the Lone Mountain area of southwestern Montana*. Bozeman: Montana State University, Institute for Applied Research, 1973.

Caro, F. G. (Ed.). *Readings in evaluation research*. New York: Basic Books, 1971.

Carruthers, G. E., Erickson, E. C., & Renner, K. N. *Delivery of rural community services: Some implications and problems*. Las Cruces: New Mexico State University, Agricultural Experiment Station, 1975 (Bulletin 635).

Catton, W. R. Can irrupting man remain human? *Bioscience*, April 1976, *26*(4), 262–267.

Chadwick, G. *A systems view of planning: Toward a theory of the urban and regional planning process*. Oxford: Oxford University, 1971.

Chin, R., & Benne, K. D. General strategies for effecting change in human systems. In W. G. Bennis, K. D. Benne, & R. Chin (Eds.), *Planning of change* (2nd ed.). New York: Holt, 1969.

Ciriacy-Wantrup, S. V. *Resource conservation* (rev. ed.). Berkeley: University of California Press, 1963.

Clapp, J. A. *New towns and urban policy: Planning metropolitan growth*. New York: Dunellen Publishing Co., Inc., 1971.

Clarke, T. N. *Community structure and decision-making: Comparative analysis*. San Francisco: Chandler, 1968.

Clawson, M. *Suburban land conversion in the United States—An economic and governmental process*. Baltimore: Johns Hopkins University, 1971.

───── & Hall, P. *Planning and urban growth: An Anglo-American comparison.* Baltimore: Johns Hopkins University, 1973.

Committee on Public Participation in Planning. *People and planning.* London: Her Majesty's Stationery Office, 1972.

Commoner, B. Alternative approaches to the environmental crisis. *Journal of the American Institute of Planners,* May 1973, *39,* 147–62.

─────. *The closing circle: Nature, man & technology,* New York: Knopf, 1971.

Constandse, A. K. The ijsselmeerpolders: An old project with new functions. *Tijdschrift voor Econ. en Soc. Geografie,* May–June 1972.

─────. Personal conversation, Wageningen, The Netherlands, 1973.

Council of State Governments. *Land: State alternatives for planning and management.* Lexington, Ky., 1975.

Countryside planning act. London: Her Majesty's Stationery Office, 1968.

Davis, T. L., & Sorenson, D. M. *Land use planning handbook.* Fort Collins: Colorado State University, 1973.

Dillman, D. A., & Dobash, R. P. *Preferences for community living and their implications for population redistribution.* Pullman: Washington State University, Agricultural Research Center, 1972 (Bulletin #764).

Ditwiler, C. D. Private memorandum, November 1974.

───── & Barron, J. C. *Community planning: Criteria, structures, processes and implementing strategies.* Pullman: Washington State University, Agricultural Research Center, 1973 (Research Project Outline).

─────, Lassey, W. R., & Barron, J. C. *The impact of mandated legislation on local planning activity in the state of Washington.* Pullman: Washington State University, 1976 (Agricultural Research Center Circular #596).

Dolliver, J. Land use issues at the state level. In James C. Barron (Ed.). *Land use policy.* Pullman: Washington State University, Cooperative Extension Service, 1974, pp. 3–8.

Dorney, R. S. Role of ecologists as consultants in urban planning and design, *Human Ecology,* March 1973, *1*(3), 183–199.

Eberts, P. *A theoretical perspective toward an action-oriented model of community change and development.* Paper presented to the Workshop on New Brunswick Newstart, Ottawa, Ontario, Canada, November 4–5, 1971.

─────. NE-47, Consequences of changing social organization in the Northeast. In *Papers of the workshop on current rural development regional research in the northeast.* Ithaca, N.Y.: Northeast Regional Center for Rural Development, 1973.

Egler, F. E. Ecology and management of the rural and suburban landscape. In Pierre Dansereau (Ed.), *Challenge for survival.* New York: Columbia University Press, 1970, pp. 81–102.

Ewald, W. R., Jr. (Ed.). *Environment for man: The next fifty years.* Bloomington: Indiana University Press, 1967.

Fairbrother, N. *New lives, new landscapes.* New York: Knopf, 1970.

Festinger, L. *A theory of cognitive dissonance.* Evanston, Ill.: Row, Peterson, 1957.

Finkler, E. Big Sky, *Planning* (The ASPO Magazine), May 1973, pp. 16–22.

Finley, J. R. *A study of interorganizational relations.* Unpublished Ph.D. dissertation, Cornell University, Ithaca, N.Y., 1970.

Florea, B., & Scott, K. *Agriculture in an urban environment: King, Kitsap, Pierce, and Snohomish counties, Washington.* Pullman: Washington State University, Cooperative Extension Service, 1973.

Friedmann, J. Notes on societal action, *Journal of the American Institute of Planners,* September 1969, *35,* 311–18.

———. *Retracking America: A theory of transactional planning.* New York: Doubleday, 1973.

Fuguitt, G. The places left behind: Population trends and policy for rural areas, *Rural Sociology,* December 1971, *36*(4), 449–470.

Gallatin County Tribune, Bozeman, Mont., 1971–1972.

Gessaman, P. H. *A conceptual framework for rural development.* Paper presented at the 1974 Seminar of the Great Plains Resource Economics Committee. Lincoln: University of Nebraska, Department of Agricultural Economics, 1974.

Glikson, A. *The ecological basis of planning.* Lewis Mumford (Ed.). The Hague: Martinus Nishoff, 1971.

Graham, R. J. *Fisherman use and fish harvest on the Gallatin River, Montana.* Bozeman: Montana State University, Institute for Applied Research, 1973 (Research Monograph No. 5).

Gray, W. H. *Methods of agricultural land preservation.* Pullman: Washington State University, Cooperative Extension Service, February 1975 (Extension Monograph 3906).

———. *Agricultural land use in Washington: Conversion or preservation.* Pullman: Washington State University, Cooperative Extension Service, April 1975. (Extension Monograph 3935)

Green, R. J. *Country planning, the future of rural regions.* Manchester, United Kingdom: Manchester University, 1971.

Groot, J. P., & van Dusseldorp, D. B. W. M. *The guiding image and rural physical planning.* Wageningen, The Netherlands: Department of Nonwestern Sociology, The Agricultural University, 1970.

Hahn, A. J. Planning in rural areas. *Journal of the American Institute of Planners,* January 1970, *36,* 44–49.

Hand, I. *Environment and change: The next 50 years.* Bloomington: Indiana University, 1968.

Hansen, N. M. *Rural poverty and urban crisis.* Bloomington: Indiana University, 1970.

Hanton, S., Lassey, W. R., & Williams, A. S. *Organizing for area development: A case study.* Bozeman, Mont.: Agricultural Experiment Station, 1972 (Research Report #27).

Harder, J. K. *Student internships.* Chicago: American Society of Planning Officials, 1969 (Report #246).

Hartman, C. W. Reshaping planning education. *Journal of the American Institute of Planners,* July 1970, *36,* 218–221.

Hehn, E. Effect of campsite use on the environmental quality of the Gallatin Canyon. Bozeman: Montana State University, Institute of Applied Research, 1973.

Hightower, J. *Hard tomatoes, hard times.* Washington, D.C.: Agricultural Accountability Project, 1972.

Hillhorst, J. G. M. *Regional planning: A systems approach.* Rotterdam, The Netherlands: Rotterdam University, 1971.

Hobson, D., & Lassey, W. R. *Summary of state and local planning programs in the northwest region and summary of current planning positions in counties and regions.* Preliminary survey results from local, state, and federal agencies in Washington, Montana, Idaho, and Oregon, September 1974.

Hofstee, E. W. Land ownership in densely populated and industrialized countries. *Sociologia Ruralis*, 1972, *XII*, 6–36 (Special Issue).

Isard, W., et al. *Ecological-economic analysis for regional development.* New York: Free Press, 1972.

Jezeski, James J. (Ed.). *Impacts of large recreational developments upon semi-primitive environments.* Vol I, *Integrated report.* Bozeman: Montana State University, February 1973.

———. *Impacts of large recreational developments upon semi-primitive environments.* Bozeman, Mont.: Center for Interdisciplinary Studies, June 1973 (Research Monograph #1).

———. *Impact of large recreational developments upon semi-primitive environments,* Vol. I, *Integrated report* (rev. ed.). Bozeman, Mont.: Center for Interdisciplinary Studies, September 1973.

——— et al. *Impacts of large recreational developments upon semi-primitive environments,* Vol. II, *Disciplinary appendix.* Bozeman: Montana State University, February 1973.

Kelman, H. C. The process of opinion change. In W. G. Bennis, K. D. Benne, & R. Chin (Eds.), *Planning of change.* New York: Holt, Rinehart and Winston, 1969.

Kelso, M. M. Management & use of land as a public good. In *Increasing understanding of public problems and policies—1972.* Chicago: Farm Foundation, 1972.

Klein, D. Some notes on the dynamics of resistance to change: The defender role. In Goodwin Watson (Ed.), *Concepts for social change.* Washington, D.C.: National Education Association, 1967.

Kraenzel, C. F., & Macdonald, F. H. *Follow-up of patients discharged from Warm Springs hospital to select Montana counties.* Bozeman, Mont.: Agricultural Experiment Station, 1971 (Bulletin #646).

Kulp, M. *Rural development planning: Systems analysis and working method.* New York: Praeger, 1970.

Lambert, A. *The making of the Dutch landscape.* London: Seminar Press, 1971.

Lassey, W. R. Combining methods of social research in underdeveloped areas. *Rocky Mountain Social Science Journal*, October 1968, *5*, 106–118.

———. *Planning for rural health systems: The case of eastern Montana.* Paper presented to a conference sponsored by Western Social Science Advisory Committee. Portland, Ore.: Agricultural Experiment Stations, 1970.

———. *Rural and regional planning: Conceptual and operational models; organizational, implementing, and decision-making processes.* Pullman, Wash.: Agricultural Research Center, 1973 (Research Project Outline).

———. *Rural planning, ecology and rural development: Models from Dutch and British experience.* Paper presented to the Annual Meeting of the Rural Sociology Society, University of Maryland, 1973.

——— (Ed.). *Human resource planning.* Pullman: Washington State University, Cooperative Extension Service, 1974 (Proceedings of a seminar).

———. *The organization of planning programs in the state of Washington.* Pullman:

Washington State University, Cooperative Extension Service, Bulletin Department, 1975 (Extension Monograph #3982).

——— & Ditwiler, C. D. Public involvement in federal land use planning. *Environmental Law*, Spring 1975, *5*(3), 643–59. Portland: Lewis & Clark Law School.

——— & Navratil, G. *Government, organization, and public policy issues: The Gallatin Canyon and Big Sky of Montana*. Preliminary report on planning issues related to *Impact of a large recreation development on semi-primitive environments*. Bozeman, Mont.: Center for Interdisciplinary Studies, 1972 (Mimeographed).

——— & Fernandez, R. R. *Leadership and social change* (2nd ed.). La Jolla, Calif.: University Associates, Inc., 1976.

——— & Williams, A. S. *Multi-county areas as a tool for development in Montana*. Bozeman, Mont.: Agricultural Experiment Station, 1970 (Research Report #2).

——— & ———. *The environment, development and planning*. Paper presented to the Annual Meeting of the American Sociological Association, Denver, Colo., 1971.

———, Williams, A. S., & Gilchrist, J. C. *Leadership orientations in a multi-county area*. Paper presented to the Annual Meeting of the Rural Sociological Society, Baton Rouge, La., 1972.

———, Barron, J. C., & Ditwiler, C. D. *County and regional planning in Washington state*. Draft report, based on research involving interviews with county and regional planning directors in all Washington counties or planning regions, September 1974.

Lewis, P. H., Jr. *Regional design for human impact*. Springfield, Ill.: Thomas Publications, 1969.

Lippitt, R. The use of social research to improve social practice. In Goodwin Watson (Ed.), *Concepts for social change*. Washington, D.C.: 1967.

Malone, M. P. The Gallatin Canyon and the tides of history. Bozeman: Montana State University, Institute for Applied Research, 1973 (Research Monograph No. 4).

Mayer, R. R. Social system models for planners. *Journal of the American Institute of Planners*, May 1972, *38*, 130–139.

McBroom, W. *Illness and medical care*. Missoula, Mont.: Institute for Social Science Research, 1971 (Publication #3).

McCresky, W. A report on structures in the Gallatin Canyon: 1970. Bozeman: Montana State University, Institute of Applied Research, 1970.

McEntire, D. Alternative models of regional organization. Paper presented to the Annual Meeting, Rural Sociological Society, Baton Rouge, La., August 1972.

McHarg, I. L. *Design with nature*. New York: Natural History Press, 1969.

McLoughlin, J. B. *Urban and regional planning: A systems approach*. London: Faber & Faber, 1969.

Meadows, D. H., et al. *The limits to growth: A report for the Club of Rome's project on the predicament of mankind*. New York: New American Library, 1972.

Moe, E. O. *Agency collaboration in planning and service*. Paper presented to the National Conference on Social Welfare, Centennial Forum, Atlantic City, N. J., May 31, 1973.

———— & Tamblyn, L. R. *Rural schools as a mechanism for rural development.* Las Cruces: New Mexico State University, 1974 (ERIC-CRESS).

Montagne, J. The role of geology in interdisciplinary studies of the Gallatin Canyon area, Gallatin County, Montana. Guidebook, 21st Annual Field Conference, Crazy Mountains Basin, Montana Geological Society, 1972, pp. 187–190.

Murray-McCormick Environmental Group. *The Gallatin Canyon planning study: Final report.* Sacramento, Calif.: Applied Science and Resource Planning Division, Murray-McCormick Environmental Group, 1972.

National land use policy: Background papers on past and pending legislation and the roles of the executive branch, Congress, and the states in land use policy and planning, United States Congress, Senate Committee on Interior and Insular Affairs, Committee Print. Washington, D.C.: U.S. Government Printing Office, 1972.

National land use policy legislation, 93rd Congress, Committee on Interior and Insular Affairs. Washington, D.C.: U.S. Government Printing Office, 1973.

Odum, E. P. *Fundamentals of ecology* (3rd ed.). Philadelphia: Saunders, 1971.

Olson, J., Leeson, B., & Nielson, G. E. *Soil interpretations for land use planning and development in the Gallatin Canyon area.* Bozeman, Mont.: Agricultural Experiment Station, 1973 (Research Report #10).

Perloff, H. S. The evolution of planning education. In David R. Godschalk (Ed.), *Planning in America: Learning from turbulence.* Washington, D.C.: American Institute of Planners, 1974.

Picton, H. D. Elk, economics and recreational development. *N.W. Section—The Wildlife Society,* 1972.

————. The Gallatin human-wildlife community: A synopsis. *N.W. Section—The Wildlife Society,* 1974.

Price, I. *Buying country property.* New York: Harper & Row, 1972.

Reich, C. A. *The greening of America.* New York: Random House, 1970.

Reilly, W. K. (Ed.). *The use of land: A citizen's policy guide to urban growth.* New York: Thomas Y. Crowell Company, 1973.

Revenue sharing and the planning process: Shifting the focus of responsibility for domestic problem solving. Report of the Subcommittee on the Planning Process and Urban Development. Washington, D. C.: Advisory Committee to the Department of Housing and Urban Development, National Academy of Sciences, National Academy of Engineering, 1974.

Roemhild, G. *Aquatic invertebrates and water quality: The effect of human ingress in a semi-primitive area,* Bozeman: Montana State University, Institute of Applied Research, 1973.

Rogers, E. M., & Shoemaker, F. F. *Communication of innovations.* New York: Free Press, 1971.

Rose, D. K. *An interim report on the Montana State University travel research project in the Gallatin Canyon.* Bozeman: Montana State University, 1971.

Rural development act of 1972, 92nd Congress, Public Law 92-419, 1972.

Second report on physical planning in the Netherlands (condensed ed.). Part I: Structure of planning in the Netherlands, Part II: Future pattern of development. The Hague, The Netherlands: Government Printing Office, 1966.

Sennet, F. Proposal for an integrated social services program for northeast Montana. Helena, Mont.: Department of Social and Rehabilitative Services, 1972.

Sharp, E. L. Relation of air ions to air pollution and some biological effects. *Environmental Pollution*, 1972, *3*, 227–239.

Sismondo, S. *Measurement instruments for community structure research in Kent County, New Brunswick, Canada*. Richibucto, New Brunswick: New Brunswick Newstart, Inc., 1972 (Monograph).

———. *Applications of structural indicators for the measurement of development: Selected findings for rural communities in Kent County*. Richibucto, New Brunswick: New Brunswick Newstart, Inc., 1973.

Spiritis, G. L., Jones, C. F., Parish-Speights, J., & Carbaugh, F. *Student internship manual*. Chicago: American Society of Planning Officials (undated).

State of Washington. *Planning enabling act*. Chapter 36.70. Olympia, Wash.: State Library, Rev. Codes of Washington, 1972.

Steinhart, J. S., & Steinhart, C. B. Energy use in the U.S. food system. *Science*, April 1974, *181*, 307–316.

Stocks, D., & Sedlacek, S. An approach to community development: Hill County. In William R. Lassey and Anne S. Williams (Eds.), *Community development in Montana: resources, methods, case studies*. Bozeman, Mont.: Big Sky Books, 1970.

Strong, A. L. *Planned urban environments: Sweden, Finland Israel, the Netherlands, France*. Baltimore: Johns Hopkins, 1971.

Stuart, D. G., et al. *Impacts of large recreational developments upon semi-primitive environments: The Gallatin Canyon case study*. Bozeman: Montana State University, Institute of Applied Research and Agricultural Experiment Station, 1974.

Taylor, J. L. *Instructional planning systems: A gaming-simulation approach to urban problems*. Cambridge, United Kingdom: Cambridge University, 1971.

Thompson, L. S., & Hash, C. T. *Price effect of changes in land use in Gallatin County, Montana: A case study*. Bozeman: Montana Agricultural Experiment Station, 1973 (Research Report 44).

Toffler, A. *Future shock*. New York: Random House, 1970.

Town and country planning act. London: Her Majesty's Stationery Office, 1972.

Tubbs, C. R., & Blackwood, J. W. Ecological evaluation of land for planning purposes. *Biological Conservation*, April 1971, *3*, 169–172.

United States Senate. *Land use policy and planning assistance act of 1973*. 93rd Congress, 1st session, Senate Bill 268, 1973.

United States Department of Agriculture. *Land use planning assistance*. Washington, D.C.: U.S. Government Printing Office, February 1974.

Warner, W. K. The structural matrix of development. In G. M. Beal, R. C. Powers, & E. W. Coward, Jr. (Eds.), *Sociological perspectives on domestic development*. Ames: Iowa State University, 1971, pp. 94–115.

Warren, R. *The community in America* (2nd ed.). Chicago: Rand McNally, 1972.

Watson, G. Resistance to change. In W. G. Bennis, K. D. Benne, & R. Chin (Eds.), *Planning of change*. New York: Holt, 1969.

Weaver, T., & Dale, D. Trampling effects on vegetation of the tract corridor of north Rocky Mountain forests. Bozeman: Montana State University, Institute of Applied Research, 1973.

Weller, J. *Modern agriculture & rural planning*. London: Architectural Press, 1967.

Wibberly, G. Personal conversation, London, United Kingdom, 1973.

Williams, A. S. *The impact of a large recreation development upon a semi-primitive environment: A case history of canyon planning efforts*. Bozeman: Montana State University, Institute of Applied Research, 1972.

———— & Gilchrist, C. J. *A typology of property owners: A case study of a planning effort*. Bozeman, Mont.: Center for Interdisciplinary Studies, 1973 (Research Monograph #3).

———— & Lassey, W. R. *Regional planning and development: Organization and strategies*. Bozeman, Mont.: Agricultural Experiment Station, 1974 (Research Report #58).

————, Nielsen, G. E., Reuss, J. W., Stuart, D. G., & Shovic, H. F. *Problems of interdisciplinary, applied research in a university setting*. Bozeman: Montana State University, Institute of Applied Research, 1974.

————, Meldahl, N., Dick, K., & Navratil, G. *The sociology of residential and recreational uses of the Gallatin Canyon*. Bozeman: Montana State University, Institute of Applied Research, 1972.

Williams, T., & Hanson, T. Hydrologic measurements and water use studies in the West Fork area. Bozeman: Montana State University, Institute for Applied Research, 1973.

Index

Index

Dr. William R. Lassey is Rural Sociologist
and Professor of Sociology and Environmental Science at Washington State
University. Responsible for extension and
research activities focused on land use
and rural planning in the state of Washington, Dr. Lassey has had wide experience
in rural planning both in the United States
and abroad. He has undertaken major
studies in rural planning and development
in Central and South America. He was
director of a series of programs designed
to improve community planning and development in rural areas which were supported by the Community Services and
Continuing Education Program under
Title I of the Higher Education Act of
1965. In 1968 he was appointed director
of the new center for planning and development which focused on research and
consultation with rural and urban regions
throughout the state of Montana and in
neighboring states. During the 1972-73
academic year, Dr. Lassey was a visiting
professor at the National Agricultural
University of the Netherlands and at the
University of Reading and University College of the University of London. During
this period, his activity was focused on
research on rural planning programs in the
Netherlands and United Kingdom. Dr.
Lassey is the author of some 25 major publications including two previous books,
Community Development in Montana and
Leadership and Social Change.